POLICING POST-CONFLICT CITIES

ALICE HILLS

ZED BOOKS
London & New York

Policing Post-Conflict Cities was first published in 2009 by Zed Books Ltd,
7 Cynthia Street, London N1 9JF, UK and Room 400, 175 Fifth Avenue,
New York, NY 10010, USA

www.zedbooks.co.uk

Designed and typeset by illuminati, Grosmont, www.illuminatibooks.co.uk
Cover designed by Andrew Corbett
Printed and bound in the UK by the MPG Books Group

Distributed in the USA exclusively by Palgrave Macmillan,
a division of St Martin's Press, LLC, 175 Fifth Avenue, New York, NY 10010

A catalogue record for this book is available from the British Library
Library of Congress Cataloging in Publication Data available

ISBN   978 1 84277 969 9 Hb
ISBN   978 1 84277 970 5 Pb

CONTENTS

ACKNOWLEDGEMENTS

I have been working on these themes for some years, and am grateful to more people in more countries than I have space to mention. Even so, special thanks are due to Bruce Baker, Andrew Goldsmith, Eboe Hutchful, Otwin Marenin and Gordon Peake. Needless to say, the opinions expressed are mine alone.

ACRONYMS AND ABBREVIATIONS

AI	Amnesty International
AFL	Armed Forces of Liberia
AFRC	(Sierra Leone) Armed Forces Revolutionary Council
ANP	Afghan National Police
AusAID	Australian Government Overseas Aid Programme
CID	Criminal Intelligence Department
CIVPOL	(UN) civilian police
CPA	(Iraq) Coalition Provisional Authority
CPA	(Sudan) Comprehensive Peace Agreement
CPDTF	Commonwealth Police Division Task Force
DDR	Demobilisation, disarmament and reintegration
DFID	(UK) Department for International Development
DoJ	(US) Department of Justice
DP	Displaced person
DRC	Democratic Republic of Congo
ECOMOG	Economic Community of West African States (ECOWAS) Ceasefire Monitoring Group
EPLF	Eritrean People's Liberation Front
EU	European Union
EUFOR	European Union Force
FCO	(UK) Foreign & Commonwealth Office
FPU	Formed police unit
FSB	(Russian Federation) Federal Security Service
GNP	Gross national product

GNR	(Portugal) Republican National Guard
GOSS	Government of Southern Sudan
HRW	Human Rights Watch
IBRD	International Bank for Reconstruction and Development
ICG	International Crisis Group
ICRC	International Committee of the Red Cross
IDASA	Institute for Democracy in South Africa
IDP	Internally displaced person
IED	Improvised explosive device
IFOR	(NATO) Implementation Force
IGO	Inter-governmental organisation
IMF	International Monetary Fund
INP	Iraqi National Police
IPS	Iraqi Police Service
IPTF	International Police Task Force
IPU	Integrated police unit
IRIN	(UN) Integrated Regional Information Networks
ISAF	International Security Assistance Force
KFOR	(NATO) Kosovo Force
KPS	Kosovo Police Service
LNP	Liberia National Police
LOTFA	Law and Order Trust Fund for Afghanistan
MANPADS	Man-portable air defence systems
MDTF	Multi-donor trust fund
MNF	Multi-National Force – Iraq
MoD	(UK) Ministry of Defence
MONUC	United Nations Mission in the DRC
MoPol	(Nigeria) Mobile Police
MP	Military police
MSA	Mission subsistence allowance
MSU	Multinational specialised units
MVD	(Russian Federation) Ministry of Internal Affairs
NATO	North Atlantic Treaty Organization
NCO	Non-commissioned officer
NGO	Non-governmental organisation
NP	Nigeria Police
NPF	(Liberia) National Police Force
NPFL	National Patriotic Front of Liberia
NTGL	National Transitional Government of Liberia
OCHA	(UN) Office for the Coordination of Humanitarian Affairs

OECD DAC	Organisation for Economic Co-operation and Development Development Assistance Committee
OMON	(Russian Federation) Special police forces
OSCE	Organization for Security and Co-operation in Europe
PCRU	(UK) Post-Conflict Reconstruction Unit
PIR	(DRC) Police for Rapid Intervention
PNC	(DRC) Congolese National Police
PNH	Haitian National Police
PSC	Private security company
RNA	Rwanda News Agency
ROE	Rules of engagement
RPG	Rocket-propelled grenade
RUF	(Sierra Leone) Revolutionary United Front
SCIRI	Supreme Council for the Islamic Revolution in Iraq
SCR	(Rwanda) Central Intelligence Service
SFOR	(NATO) Stabilisation Force
SIDA	Swedish International Development Agency
SJSR	Security and justice sector reform
SLP	Sierra Leone Police
SNF	Somali National Front
SOBR	(Russian Federation) Special rapid response units
SOD	(Liberia) Special Operations Division
SPC	Standing police capacity
SPF	Somali Police Force
SPLA/M	Sudan People's Liberation Army/Movement
SPU	Special police units
SSAJ	Safety, security and access to justice
SSPS	Southern Sudan Police Service
SSR	Security sector reform
SWAT	Special weapons and tactics
TSU	Tactical support unit
UDA	Ulster Defence Association
UNAMIR	United Nations Assistance Mission for Rwanda
UNDP	United Nations Development Programme
UN DPKO	United Nations Department of Peacekeeping Operations
UN FAO	Food and Agriculture Organization of the United Nations
UNHCR	Office of the UN High Commissioner for Refugees
UNICEF	United Nations Children's Fund
UNITAF	(Somalia) Unified Task Force
UNMIL	United Nations Mission in Liberia

UNODC	United Nations Office on Drugs and Crime
UNOSOM	United Nations Operations in Somalia
UNPOL	United Nations Police
UNRWA	United Nations Relief and Works Agency for Palestine Refugees in the Near East
USAID	US Agency for International Development

I

ORDER IN AN URBAN CENTURY

Almost every post-conflict city experiences acute insecurity. Baghdad, Kabul, Mogadishu, Monrovia and Sarajevo all saw an increase in looting, revenge attacks, armed robbery and kidnappings. Street-level security was minimal as factional leaders positioned themselves, occupying militaries protected themselves, and indigenous police burned their uniforms, or hid in their neighbourhoods. Later, Western attempts to reconstruct indigenous security forces on democratic lines ended in failure. Yet none of these cities has disappeared. Some were partially destroyed and their inhabitants displaced, but none experienced anarchy, and all offered business opportunities to men such as Osman Ato, who in the early 1990s controlled much of Mogadishu's qat trade, provided many of the vehicles used by the militias and owned most of the houses rented by NGOs.[1] This book is about the re-emergence of order in such cities, and the challenges of managing it.

It is impossible to explain how and why order re-emerges after conflict without considering cities, for they have a political, cultural and physical significance that rural areas lack. Above all, cities are significant because their known history means that they offer a labora-tory in which to trace the social and political continuities moulding the re-emergence of order. They represent units of analysis for examining the interface between order and security, which is typically made visible by the activities of their police, and they offer discrete case studies of order and security; of who provides it, and how, and whose needs are prioritised. Based on developments in a range of cities, I argue that – and this is my central thesis – order and security are interwoven, but that, while security facilitates order, order is necessary for meaningful security. In other words, security is best understood as a process and a variable within order, rather than its end.

The topic is given urgency by the failure of US-led operations in Afghanistan and Iraq, but it is of broader relevance than this suggests. Not only do these issues present themselves acutely in cities, but also their development suggests explanations for the meaning of security, the nature of policing, and the relationship between security and development more broadly. And they emphasise the extent to which Western understanding remains rooted in historically specific forms of Westphalian order: law and order are invariably seen as the primary means for managing post-conflict disorder and insecurity.

To see how the processes of order and security relate to one another and are managed in major cities that are emerging from conflict (hereafter 'post-conflict cities'), we need first to relate developments to the broader urban environment; that is, to the context in which order and security are to be created. This chapter offers an overview of cityscapes before considering what is meant by security and order, and their supporting concepts of power and stability.

CITIES

Contemporary conflicts display an urban bias. Although most wars are fought in rural areas where the state has little oversight or presence, and where the infrastructure is easily destroyed, cities are usually a target for belligerents, and the size and density of their population and its associated infrastructure mean that the political significance and societal impact of conflict are typically greater in them than in rural areas.

All wars are brutal, and some of the most appalling operations of recent years have taken place in jungles and villages out of sight of the international media, yet urban war seems to have a particularly vicious logic of its own, especially when (as in Algiers, Grozny and Haditha) it involves military forces acting as police in internal security operations (Hills 2002). Many professional soldiers believe that urban operations are merely a subclass of tactics and do not deserve special attention, yet it is generally agreed that many aspects of operating in cities are unique. Also, current military thought, decision-making and logistics are designed for (and work best in) open area operations of the type conducted in the countryside, and operating in a man-made physical terrain superimposed onto natural terrain exacerbates existing tactical and logistical challenges. More importantly, cities are rarely empty, so securing a city means troops must operate among civilians to a far greater extent than they would in open countryside. Further, short-term tactical advantage usually lies with the side having least regard for casualties. Consequently, urban war is not only the most operationally and politically challenging of all military operations, but also it is the closest that most conventional militaries come to pre-industrial forms of conflict. The traditional core capability of aggressive close combat – the hunter-killer philosophy of 'What I find, I can kill' – remains essential for successful operations, and casualties are usually high. Lastly, urban war is special because of the stakes involved: cities are important political prizes in a way that villages, forests, lakes and deserts are not.

Today's emphasis on urban operations is unsurprising, for one of the most notable transformations of recent years has been the change from a predominantly rural world to an urban one: there are more cities today and they are getting bigger. It has been estimated that in 2015 the world's population will be 7.2 billion; that is, 1.1 billion more than in 2000 (Nichiporuk 2000).[2] Approximately 95 per cent of the increase will be in developing countries and almost all of it will occur in cities, making urbanisation one of the major developmental challenges of the twenty-first century (IBRD 2000: 47). And rapid or large-scale urbanisation often prompts conflict. Urbanisation implies social relationships, but also it means tensions and inequality. Civil wars, famine and poverty push people to cities, which lack the resources to absorb them, while the institutions, social capital and politics that served a dispersed rural population rarely transfer. Expectations rise, and second- and third-generation urban residents begin to organise themselves and make demands of governments that do not have the political and social mechanisms to meet them (Milbert 2006). A rapidly expanding population, inadequate access to basic services, declining standards of infrastructure, bigger slums, social exclusion, criminalisation, and ethnic and sectarian tensions can lead to disorder and insecurity. In most cases, urbanisation is associated with demographic changes – youthful but alienated populations are linked to instability from Northern Ireland through the Middle East and West Africa to South Asia – and growth is commonly accompanied by crime, corruption, pollution and urban decay.[3]

There are no standard definitions of cities, and countries define them according to a range of administrative criteria, population size and density, or economic characteristics. The World Bank, for example, states:

> The formal definition of urban areas describes them as concentrations of nonagricultural workers and nonagricultural production sectors. Most countries call settlements with 2,500–25,000 people urban areas. The definition varies from country to country and has changed over time ... A city has a certain legal status (granted by the national or provincial government) that is generally associated with specific administrative or local government structures. (World Bank 1999: 127)

Technically, 'city' denotes a statistical grouping of people in a single area, while 'urban' refers to the patterns of social and cultural behaviour that appear to be unique to city life.

The dominant features of cities are easier to identify, being their man-made construction, high population density and urban nature. Physically, most differ more in degree and style than in structure. In some cities elites have taken over the centre and the poor are pushed out to the suburbs; in others the middle class live in the suburbs and abandon the city centre to the poor. Most (including Mogadishu and Kinshasa, capitals of Somalia and the Democratic Republic of Congo, DRC) have – or had – European characteristics such as central boulevards, combination street patterns, high-rise buildings of reinforced concrete and a framed construction in a city core, residential suburbs, and distinct economic, social and ethnic sectors (Hills 2002). Many have shantytowns of one-roomed shacks without running water, sanitation or electricity where the state has never had a presence even though they encroach on central districts. Even before the US invasion of 2003, areas of south-west Baghdad resembled Kinshasa, complete with sewage, filthy rubbish, beggars and flea markets.

SPECIAL FEATURES

Regardless of definitional issues, major cities are special. They are symbols of national existence or religious identity, and visible expressions of states, governments and ethnic groups. They are destination points for extremists and criminals, and sanctuaries or battle spaces for insurgents and terrorists. They are a focus for national and international attention because politicians live in them, and foreign troops, officials and journalists are based there. This can make cities in conflict-prone regions either safer or dangerously insecure.

Take the case of Freetown, Sierra Leone's capital, in the late 1990s. Sierra Leone had for long been divided into Freetown and the rest of the country. During the 1970s and 1980s power became concentrated in the hands of the president, so all decisions were taken in Freetown, and all resources were distributed within it. By the late 1980s there were no state institutions in the provinces (the notoriously authoritarian and corrupt Sierra Leone Police collapsed), and the presidency became the prize. After the war, the UK focused its attention on Freetown because that was where the government of its protégé, President Ahmad Kabbah, was based. Contrast the situation in Afghanistan. The Taliban's tactical focus on bombing buses and markets in Kabul was straightforward: 'Kabul is the capital city and the foreign troops are concentrated there' (BBC 21 June 2007).

Cities are not neutral environments. They can exacerbate existing tensions because they introduce 'a set of characteristics – proximate ethnic neighbourhoods, territoriality, economic interdependency, symbolism, and centrality – not present to such an extent on wider geographic scales' (Bollens 2000: 326). Also, they are political organisms. Not only do political elites live in them, but also they contain production and storage facilities, seaports, airports, ground transportation hubs and financial centres. Cities in the South (where most contemporary conflicts occur) hold most of a country's economic resources, infrastructure and flows of development aid. Dili, capital of Timor Leste, is a case in point. Around 40 per cent of the population lives on less than 55 US cents a day (this is the UNDP's poverty line for the country). In theory, relieving poverty should be easy – Timor receives energy revenues of some $158 million a year – but the government spends most of that money in Dili, and less than a fifth of state-provided goods and services go to the rural areas where most people live. Cities are often links in the global production chain too. They are targets for foreign investment, and account for an increasing share of national income; typically they generate around 55 per cent of gross national product (GNP) even in low-income countries in conflict-prone regions.[4] They are prizes worth fighting over.

And cities are notoriously violent even in peacetime. Take the case of Brazil's main cities. Levels of violence and crime are especially high in the favelas, or temporary shantytowns, which lack all basic services and are inhabited mainly by black, mixed-race or internal migrants from the poor north-east of the country. The favelas' socially excluded inhabitants are caught between the criminal violence exercised by drug gangs, the violence imposed by groups of vigilantes offering alternative justice, and the violence used by the police. For example, in June 2007, 1,300 police entered the slum stronghold of a prominent gang of drug dealers in Rio de Janeiro, where more than 100,000 people live (BBC 28 June 2007). The operation was officially part of a move to make the city safer before it hosted the Pan-American games, but it actually formed part of a recurring pattern whereby the police's main contact with slums takes the form of violent invasions. In this case, officers were supported by guns, grenades, armoured vehicles and helicopters. Policing in such circumstances is a high-risk occupation, with inadequately trained and resourced officers regularly confronting heavily armed criminal gangs. Against that, police kill about 2,000 people a year in Rio de Janeiro and São Paulo, many of them by extrajudicial execution and torture (Amnesty International 2005).

The reluctance of most police to enter shantytowns except on raids or in search of bribes results in security voids that are commonly filled by gangs, vigilantes and militia groups. One consequence is that some big cities see war-like levels of violence between territorially based gangs. It is true that cities are insecure places even in peacetime, but powerful weapons are easier to access in a post-conflict city such as Belgrade or Beirut, and there is a greater readiness to use them. Even so, the distinction between pre-conflict and post-conflict conditions may not mean much, especially in a city such as Brazzaville in the Republic of the Congo. In the mid-1990s, more than 62 per cent of Congo's 3 million population lived in urban areas, but roads were scarce and urban infrastructure was at best fragile.[5] The fighting of 1997, which was confined to the capital and its surrounding suburbs, was effectively 'conventional mob warfare' (Geibel 1998: 17–20), but it resulted in widespread destruction because major weapon systems such as tanks, helicopter gunships and fighters had been used in addition to the more usual rocket-propelled grenades (RPGs), mortars and artillery. Yet for many people the end of conflict made little difference to everyday levels of security.

As this suggests, it is difficult to develop a baseline against which to judge conditions once conflict ends. Assessments are skewed by the significance of the city concerned, the extent of its physical destruction, social and ethnic tensions, international advocacy, or by media reports. Some cities are destroyed, but others emerge relatively unscathed. In some places the routines of daily life remain structured while elsewhere social hierarchies and control mechanisms are destroyed. Nevertheless, one thing is clear: the need for physical security dominates life. With it, people can rebuild their lives, houses, businesses and institutions. Without it, occupying troops overreact, policemen hide and ordinary people are not safe in their houses, let alone outside them. Finding food, earning a living, seeking medical assistance, staying cool or keeping warm, avoiding kidnappers, all become difficult or impossible when gangs or militias control the streets, hospitals are looted and power-generation plants are destroyed. Fear and violence destroy not only the physical security of individuals but also the social networks and technical infrastructure sustaining cities. That is, their order.

SECURITY

Anyone considering post-conflict cities is struck by the extent to which security is the central point around which debate and competition take place: security dominates despite being absent. At its most basic, security means that inhabitants are not forcibly displaced, raped, robbed, kidnapped, mutilated, tortured or killed. Definitions of security are now commonly stretched beyond this to incorporate a range of meanings that include food, water, health and environmental issues. Security is undoubtedly a multifaceted social phenomenon, incorporating individual and public aspects and spaces, so today's broader understanding offers a useful corrective to traditional definitions relying on statist notions. Also, security is always defined situationally and contextually, and its meaning shifts to reflect contingencies. This happened in Gaza City a few days after Hamas overran Fatah strongholds in June 2007. Concerns about physical safety were quickly replaced by worries about food supplies, and Gazans began stockpiling food after Israel closed the crossing points that are Gaza's supply lines, only for fears to swing back at the first sign of renewed fighting. Nonetheless, the fact remains that notions such as 'human security' (considered in more detail in Chapter 3) are derived from, and possible only in the absence of, physical violence. This makes their application in post-conflict cities of questionable value, for the principal political weapons in most post-conflict cities are intimidation and violence. Threats are usually physical, and to do with the elusive notion of 'survival', especially when cities are divided into ethnic or sectarian areas, or when security's referent object is an identity or group (Ayoob 1995; Krause 1998: 25).

Territoriality is an additional facet of security's physical dimension. It is about asserting control over specific localities in order to expand a dominant group's space or restrict that of an adversary, and it often results in a ghettoisation of security (Caldeira 2000; Davis 1998; Hoffman 2007a; Seekings 2001). Thus territoriality prompted the use of communal terror to remap Vukovar, Sarajevo and Mostar after the Balkan wars, just as it expressed sectarian ambitions of fears in Baghdad in 2003. Its influence is equally evident in the actions of conventional security forces. It drove the US seizure of Iraq's symbols of regime power (including police headquarters) in 2003, and it underpins the Israel Defense Forces' attempts to control Palestinian movement by the destruction of Palestinian houses, infrastructure, and cultural and administrative facilities.

PERSPECTIVES

Perhaps the greatest potential insight into the meaning of security in cities remains that associated with the classic question, 'When do I feel safe?' For the nature, shape, functions, and dynamics of functional security are determined by cities being a uniquely human environment, and by most people valuing the safety of their life and/or property. This may be a reason for the West's assumption that police have a role to play, for in the West the police role is oriented to answering two questions: 'How safe am I in the here and now?' and 'How well ordered is my immediate environment?' (Innes 2004). But this is not the case in post-conflict cities.

Multiple perspectives and understandings of security exist in cities. There are marked differences between the security priorities and practices of military forces, international police advisers, indigenous police and the populace, so the key questions become whether or not they may be combined into a coherent and meaningful whole, and whether one is dependent on the other. These questions are addressed in the course of Chapter 4's discussion of policing Basra. Indeed, the policing of Iraq since 2003 is the point of departure for this book. For Iraq raises a number of important questions about public security in post-conflict cities, most of which have theoretical, analytical and policy-relevant implications. These include whether the concerns of the state should be prioritised over those of individuals or of groups based on religious divisions, and individuals over groups or vice versa. Developments in Baghdad and Basra enable us to explore questions concerning security in terms of for whom and from what. But for now it is sufficient to note the main differences between the approaches of international militaries and indigenous police.

Conventional militaries are primarily concerned with protecting their troops, vehicles and installations from attack, whereas police officers focus on their own physical safety. But there are other differences too. For example, many of the operations multinational militaries undertake in the aftermath of conflict (such as humanitarian assistance, peacekeeping and non-combatant evacuation) occur in cities because they are the location of the port facilities and airfields expeditionary forces need, or because the city concerned is strategically significant. This matters little to police. Both military and police are affected by the close and multidimensional nature of the urban environment with its alleys, cellars and rooftops, and by the speed and scale of change associated with operating in and around civilians. This ensures that cities have a magnifying effect on the complexity, rate, scale and range of security operations. But this is usual for police. In contrast, militaries prefer to operate in open countryside. Indeed, operating in cities in the immediate aftermath of conflict is particularly difficult for militaries. It is, for instance, challenging for Western troops to transition from a war-fighting to a policing mode in which the environment becomes less important than the populace, about which they rarely have sufficient intelligence.

Lack of intelligence matters because the objective of most militaries is population identification and control. Troops focus on a city's terrain and density, and are suspicious of non-combatants who may be hiding fighters. In contrast, indigenous police, where they exist, are static and inert, and are most aware of threats to their own safety, ethnic tensions and local power relations. The conventional military view is that cities – and their inhabitants – are to be avoided wherever possible, but cities are the police's workplace and livelihood. Similarly, international militaries must control city infrastructure wherever possible because power-generation plants, water supply systems and police stations have an operational significance not found in other operations. But police stations are significant for indigenous police primarily as fortresses in which to hide, or keep prisoners. Retaining or controlling territory or key points is less important for police.

There is nothing new about this. The problems confronting US soldiers and Iraqi police in Baghdad in 2003 are not dissimilar to those facing French paratroopers and Algerian police in Algiers in 1956, and most conflicts end with looting, revenge attacks and the disappearance of those designated war criminals. What is new is today's debate about who should provide public or city-wide security in the aftermath of international interventions, and the models on which it should be based.

It used to be that occupying troops enforced basic order before handing over to reconstituted national authorities and a purged police. Militaries sometimes retained a degree of oversight, but were more concerned to leave a city than rebuild, restructure or reform its police on 'democratic' lines. This changed in the 1990s when security definitions were broadened, international peacekeeping operations routinely involved UN police, and police reform became a policy goal. The West's understanding shifted again in the aftermath of the US-led invasion of Iraq in 2003. Indeed, the security vacuum that seemingly developed in Iraq will influence the way security in cities is assessed for years to come. For security dominated the calculations of everyone involved. Force protection shaped US military tactics, yet Washington had no taste for the nation-building that might have mitigated insecurity, and operationalised broadened definitions of security. The UN, meanwhile, played no part in managing Iraq once it became a terrorist target (its chief envoy, Sergio Vieira de Mello, was killed in 2003). Five years after the US invasion, international attempts to create an effective military and police had failed, and street-level security was left to sectarian militias. The only certainty in cities such as Baghdad is that security means whatever the strongest actors make of it.

ORDER

Order, like security, is a fetishised concept (Neocleous 2000: xii). Both are open-ended and multi-layered concepts that are difficult to handle, though order, unlike security, is currently unfashionable: there is no critical order studies. Hobbes was in no doubt as to the significance of order; without it, he argued, 'there is no place for industry, because the fruit thereof is uncertain; and consequently no nurture of the earth; no navigation, nor use of the commodities that may be imported by sea; no commodious buildings ...; no knowledge ... no arts; no letters ... and what is worse of all, continual fear, and danger of violent death' (Hobbes 1962: 368). Yet order is neglected by post-structural studies, and analyses of power fail to reference it (e.g. Hansen 2006; Goverde et al. 2000). In the 1960s, the institutionalisation of order was seen as a critical defence against mobilisation (Huntingdon 1968), but the legitimation of intervention by international forces during the 1990s shifted attention towards humanitarian claims and away from order with its connotations of conventional political and social arrangements. Indeed, rather than treat the analysis of order as a relatively neutral evaluation of existing patterns, many exponents of critical security studies treat it as a specifically political move aimed at the defence of the (coercive) state (Booth 2005). The Bush administration's strategy of regime change in Afghanistan and Iraq briefly rebalanced the emphasis (the removal of the repressive order associated with the Taliban and Saddam Hussein was initially welcomed), but Washington's inaccurate assumptions, reinforced by threats from international terrorists, ensured that attention soon swung back to security. The notion of order is rarely invoked.

Colloquially, order implies a degree of predictability, regularity and stability to social and political relationships, institutions and behaviours. Ideally, it refers to arrangements that ensure that each element in a political whole is arranged in equilibrium according to a known scheme, and that each has a proper function. But it is misleading to say that order refers primarily to the 'requirement to lay in place a basis for preventing renewed conflict and to reduce/minimise the role of armed violence in a society' (Siegel 2000: 36). Rather, order requires the existence of an agreed set of rules; order refers to orderly and predictable procedures, which may be repressive or democratic. In other words, disorder results from the absence of agreed rules, rather than from institutional collapse or insecurity per se.

The part played by order in the post-conflict phase varies according to cultural context, personalities and time scale. Order was not a priority for Mohammed Aideed in Somalia or Charles Taylor in Liberia, but it is for Western forces, especially when there are significant levels of destruction or distress, no internationally recognised government exists, and an exit strategy is required. Tenacious forms of alternative order may also exist. For example, the gangs involved in Nicaragua's slum wars enforce a predatory version of social order through the imposition of localised regimes of terror based on an ethos that a gang member summarised as 'we give the orders here' (Rodgers 2007). Rodgers describes how gang members are an intimidating presence, displaying their guns and machetes, and verbally threatening residents with violent retribution if they denounce them or those involved in the local drugs trade. The threats are frequently backed up by multiple random acts of terrorising violence.

Localised order is especially common in the aftermath of conflict, yet it does not exist in a vacuum. It forms part of a broader pattern of political response, or (more typically) lack of response, for, despite the presence of localised forms of order, the state remains the primary and most significant security actor. With the exception of a Mogadishu, with its fragmented and centrifugal politics, the existence of recognisable forms of order offering security across the city usually depends on the activities of state-sponsored agents; only they can provide the coordination and levels of social control required. One reason for this is because, as Lee noted in 1969, civil order is essentially the result of a respect for the limitations of violence (Lee 1969: 23). Understood in this sense, order is the result of an agreed set of rules.

What, then, is needed to reach this stage? How should or does it proceed? How does it relates to what happened earlier? Previous experience is particularly significant because post-conflict cities are affected by what has gone before, and the causes and consequences of government collapse are usually relevant to the conditions a city finds itself in. Ineffective transitional governments may rely on coercion to impose order precisely because government institutions are missing, or because there is no longer a belief in the utility or desirability of such institutions (Jackson and James 1993). Further, if Zartman is right to characterise state collapse as a long-term degenerative disease (1995: 8), then it is probable that the populace will have developed alternative forms of order and security; collapse and conflict usually involve the breakdown of social structures as strongmen and political entrepreneurs use private militias, trafficking and violence to enforce their own versions of order. But collapse, like disorder, is difficult to measure. It is not about crime rates and casualties per se, except in so far as these are evidence of the absence of agreed rules. It is not about degrees of personal violence either, because blood feuds may be an accepted way of settling disputes. The emergence of order is similarly problematic.

A further question arises: is the order that emerges in a Basra or Freetown the negation of a previous order, or is it a more complex mix of rejection, destruction, negotiation and adaptation? After all, the desire to enforce specific forms of order commonly prompts, drives and shapes wars and their aftermath. Freetown is a case in point. In the mid 1990s, both the Armed Forces Revolutionary Council

(AFRC) and the Revolutionary United Front (RUF) claimed they were fighting to change the existing order (that is, forms and structures of government), which had not only institutionalised corrupt governance, but also embedded corruption throughout society, and concentrated power in Freetown. Ironically, Richards argues that Sierra Leone's war was a crisis of modernity fought by teenagers whose aspirations were for schools and jobs (Richards 1996: xx, 103.; cf. Keen 2005); that is, for a specific form of order (compare Hoffman 2007b).

Order may be negation when the belligerent enforcing regime change caused the conflict, but it is more commonly a nuanced mix. This suggests that the dynamics of post-conflict cities are better understood in terms of power relations than as a matter of security. The reason is that security and power, like order, cannot be treated as a substantive entity, institution, possession or capability separate from the relationship in which they are exercised. From this it follows that the purpose and objectives of order vary according to context. Political actors use it as a goal for a multitude of overlapping and sometimes contradictory purposes, but it rarely if ever emerges as an unexpected by-product. Indeed, it usually requires that various functional elements be coordinated. For this reason it is arguable that order shares a unique feature with security (and policing), which is that both it and the problem it seeks to address (disorder and insecurity) are socially constructed (Loader and Walker 2007: 186).

To summarise, order concerns behaviour and consequences that display predictability in the rules that govern them. The resultant interactions are predictable partly because the actors concerned have tacit knowledge of the rules regulating behaviour and its consequences in their cities, and partly because the existing distribution of power lends predictability to their actions; they and their audience act in the light of their knowledge.[6] This suggests that order, like security, is ultimately about relations of power and the patterns they form. Neither is absolute or static. Both are shaped by contingencies, and derive their meaning from relational contexts. The need in this book, therefore, is to identify what commonly obstructs order, what facilitates it, which actors are most important, and where the critical points of interface between order and security are.

POWER

This chapter focuses on order and security, but of all the concepts introduced here, power is arguably the most fundamental in the post-conflict city: it underpins, and is expressed through, order and security. At its most basic it refers to the ability to influence others in some way, and to bring about significant change by real or potential action. Weber's definition encapsulates this understanding: 'By power is meant that opportunity existing within a social [relationship] which permits one to carry out one's own will even against resistance and regardless of the basis on which this opportunity rests' (Weber 1962).

Power in the post-conflict city exists at a number of levels. These may be vertical or horizontal, but all are ultimately based on coercive (usually military or paramilitary) capabilities, though referring also to non-military elements such as religious authority. Power is about resources, rather than rules, and it is primarily an empirical matter. It is about capacity, or the ability to carry out one's will in a social relationship (Goverde et al. 2000: 17–22; 41–2). It is about the socially structured and culturally patterned behaviour of groups, and – this is key – it is always a relational phenomenon (Goverde and Tatenhove 2000: 106–7). Thus power, like security, is always located somewhere and never exists in isolation: 'Power refers to the capacity of agents, agencies or institutions to maintain or transform their environment, social or physical; and it concerns the resources which underpin this capacity and the forces that shape and influence its exercise (Held 1995: 170).

This suggests that unless one party to the conflict has won an outright victory, or gains independence, the re-emergence of order depends on power sharing, and on agreement on basic rules. In other words, order, like security, is a matter of power relations. It involves negotiation, bargaining and concessions between warlords, factional leaders, international militaries and officials, and neighbouring leaders or governments, each of which pursues its own agenda.

POWER RELATIONS

Power, security and order emerge from, and are reproduced in, inter-action, and the power that accrues to certain individuals or groups is exercised, accumulated, invested, traded or lost.

The notion of power relations encapsulates this by referring to the horizontal and vertical patterns of negotiation and imposition existing between individuals and groups. It alludes to the intent and ability to manage conduct, identity and territory. The resultant relationships are interconnected and always have a purpose.

This dynamic is especially marked in cities because urbanisation implies social relationships. It also implies that the most effective actors have tacit knowledge of the rules governing life in the city, and of the relational and structural phenomena underpinning it. This was evident in Falluja, a city of some 284,000 in Iraq's so-called Sunni triangle, when in 2004 American forces attempted to use their military power to punish the city and shape its political environment, even though historical experience suggests that military capabilities have only a limited capacity to mould the conduct and self-awareness of a populace. For power in a city such as Falluja concerns the ability to influence and protect, as well as to coerce, constrain, punish, destroy, or intimidate (Hills 2006). This cannot be understood in isolation from the networks of social structures underpinning relationships (Findley and Edwards 2007).

Falluja, like most post-conflict cities, shows that power cannot be treated as a discrete entity or possession, least of all in a political war in which the objective is control. It emphasises that power is often a matter of leverage and relationships, as when Falluja's civic leaders were expected to exercise some influence or control over the insurgents. Paradoxically this is something that Falluja's insurgents were seemingly more aware of than the US forces that sought to control them. They evidently understood that hierarchical structures of domination in and of a city depend on, and operate through, local low-level capillary circuits of power relationships. Certainly the radical Islamists elsewhere in Iraq were successful at using alternative or soft forms of power – witness the political-social welfare networks organised through Shi'ite mosques in the poorer areas of Baghdad and Najaf.

A number of issues arise from this interpretation. It is necessary to identify the formal and informal actors who are most influential in promoting order and security, and to ascertain their knowledge, resources and capabilities. It is also necessary to know how they understand order and security, how they measure success (no one doubts the meaning of failure), and how they relate to one another. Additionally, localised forms of order and (in)security must be related within the broader context of the city.

STABILITY

Power underpins order, but stability expresses its desirability. Like 'order', the term 'stability' is academically unfashionable, yet it is regarded as important in policy circles. The UK's Department for International Development (DFID) states that without it 'development cannot progress', while the Dutch Clingendael Institute's Stability Assessment Framework asserts that stability is 'a very important link exists between peace, security, and development' (DFID 2005a: 6; Clingendael Institute 2005: preface). Such statements imply that stability refers to an environment in which factional militia and violent gangs are subordinated to legitimate government authorities before being reintegrated into society.

This may be the long-term goal of many donors, but the essentials of stability have more to do with predictability and are better conveyed by the American Cold War analyst Herman Khan. He defined stability as a situation when 'stresses or shocks do not tend to produce large, irreversible changes. This does not mean the system does not react when subjected to stress or shock. ... Stability means that the reaction is one of a limited, and perhaps predictable nature and that the changes are not reversible or lead to a new balance not essentially different from the original' (Khan 1965: 38). Manwaring and Corr's state-oriented stability equation supplement Khan's approach. They argue that three elements are necessary for long-term stability (S) in conflict-prone environments: a military/police capability (M) to provide acceptable levels of security; an economic ability to generate socioeconomic development (E); and the political competence (PC) necessary for developing a type of governance to which people can relate and support. This is expressed as $S = (M + E) \times PC$. The critical variable is PC (Manwaring and Corr 1996: 40).

Khan's emphasis on predictability and adjustment implies that the re-emergence of order is *not* the fundamental problem in contemporary cities: order always emerges in one form or another. Rather, it is the ways in which order is managed. For cities are places 'occupied and used by many actors' (Marcuse and van Kempen 2000: 265), many of whom do not value stability.

SECURITY AND ORDER

Mapping the links between security and order is difficult. It is usual to claim that without security there can be no order – someone must stop looting or riots, and separate belligerents. Until this happens, it is said, progress towards security or stability is difficult: 'A return to any sense of normalcy and/or order depends on the provision of security. Refugees and internally displaced persons will wait until they feel safe to go home; former combatants will wait until they feel safe to lay down their arms ...; farmers and merchants will wait until they feel that fields, roads and markets are safe before engaging in food production and business activity' (Stromseth et al. 2006: 142). It is difficult to disagree. However, security (unlike order) is rarely city-wide, so the debate may merely reflect the difficulty of deciding whether security is a common or a selective project. Much depends on time frames. On the one hand, security can be enjoyed by a few in isolation in the short term, even if this creates the conditions for insecurity in the long term. On the other hand, most strongmen do not think in the long term. In reality, common security projects, or projects that can be extended to all inhabitants, are rare.

The question then arises as to how this relates to order's re-emergence, the foundations of which are laid in the days after conflict ends. For, as this book will show, just as violence seems to be integral to state building (Tilly 1985: 170; Broadhurst 2002) so insecurity is probably linked to the re-emergence of order. In the long term, security and order can be meaningfully defined only in terms of the system of political competition that has grown up inside the city or country concerned (Lee 1969: 9). But in the short term, strongmen and sectarian militias fight in order to gain access to city (that is, state) resources, and consciously attempt to shape the conduct of individuals, groups and the population in furtherance of specific objectives. Further, security is usually seen as symbolising political objectives.

Most discussions of security focus on the concerns associated with either state security or individual security even though the web of linkages and dependencies between the two often makes it difficult to meaningfully distinguish between them. Yet the provision of security has never been a state monopoly; there has always been a pluralised field of delivery, and the delivery of security – whatever the term is taken to mean – usually takes place through the practices of states, factional interests, locally based groups, non-governmental actors and commercial interests. Negotiations between the various groups will be significant.

Formal security arrangements are rare in the immediate aftermath of conflict, but this is the period in which power relations are adjusted and developed. There may be several central formal points of power, of assured security, but it is more probable that both will flow from a bond or link between connected (but not necessarily coordinated) agents. The goal for international organisations then becomes one of identifying who can offer or provide effective security, on what issues, under what conditions, and with what effects. Only then can the re-emergence of security be planned and order mapped. (It may also throw light on the ways in which the referent object of security is determined, and on the processes by which security is represented.) In practice, however, the conclusion is a foregone matter: security will be provided by conventional military forces, international and/or local, who will hand over to public police (indigenous though usually mentored or trained by international officers) as soon as it is functionally or politically appropriate to do so. This conviction drives both theoretical and empirical analyses.

RELEVANT LITERATURE AND PROGRAMMES

A body of literature now exists on the actual and potential role played by police in post-conflict environments. Prompted initially by the need to reform South Africa's post-apartheid police, and the USA's concerns regarding repressive policing in Latin America, but driven primarily by the USA's and EU's desire to restructure and reform police in the aftermath of the Balkans wars in the early 1990s, innumerable academics and policy analysts examined and promoted police reform (Brogden and Shearing 1993; Holme and Eide 2000; Peake 2004; Perito 2003; Ziegler and Neild 2003).

Most of these publications were written in response to, or were prompted by, the policy requirements and liberal concerns of the day. Further, most of the research on what became known as 'security sector reform' (SSR) focused on the military (particularly those in the former Warsaw Pact); the police (who were invariably seen as inferior in every way) were neglected. This changed at the end of the 1990s, at which point police reform became a cottage industry. Some of the resultant work is insightful (e.g. Edmunds 2007; Rauch and van der Spuy 2006), but much is normatively driven, self-consciously 'critical', or, more commonly, uncritical. Too many commentators assume the value of 'democratic policing' to be self-evident; too many assume that what applies to the military also applies to police; and far too many repeat the unsubstantiated assertions and jargon of donor orthodoxy. This situation prompts a second concern, which is that insufficient attention is paid to the body of literature produced by scholars (mainly American) working on comparative policing.

The 1990s also saw researchers from architecture, criminology and geography considering the intersecting problems of cities and security governance. But most of those addressing police reform worked within the confines of their own subfield. This was understandable in that conflict, police and urban studies belong to distinct research and policy traditions; they are organised by different sets of scholars and professionals using different jargon. As a result, articles on the role of UN civilian police in Haiti or executive policing in Kosovo ignored the work of Chan or Marks on police culture (Dwan 2002; Chan 1997; Marks 2000). Even now too many articles and reports offer remarkably positive assessments of what has been achieved, or they consist of lists of what must be done. Insufficient attention is paid to relevant studies on other forms of policing in extreme circumstances such as colonial policing, occupation policies during the 1940s, and counterinsurgency and counterterrorism operations in the 1960s (Donnison 1966; Kitson 1971; Sinclair 2006). At the same time, however, there has been a wealth of studies covering aspects of reconstruction from the perspective of architecture, social policy, urban policy and political geography (Barakat 2005; Graham 2004). And increasingly urban areas are seen as important for military-based policing operations (Hills 2002), and for policing and the politics of reform (Hinton 2006). Even so, most commentators on police reform neglect to distinguish between the policing challenges of urban as opposed to rural areas, or West Africa rather than the Balkans.

Little has changed since the late 1990s. The failure of US-led programmes to create a reformed Iraqi police has not resulted in publications furthering our knowledge of the relationship between police and the state, or between state and locally based policing. There are now a range of programmes addressing order, reconstruction, conflict resolution and reconstruction in universities such as Bonn and Duisberg-Essen, and Yale, and postgraduate programmes on conflict, security and development are increasingly popular in English-speaking universities. Yet publications addressing the relationship between policing, internal security and the Ministry of the Interior in Iraq, for example, are invariably driven by government requirements, rather than any desire to understand the dynamics of police change, or the relationship between police and the state (e.g. Jones et al. 2005). Meanwhile critical security studies continue to focus on issues such as human security and 'gender'.

This is not to suggest that policy publications are analytically flawed, and it is not to deny the existence of informative and thought-provoking articles, many of which acknowledge that the police are an important resource on which societies can draw. But there is remarkably little investigation of the role of the police in the reproduction of state order or urban development.[7] Crucially, what is missing is analysis showing how the discrete process of policing relates to the broader environment of which it is part.

Ironically, this is where potential research projects (and funding) probably lie. For the topic is directly relevant to the cross-cutting question of whether there is, or is not, a conceptual link or causal connection between insecurity, state failure and poverty. Anecdotal evidence suggests there is, and governmental institutions such DFID and the United Nations Office on Drugs and Crime (UNODC) assume it to be the case. So does the now substantial literature on violence and repressive policing in the Americas. As Koonings and Kruijt say of Latin American cities, 'persistent social exclusion, linked to alternative extra-legal sources of income and power, combined with an absent or failing state in particular territorial/social settings, will provide means and motives for violent actions' (Koonings and Kruijt 2007: 13). However, the topic has yet to receive the systematic comparative analysis it deserves. It remains unclear whether we should generalise from a Medellín to a Grozny or Monrovia.

METHODOLOGY

I use case studies to explore such issues because real-world issues can enhance our theoretical understanding of why things happen as they do (Jentleson 2002: 8). Additionally, it enables me to use a variety of sources, and this matters for my argument for two main reasons. First, hard and/or open source evidence is often difficult to find, so secondary news reports and personal accounts are important, if partial, sources of information. Consequently, my analysis relies on UK broadsheets, local newspapers (many of which are in English and available on the Internet), news publications and specialist reports from advocacy groups, supplemented by accounts from former officials and journalists. This is not ideal, but it offers insights into social dynamics and individual behaviour. Second, although I have discussed policing post-conflict cities with an internationally representative range of senior and mid-ranking police and military (in the UK and at international venues) for some years, I have not directly observed it. Being able to compare a range of material is therefore important, and case studies offer a way to do this systematically. My judgement of what is or is not plausible is further informed by insights gained from the literature on urban operations since 1945, and on public police and policing more generally. Inevitably, my choice of case studies reflects my research bias, but each example has been influential, and together they suggest the complex social phenomena that is policing in the post-conflict city. This approach has the added advantage of placing Western orthodoxy on democratic-style policing in perspective.

The question of order is addressed here primarily in terms of indigenous police, and the answers offered are based on functional developments. Nevertheless, I use 'policing' and 'security' as more than simply descriptive terms: they represent a broad analytical (and functional) approach to addressing significant contemporary questions. My approach has an explanatory, rather than normative focus, and my analysis builds on current trends and immediate expectations, rather than on what should be possible.

CASE STUDIES AND RESEARCH QUESTIONS

Given the book's focus on the re-emergence of order, and its cross-cutting themes of security, police and policing, it is important to consider developments in a range of cities. Post-conflict cities typically share a number of common traits, but, given that policing reflects its host society, it makes sense to look at specific examples. The best way to do this is to use exemplars or case studies, supplemented by case instances. Only then can we see how actors and agencies understand the predicament of post-conflict cities, and how and why they invent strategies that allow them to manage (or evade) the problems associated with disorder and insecurity. Analysing the problem in this way emphasises the recurring dynamics typical of the field, and makes it easier to identify some of the broad principles that structure the ways in which people think and act. Also, it avoids forced comparisons between dissimilar examples.

The cases are (in alphabetical order) Basra, Baghdad, Freetown, Grozny, Juba, Kabul, Kaduna, Kigali, Kinshasa, Mogadishu, Monrovia and Sarajevo. Inevitably, many significant cases (Beirut, for example, and Dili) are omitted, while others (such as Kano and Mostar) provide case instances, rather than studies as such. There is a strong emphasis on Africa, and Africa's experience is not universally applicable, but I think it justified: my selection covers the main trends in – and tensions between – liberal and non-liberal approaches to policing. Also, state failure is a primarily African phenomenon (Englebert and Tull 2008), and more than 40 per cent of the UN police deployed in peace missions in mid-2007 were in Africa. Of course, policing is socially specific. Nevertheless, a degree of generalisation is appropriate. Looting, for example, is discussed here mainly in relation to Baghdad, but it is relevant in many other cities too, and secondary illustrations of it in, say, Monrovia enrich the picture. Similarly, cross-cutting themes such as the role of youths occur in my account of Baghdad, and are further illustrated by reference to Freetown and Gaza City.[8]

In each case, the central process under discussion is that of policing, while the larger process is that of transitional cities in the aftermath of conflict. The 'units' of analysis are cities, police, and policing operations. This means that while the role of individual police (the micro level of policing) is addressed, and the internal reforms imposed on the police as an institution (the meso level) are noted, the focus is on the redistribution of power and its broad implications (the macro level). However, boundaries between the three levels and the phases they represent cannot be sharply delineated. They may be clear in Bosnia, but they are less so in Baghdad or Kabul, where levels of insecurity fluctuate and a spider's web of political alliances connects the three (Wisler 2007).

The primary research questions for each case are:

- What does order mean?
- When is order visible, and what variables affected its emergence?
- What determines its policing?
- What is the relationship between order and security?

Supplemental questions include:

- Did the presence of international actors affect the outcome?
- Is the police's primary function to manage the accommodation and socialisation (between winners and losers) required for order?
- What is involved in policing? How does it relate to what happened earlier? How does it proceed? Is it the negation of previous order, or a mix of rejection, destruction and adaptation?

Five premisses underpin these questions:

- Policing is a symbolic activity offering insight into the emergence of order, and the causal regularities underlying the development of state and social structures.
- The state retains a role in post-conflict cities.
- The presence or absence of police as a specific organisation is critical to the ability of state authorities to undertake specific tasks.
- Order and security are based on relations of domination and coercion, rather than shared norms.
- The various elements underpinning policing in post-conflict cities modify each other through feedback relationships, and a change in one can set in motion a cascade of reflexive changes.

2

CONTROLLING CITIES

This chapter identifies the main features of the post-conflict city, the factors that alleviate or intensify insecurity, and the indicators marking the re-emergence of order. For – and this is its foundational hypothesis – order re-emerges, rather than emerges. This is not just semantics, for order is dependent on what went before. It is the reconfigured complex of interlocking structures, processes and relationships composed of pre-existing elements and habits, only some of which will be revised and reoriented by new pressures and new or modified contexts. My purpose here is to note the broad patterns and signs of this, and assess the effect of continuities in relation to policing. Contrary to Donald Rumsfeld's notorious statement, 'stuff' rarely 'just happens'.

POST-CONFLICT CITIES

War undermines or destroys the political and physical order and social networks through which cities function. Urban life is the result of a complex web of social forces, institutional settings and interpersonal relationships, which conflict suspends, fragments or destroys. Chronic violence, factional issues and informers further undermine personal and associational ties, and scale is condensed down to the clan, family, individual, street or building (Hills 2003).

to Kinshasa, where a very different form of order operates beneath state-sponsored forms.

Chapter 7 supplements these accounts of the re-emergence of order with four instances where alternative forms of order and policing parallel statist organisations, thereby emphasising the significance of continuity, rather than change. First, the accommodation required of an established Southern police is discussed by reference to policing in the Nigerian cities of Kano and Kaduna in the aftermath of sectarian conflict. Second, the small Sudanese capital of Juba is used to illustrate the adaptive stages policing typically experiences during the creation of a new order after civil war. Third, and in sharp contrast to the previous examples, developments in the industrialised Caucasian city of Grozny illustrates what can happen when non-negotiable forms of order are imposed, only to be accommodated according to established rules. This adds another dimension to the debate. Lastly, Chapter 8 provides an overview of findings, trends and unresolved issues before concluding that order results where there is agreement about the rules governing the city concerned, irrespective of the precise state of security obtaining.

the fourth theme, policing, forms the central cross-cutting process, and is discussed as such in Chapter 2.

Chapter 3 focuses on the liberal orthodoxy that drives today's interest in reconstruction, shapes contemporary assessment and understanding, and is expressed in donor projects. Such projects promote a fundamental reconstruction of order and policing based on a culturally specific interpretation of order and change. Most offer an ideologically based explanation of the putative conceptual and policy-relevant linkages between order, security and development while failing to acknowledge the power relations that lie at their heart. This matters because, as the case studies in Chapters 4–7 show, order re-emerges through processes of adaptation and accommodation. In other words, order and security represent a process of negotiation, adjustment and assertion as much as an outcome, and Western notions such as the rule of law are merely one of many possibilities.

This is evident in Chapter 4's account of the tensions between international and indigenous power projects in the Iraqi cities of Baghdad and Basra since 2003. However, liberal orthodoxy cannot be understood in the light of Iraq alone, so Chapter 5 compares five counterbalancing examples, which emphasise the extent to which the West underestimates the role of social continuities in the production of order. The relatively successful (and very influential) experience of international operations in the Bosnian city of Sarajevo are compared and contrasted with projects in the Bosnian town of Mostar, and with attempts at police reform in the Afghan cities of Kabul and Kandahar. The significance of continuity is then highlighted by reference to the state-dominated order of Kigali in the aftermath of the Rwandan genocide.

The limitations of current orthodoxy are, however, most evident in cities where Western notions of order and state capacity have little resonance. Chapter 6 considers four situations where powerful factions make their own rules. The implications of an extreme case – Mogadishu – are discussed first. Typical tensions are then explored by reference to Monrovia, which illustrates the strains that exist between state and non-state, international and indigenous understandings of policing. Lastly, alternative possibilities are noted by reference

OVERVIEW

What follows is a discussion of the ways in which order re-emerges in major cities. It shows that causal relationships are more ambiguous than liberal orthodoxy suggests, and order and security cannot be stage managed in terms of cause and effect; order frames security and gives it meaning, but also security frames order and gives it meaning. Security is for this reason identified as the dependent variable; it is a necessary (though not essential) precondition for order, and policing is its functional means. The reason is simple: insecurity may be instrumentalised, but when there is no order there is no security and little policing. Conversely, while it may be necessary for troops to enforce security, and factional militias to provide policing, some form of police is usually seen as the appropriate way to maintain order. And police are usually regarded as having primary responsibility for social order once acceptable levels of stability are reached. There are few exceptions to this general rule.

My point of departure is today's debate about regime change and state reconstruction, and my purpose is to trace the rationalities, commonalities and discrepancies shaping the emergence of order. But *Policing Post-Conflict Cities* is neither a history of the present nor genealogical. It does not give an account of the administration of war-torn territories or an assessment of donor programmes, and it does not explicitly address policing in relation to the US-led war on terror. The post-2001 debate has been influential on Western attitudes to police reform and police assistance, but its relevance elsewhere is less clear. Similarly, although I link phenomena from the new security agenda to more conventional security issues – only then can security remain a meaningful concept – I doubt whether it is possible to develop a single coherent concept of security covering every aspect of urban life. In other words, my analysis builds on current trends and immediate expectations, rather than on utopian goals of what is, or should be, possible.

Based on the premise that the constituent elements of order are most visible in post-conflict environments, each chapter presents a set of related thematic and/or analytical issues, which are explored by reference to specific cities. This chapter has introduced the core explanatory themes of urbanisation, security, order and power, while

It could not be otherwise in a city such as Grozny, where in 1996 approximately 10,000–40,000 of the pre-war population of 490,000 hid in damp cellars with little heat or food. Two years later Grozny was still deadlocked in an attritional war, and most inhabitants found themselves trapped between Russian brutality and retribution by rebels if they collaborated with Moscow's attempts at restoration. Or take the case of Sarajevo, the site of a four-year siege in which the buildings associated with the pre-war order were deliberately destroyed by systematic bombardment (Coward 2004). In both cases, the pre-war order was targeted. Whether it was destroyed is another matter. Subsequent developments suggest that it was not.

Categorising the period that follows the end of such conflicts is to some extent arbitrary. War may be the opposite of peace, but the dividing line between the two is difficult to determine, especially at the margins. Ceasefires may not be kept, and military victory does not necessarily mean the end of conflict. Baghdad, for example, experienced more insecurity in the years following President Bush's May 2003 announcement that war-fighting had ended than it did during the war itself; 3,700 coalition soldiers and tens of thousands of Iraqis died in the four years after Saddam's fall.[1]

Precise and accurate categorisation may be best left to historians, but definitions matter for operational, legal and political purposes, and there have been many attempts to define post-conflict by analysts seeking to develop a framework for stabilisation operations. Some incorporate negative features (such as the absence of physical or direct personal violence) and some positive aspects (such as the absence of structural or indirect violence), but the term is as elastic as conflict prevention (Galtung 1969). Most conflicts do not end in a straightforward or identifiable manner, with a clear victor, and even when they do the ensuing changes may result in the emergence of violence that feeds on existing or latent grievances. Conflicts may be temporarily frozen, only to resume later, or they may drift into other manifestations. Insecurity may even become more extreme after the end of conventional conflict.

Freetown illustrates all these issues. It was repeatedly occupied in the 1990s despite the existence of peace accords and agreements. Early 1998 saw a Nigerian-led West African intervention force,

ECOMOG, drive Foday Sankoh's RUF rebels away, and President Kabbah return. Less than a year later rebels backing Sankoh retook parts of Freetown from ECOMOG, burning neighbourhoods to the ground, and mutilating, raping and killing some 5,000 inhabitants. The rebels were subsequently driven out, and UN troops arrived to police a peace agreement, but the ceasefire soon failed, and it was not until November 2000 that government forces backed by British forces decisively defeated the rebels as they again closed in on Freetown. There was no sign of sustainable political order before then; the rebels failed to develop a credible political agenda, while the government was notorious for mismanagement and corruption. It was not until after the elections of 2002 that Kabbah – by then firmly located in Freetown – was able to tell a jubilant crowd, 'War don don' (IRIN 2002).

By post-conflict I mean here the period following a ceasefire agreement, a military victory, or a rout, which is usually accompanied by a lessening of the incidence and intensity of military operations, killings and overt destruction. The time periods I use are three months for the immediate aftermath, up to two years for the short term, and three to five years for the medium term. Beyond that (up to ten years) is long-term.

INFLUENTIAL FEATURES

Just as it is difficult to define post-conflict, so there is no typical post-conflict city on which to base discussion, for size, geopolitical and cultural context, temporal span and place make a difference, as do the type of conflict and its manner of ending. But although there is no typical post-conflict city, there are some general factors affecting the situation, of which the most influential are the nature of the conflict and the way it ends.

Most of today's conflicts are civil wars occurring in fragile or failed states where governance capacity is low, irregular forces play a significant role, and there are no clear distinctions between combatants and non-combatants. Civilians are targeted and conflict is protracted because none of the belligerents has the desire – or capacity – to win a decisive victory, let alone govern. Conflict may be terminated, but it is more common for it to be frozen or contested.

None of this is new. Indeed, it is easy to overstate the differences between the wars of the post-Cold War era and their predecessors. Intrastate conflict is nowadays more common than interstate war, and today's 'new' wars often appear to be criminal, rather than political, phenomena (Kaldor 1999). Yet few wars are driven by criminal imperatives, for criminals are interested in personal profit, rather than identity or territorial aggrandisement. Also, conflict has always represented a business opportunity for criminals, as the activities of the Dagmoush clan of northern Gaza illustrate. It kidnapped a BBC journalist in June 2007 just as war broke out between Palestine's two main factions, Hamas and Fatah, and demanded a ransom of £1.25 million, land in a former Israeli settlement, and the release of al-Qaeda militants imprisoned in the UK and Jordan. But the Dagmoush had long been involved in crime and smuggling, and had accrued power by selling themselves as guns for hire to rival factions. By 2007 they were rich, owned prime property in Gaza City, and were well placed to profit from (rather than drive) insecurity (*Sunday Times* 24 June 2007).

The type and temporal and physical scale of conflict shape the environment and conditions of the populace. Wars do not necessarily usher in dramatic change, though physical destruction often compounds social and cultural dislocation, and civil wars are particularly destructive of established forms of order, its representatives and its physical constructs. Punitive internal policing operations can be equally so. Thus the destruction of Grozny in 1994 combined with the nature of the Chechen conflict to ensure that the post-war order was brutal. Moscow sought to crush opposition to its chosen order even as Chechen nationalists promoted a separatist alternative, and the warlords and gang leaders who profited from the criminalisation of the city's economy sponsored insecurity.

Ten years of war are more likely to result in a generation of uneducated and alienated youths than are a series of intense but short-lived clashes. Lengthy war also results in demographic imbalance; males of fighting age are usually the first to leave or die, leaving a population of the old, infirm, women and small children. More generally, years of violence and crumbling public infrastructure may make a city dangerously fragile or resilient. The effects may be illustrated by cities in Germany in 1945 and Croatia in 1991, which recovered from rubblisation remarkably quickly.

When the Allies crossed the Rhine into Germany in March 1945, after five years of total war, their immediate priorities were security, displaced persons (DPs) and public health (Donnison 1961; Margry 1999: 15). Hanover, for example, was three-quarters destroyed; half a million people inhabited its ruins, lice and scabies were common, and there were fears of typhus, for the water supply was, when functioning, heavily contaminated with sewage. 'It was a town of looting, drunkenness, rape and murder as forced labour took its revenge' (Moseley 1945). Compare this scale with that of the small Croatian town of Vukovar, which was destroyed by Serb forces in 1991. The town centre had been subject to sporadic bombardment from August onwards, by which time only 15,000 of the original 50,000 population remained (Silber and Little 1995: 194f; Udovičkii and Ridegway 1997: 142–3). Bombardment and two weeks of hand-to-hand fighting meant that hundreds of bodies remained uncollected in the last days of the siege. The town was then levelled, house by house. Significantly, both cities were rebuilt remarkably quickly.

DOMINANT CHARACTERISTICS

Such cities are insecure places in which to live or operate. Indeed, this is probably their dominant characteristic. Just as Hanover and Vukovar experienced revenge attacks, looting and violent crime, so a referendum for independence in East Timor in 1999 resulted in militias killing more than 1,000, and looting and destroying nearly 70 per cent of Dili. The destruction of the Panamanian Defence Force during the 1989 US invasion triggered similar waves of disorder and looting.[2]

The experience (or fear) of violence destroys not only the physical security of individuals, but also the social networks on which they might otherwise depend, leaving areas in something approximating to a temporary limbo as factional leaders jockey for position and resources, and peacekeepers gain or lose credibility. This affects not only people's perceptions of what is permissible, but also the infrastructure that could have acted as indicators of order; police stations and power plants are meaningless if they are unprotected or empty of officers and cabling. The effects are intensified by the volatility and unpredictability of urban disorder, which is magnified by population density. Most riots are large-scale and organised (Stanton 1996), but even small incidents can see threatened security forces reverting to heavy-handed tactics that intensify insecurity. Hundreds may storm food stations.

This is not to suggest that cities present a uniformly negative picture, for their resilience is often remarkable. The numbness or optimism felt by the populace quickly wears off, and markets and stalls re-emerge because people have to trade to eat. Stallholders in Mogadishu's Bakara market traded regardless of gun battles, fires and looters, and Baghdad's markets reappeared within weeks. Markets are in this way an indicator of localised, albeit temporary, order. Even so, cities are dangerous places. The effects of looting are addressed in more detail in Chapter 4, but insecurity is often exacerbated by the presence of displaced persons and ex-fighters, and by a sharp increase in criminality.

First, cities contain DPs, who squat in empty buildings or occupy public spaces, for conflict in the countryside prompts DPs to migrate to big cities, which may, perversely, be more secure than small towns. DPs may loot. Those in Osnabrook in 1945 did, and security was restored only when a military government detachment forcibly imposed a 24-hour curfew on the entire population.

Second, the end of conflict often leaves former fighters bored, alienated and unemployed. In Liberia, most were males between 16 and 35 years old. They had become combatants because they were forced to, or because they chose to for food or from adventurism (Ellis 1999: 127). In Sierra Leone, the existence of some 72,000 ex-fighters from civil defence groups (former pro-government militias), the army and RUF threatened the new order, for it was never clear whether they would regroup, become ordinary criminals or join the Liberian conflict.

Third, increased criminality has long been associated with post-conflict cities, especially where physical destruction or decisive defeat results in the removal of traditional forms of social control. Berlin and Vienna were as notorious in the 1940s as Mogadishu and Belgrade in the 1990s. Crime is thought to increase as a result of the legacy of wartime want and opportunism, and is often associated with specific groups. Small arms are available, factions stake claims, there are scores to settle, rumour is rife, and it does not take long for kidnapping for ransom or the payment of debts, sexual violence, and armed robbery to become common. Looting and arson are typically accompanied by opportunists moving into property belonging to the weak or members of a vanquished group, and by organised crime exploiting the unregulated environment. Indeed, low-level criminality may for some people be a better choice than ineffective peacekeepers, an externally imposed government with weak, flawed or illegitimate institutions, or an environment lacking economic opportunity, social justice and basic forms of public safety.

Also, distinctions between political and criminal agendas usually blur. For there are close and long-established links between organised crime and political leaders in many cities, and criminal resources can be quickly diverted and used to fund political action or provoke conflict. The interpenetration of crime and politics in Priština and Belgrade was notorious, and quickly undermined programmes aimed at transition or conflict prevention in the aftermath of 1999's Kosovo conflict. It prompted Paddy Ashdown's comment that 'BiH is not a dangerous country. The streets of Sarajevo are safer than the streets of London. But it is a country in the grip of corruption and organised crime' (Celador 2005: 365).

Dealing with crime is not easy. International militaries are untrained, though troops are often involved because they are present, and because police are rarely visible. When Cologne, which had a pre-war police force of 2,700, was occupied by American troops in March 1945, 'not a single policeman was found' (Donnison 1966: 279). This meant that the Allies' first task was either to recruit and train a new force, or to reassemble the old. Fifty years later, the Somali police disappeared from the streets of Mogadishu, just as Baghdad's did, leaving international troops to fill the gap.

Whether this matters is a moot point. On the one hand, the absence of police signals that the inhabitants have been abandoned by the state. On the other hand, police brutality is a prompt for many conflicts. Also, cities traditionally represent the hard edge of policing; their police are aggressive and confrontational (McConville and Shepherd 1992: 230). However, cities in the South are not critical sites of policing in the sense they are in Western democracies. In the USA and UK they are in the vanguard of developments of police powers and policing styles, but this is not the case in, say, Monrovia. Also, police are selectively present in Southern cities. They rarely enter slums, which are policed by local groups or vigilantes – and the UN–HABITAT programme estimates the proportion of slum dwellers to be 72 per cent of the urban population in Africa's conflict-prone regions, the majority of whom are young (IRIN 2007b: 4).[3]

In fact, the use of informal justice and localised or sectarian policing mechanisms is common before, during and after conflict. As Debiel has noted in relation to Afghanistan and Somaliland,

> In times of state failure, anarchic conditions hardly prevail for more than a short time, if at all. In general, collapsing state authority is superseded by a multitude of actors (e.g. militia groups, warlords, external military, but also traditional elders, Sharia courts, businessmen, etc.) who take over security and organisational functions. Emerging institutional networks are generally characterised by a hybrid nature, an overlapping of traditional or religious institutions, remainders of state facilities and new social entities that are often based on violence. The spectrum of power and authority relations is redefined; it ranges from arbitrary violence and the pathogenic collapse of social contexts (social anomy) to the re-establishment of reliable security institutions. (Universities of Bonn and Duisberg-Essen 2007)

Such groups enforce their own understanding of criminality and order. This is the case in the West too. Take the case of Belfast in the 1990s, which, although not strictly a post-conflict city in the sense used here, illustrates the use of violence by paramilitaries to discipline their members and manage order. The largest Loyalist paramilitary group, the Ulster Defence Association (UDA) claimed that its goal was the restoration of law, including in the no-go areas of nationalist Belfast; its motto 'Codenta Arma Togae' meant law before violence (Monaghan and McLaughlin 2006). It set up roadblocks, patrolled streets and gathered evidence against petty criminals. Other groups adopted similar policing roles, and most claimed to assist, rather than usurp, the police; that is, to offer a legitimate policing service.

Northern Ireland's paramilitaries recognised two types of crime. Normal crime referred to vandalism, car theft, joyriding, muggings, selling of alcohol to minors, rape, drug dealing and anti-social behaviour such as dumping rubbish, while political crime included anyone believed to be connected to, fraternising with or having sympathy for their enemies. For the Nationalists this included the British state. Significantly, the decision by paramilitaries to assume a policing role was based in part on their own security needs. That this situation existed for several decades suggests that insecurity and violence were instrumentalised.

FUNCTIONAL SECURITY

Functional security is foundational to order. But who typically provides it? When does military-based security shade into public safety? Do cities experience a security vacuum? How does this relate to governance voids? What is normal, and what levels of violence are seen as acceptable or tolerable? One of the problems associated with answering these questions is that gaining an intelligence-led overview of the city is impossible, and the significance of events or trends is not always recognised at the time. Complexity is increased when conflict shifts into a different style of violence, or becomes entangled with structural features – that is, embedded. In Iraq, for example, conventional military operations quickly transitioned into counter-insurgency as insurgents armed with rocket-propelled grenades, hand grenades and rifles fought US and Iraqi forces, and public places became targets for suicide bombers. But this situation was relatively straightforward in comparison with that in Palestine, much of which has been under military occupation since 1967. Palestine illustrates the complex dynamics of local provision, and also the extent to which insecurity can be normal.

In June 2007, Gaza, a city of some 400,000 in the Gaza Strip, became the site of a battle for supremacy between Fatah, a secular nationalist group that had monopolised power since the 1960s, and Hamas, a radical Islamist group that entered electoral politics in 2005. Hamas took Fatah's key strongholds after a week of fighting left more than 100 dead. But security operated at multiple levels: Fatah's police were numerically strong, but its central command and morale were poor, whereas Hamas was better armed and organised. However, the critical variable was Israel's approach.

Gaza also illustrates the ways in which normality and insecurity are intertwined in cities experiencing chronic insecurity. After several weeks' ceasefire, fighting resumed between Fatah and Hamas, leaving several dead. However, Gaza City appeared calm, and shops and markets reopened. Fighting then resumed, with Hamas gunmen gaining control of Fatah's strong points (the Palestinian Authority's security forces held only the police headquarters), and emptying them of weapons, computers and office furniture. There was sporadic gunfire but the next few days were relatively calm; vehicles appeared on the roads, and shops opened. The main (visible) means of control were checkpoints, and the deterrent presence of masked Hamas militants outside the presidential compound.

Hamas said that providing security in the Gaza strip was its priority. A car belonging to Hamas's military wing announced through a loudspeaker that people would be safe if they stayed at home (*Financial Times* 4 June 2007). Hamas also said they would collect weapons from the security forces, and take revenge on Fatah. However, this meant that families of the men concerned would then seek revenge. What is more, despite their victory, Hamas were unable to crush the big family clans (such as the Dagmoush) responsible for much of the racketeering, stolen cars, smuggling, kidnapping and murder that destabilised everyday life.

Elsewhere in the city, the Fatah-affiliated al-Aqsa Martyrs Brigades called for martial law. Government forces seemed to have no role, though by August law and order had improved sufficiently for a policeman in a fluorescent yellow jacket to direct traffic, and cars to stop at red lights (BBC 9 August 2007). In other words, the order imposed by Hamas was fundamentally similar to that which had existed since their electoral success in 2005, and, indeed, for much of the preceding forty years. The conditions experienced by most of Gaza's inhabitants were irrelevant so far as Hamas's leaders were concerned.

POLICING THE AFTERMATH

Policing is increasingly seen as a critical element in post-conflict reconstruction, yet the literature concentrates almost exclusively on the role of multinational militaries or UN peacekeeping operations, and on the need for police reform. The roles and views of indigenous police are ignored. This is not surprising, for comparative policing is a Cinderella subject.[4]

The multinational humanitarian interventions in the late 1990s led scholars and analysts from subfields such as international studies, peace studies, defence studies and international law to address the reform of repressive police in post-conflict countries (Holme and Eide 2000; Oakley et al. 1998; Stromseth et al. 2006). This was notably so in relation to the Balkans. Many of those involved were unfamiliar with the established literature on police and policing, and in any case most research in criminal justice and criminology focuses, as it always has, on the bureaucracy and deployment of Western police in its domestic context. It concentrates on tasks such as patrolling and crime prevention, or it assesses how deployment effects crime rates and public perceptions of security; it explores the impact of environmental design on crime, and it emphasises notions such as community, service and accountability, and the commercial provision of security.

More recently, the failure of US-led efforts to create a national police force in Afghanistan and Iraq increased interest in the use of so-called constabulary (that is, paramilitary) forces and the reform of ministries of the interior (Perito 2003; Rathmell et al. 2005). Such work is driven by US policy concerns, and has not translated into a significant programme of ground-breaking research, though there are now signs of a new interest in international or transnational policing (Goldsmith and Sheptycki 2007). More significantly, policing is increasingly analysed in terms of security governance with its associated ideas of nodes and networks (Wood and Dupont 2006). In other words, policing and police are undergoing redefinition, and there is increasing debate regarding who should perform it, as well as where policing developments should be situated in relation to broader political and societal trends. This is the context within which much of today's debate takes place.

PROVISION

The centrality of security, allied to the nature of post-conflict cities, means that the question of who should provide policing is controversial. To some extent answers depend on what we think the nature and purpose of policing are, such as whether it is a public good. If the police role is regime representation, regulation, or crime control and social order, then police have little to contribute in the immediate aftermath of conflict. If, however, its primary role is public safety, crime prevention or reassurance, then opportunities exist. Even so, their immediate role is limited because public police cannot operate independently of the state-based bureaucracy that formerly sustained them. Occasionally a police force retains a degree of local support, but it cannot operate without a judicial infrastructure of prisons and courts.[5] In such circumstances the burden of survival and protection becomes that of the individual and his or her household, and is conducted in an opportunistic or ad hoc fashion. Responsibility for security usually shifts to homeowners, associational groups, vigilantes or militias, or, in the longer term, commercial companies (Abrahamsen and Williams 2007; Avant 2006; Cilliers and Mason 1999; Reno 1998; van Creveld 1991). Self-help initiatives are the common response (Baker 2007b), and local or private security prospers wherever police are seen as unable or unwilling to deal with crime and disorder (Sheptycki 2002).

DAMAGE LIMITATION

Policing in the immediate post-conflict period is a matter of damage limitation. For international authorities, it is a task performed by militaries, rather than police, because they are armed and present, but also because police are rarely visible. This may be because officers are uncertain about their role and responsibilities, or because they fear attack. Both police and belligerents associate the police role and uniform with the state, so when the state fragments officers' incentives to remain state representatives are lost, and they discard their uniforms. They act as ordinary inhabitants, and as representatives of their ethnic or tribal group (Jensen 2007: 115); their goals are the same as their neighbours'. A few officers may attempt to police their local area, but, for most, former institutional allegiances become as meaningless as societal interdependencies.

Policing for all practical purposes depends on militaries. It makes a difference to its style and intent whether the military concerned are victorious rebel fighters, clan militias, defeated government forces, or conventional militaries operating as a national force (as British forces did in Freetown) or as part of a coalition (as in Afghanistan), but all have more pressing objectives than public safety. Their concern is with force protection, aggrandisement, control (including its components such as identification and intelligence), or gratification. Many militaries in the regions where conflict usually occurs operate on the premiss that the end justifies the means, so policing is at best a descriptive term of their control-related activities. Whatever the case, police as such are irrelevant; the institution has either fragmented or been destroyed, and without it the few officers brave (or foolhardy) enough to claim their former occupation are unable to function. Those who do appear are untrained for tasks that demand robust paramilitary capabilities, while the reputation of those who are ensures they risk lynching. This means that there are two main aspects to the functional issue of managing insecurity (that is, policing): the role played by the military (armies), and the role (by omission) of police. Generally speaking, the significance of state policing results from the political objectives it symbolises, its challenging nature, and its requirement for engagement with a populace.

In the interests of clarity, one further distinction needs to be made when discussing police work and policing. What the police (as opposed to the military) are required to do is police work and, as such, should be separate from what the military do, not least because functional ambiguity is usually part of the security problem confronting fragile societies. Thus international police in Kosovo advised on humanitarian law enforcement, and dealt with individual crimes, missing persons, war crimes, crowd and traffic control, small-scale disturbances, the formation of a civil police, and confidence building generally. The more general activity of policing refers to problem-solving activities associated with the enforcement and maintenance of internationally acceptable forms of civil law and order.

POLICING BY MILITARIES

The policing of cities as conflict ends is a matter for troops and fighters. The policing of urban societies tends to be frustrating, squalid and politicised, but it is particularly problematic for conventional Western militaries. It is all too often a tedious grind of labour-intensive patrols, searches, raids and road checks, for which soldiers are unprepared and for which sophisticated technologies are irrelevant. In Iraq it meant that US or UK troops fought a war at the same time as they completed paperwork, and balanced compensation claims and conflicting evidence.[6]

Operating in this environment is difficult for a number of reasons. The circumstances in which conflict ends and the volatility of the environment mean that the troops involved are usually war-fighters. Additionally, their transitional skills may be unequal to the demands of managing non-combatants, they probably know little about the thinking of the societies in which their operations take place, and the challenges of gaining intelligence in a densely populated city or distinguishing between combatants and non-combatants are the same today as they were for French paratroopers in Algiers in 1956. And French paratroopers hated policing (Horne 1987; Talbot 1979). They could not distinguish terrorists from innocent passers-by; so as far as they were concerned, police work meant rounding up and interrogating suspects, and their response rested on intelligence gained by physical means. The fact that they had police powers facilitated the process, and it is not hard to see how frustration and the threat of bombings resulted in their systematic use of torture.

Another problem concerns the volatile nature of urban security operations. This can be seen from developments in Falluja, which quickly emerged as a centre of opposition to the US-led occupation of Iraq. The city was never the Ba'ath Party stronghold that US spokesmen claimed, but it was known for its religious and social conservatism, and nationalist fervour, and was the scene of the first serious incidents between Iraqis and Americans: 'each new level in the Iraq insurgency seems to be tested first in Falluja' (Clover 2004). US forces never policed Falluja, but they were initially welcomed. However, clashes, often involving misunderstandings, and insensitive or heavy-handed US crowd control quickly alienated Falluja's more moderate inhabitants. On 28 April 2003, two weeks after the end of the war, angry crowds gathered outside a makeshift American barracks to protest about the delayed opening of a school, and shots were fired. US paratroopers shot into the crowd in return, killing at least fifteen demonstrators. The incident acted as a flashpoint, setting off a number of attacks against US forces across the region. The US response was to employ rules of engagement (ROE) that emphasised force protection to the exclusion of all else; anyone carrying an AK-47 outside a private home was killed.

IMMEDIATE MILITARY TASKS

Security tasks vary according to the military concerned, the nature and outcome of the conflict, belligerents' interests, local conditions, time and place, and the city's political significance. The first tasks for both conventional and non-state forces are force protection and making their presence felt. They must be seen to dominate (to possess escalation dominance), and they must control key strongholds such as the presidential palace, and round up some of their known adversaries. Looting may be permitted or tolerated as a reward, a logistical tactic, a celebration or a distraction. Control must then be reasserted.

Militaries need to separate, control and demobilise former fighters; protect favoured political leaders, significant buildings, infrastructure or institutions; and keep localised violence and crime at tolerable levels. Troops typically man roadblocks, check identities, enforce and patrol security cordons, and conduct raids. Within weeks multinational military forces are expected to escort humanitarian convoys, refugees and internally displaced persons (IDPs), patrol refugee camps, and control traffic and riots.

Sporadic acts of armed violence are not necessarily a military problem, but, in practice, most incidents demand a low-level military or paramilitary response. The challenge results from the scale of many disturbances, with whole localities being involved, and from the strategic potential of flashpoints. The potential problem is evident from riots in the Kosovan town of Mitrovica in early 2000 when 60,000 Albanians broke through to a bridge separating the Serb minority in the north from the Albanians in the south. The violence was contained by NATO-led troops firing volleys of tear gas and using batons, but not before international media accused the troops concerned of failing to provide adequate security (*Guardian* 22 February 2000). As this suggests, functional divisions between conventional military and policing duties are ambiguous primarily because militaries cannot be seen to fail. The role of even paramilitary police is for this reason limited. Policing at this stage is about control, identification and territorial management, rather than creating public confidence.

DEPLOYMENT AND ENFORCEMENT GAPS

Militaries are used for policing in multinational interventions primarily because they are present, capable and well-resourced; whereas police (international and indigenous) are absent, ineffective or sectarian. Also, militaries can deal with the practical problems of deployment and enforcement (Dziedzic 1998: 3–18). Deployment, or timing, is a straightforward matter, whereas enforcement, which is about function, is more political, and tends to arise later.

Deployment gaps arise because although basic order is a priority for multinational militaries, indigenous police have either ceased to function or are part of the problem, while multinational civilian police forces are incapable of, say, separating armed groups. This meant that the British company commander in western Priština in mid-June 1999 was military commander, chief of police and prison governor. During their eight days in Priština his company dealt with 12 hostage killings, 32 ethnic attacks, 22 ethnic shootings (resulting in 11 deaths), more than 40 lootings, and hundreds of weapons seizures. Hence the comment by Robin Cook, then British foreign secretary, that three weeks into the Kosovo operation three-quarters of KFOR's duties were police-related (Hills 2002: 107). Four years later, the troops who took Basra were expected to fill the gap left by the 16,000 Iraqi policemen who had formerly kept order in the city.

Enforcement gaps occur when militaries are required to perform functions that fall between the outer shell where the military act as a rapid reaction force, maintaining area security, and the inner shell of public security for individual crimes and small-scale disturbances that is normally handled by police. The deficiencies typically relate to non-compliance with peace processes, and are compounded by the military's lack of police skills, political ambiguity, special interests, and the weakness of UN civilian police. For example, the withdrawal of Serb forces and the absence of an Albanian police force in Priština and Mostar left NATO's Kosovo Force (KFOR) as the only agent capable of establishing any appropriate form of political order. KFOR policed by default.

Even so, the military's choice of policing activities is selective (Hills 2000). Depending on the military's remit, policing ranges from the high-profile 'arrests' of war criminals to discouraging arsonists. In between are house-to-house searches conducted in order to improve security, seize weapons, capture known criminals, create a security cordon to prevent further arms from entering an area, and support or monitor local forces. Policing is further shaped by specific problems, vested interests and fears of mission creep. In Bosnia, mission creep was invoked by SFOR (Stabilisation Force) to avoid arresting war criminals, and to explain inaction in the face of disorder. The situation was different in KFOR in that Generals Rose and Reinhardt made it clear that KFOR's purpose was to support civilian reconstruction, hence the prominence attributed to community patrolling and other policing activities intended to promote confidence (cf. Zaalberg 2006: 312).

COMBAT OR CONSTABULARY FORCES

The question of who should provide policing remains more controversial than KFOR's record suggests. Combat troops were used in the aftermath of Operation Iraqi Freedom, but there were never enough of them to police big cities, they were not trained for such work, they often used inappropriate tactics, and their reliance on technology intensified, rather than alleviated, the problem. The Pentagon's approach to policing Baghdad in April 2003 emphasises this. Driven by Rumsfeld's enthusiasm for a controversial programme for streamlining war-fighting functions known as transformation, senior officials believed that relatively few forces using firepower and information technology could police Iraq. The influential Office of Force Transformation (which had developed the original notion of transformation) had argued for a rebalancing away from capabilities for sustained war-fighting towards so-called constabulary functions and rapid-reaction forces, but the Pentagon's version of transformation dominated: US forces might have to police, but they should not offer low-level non-warfighting operations. The 'war on terror' and the Bush administration's subsequent conflation of warfighting and stability operations further reinforced the Pentagon's preference, leading to US forces losing control of swathes of Iraq's cities.

Nonetheless, there is a consensus among international commentators that more military police, civil affairs officers and manpower generally are needed once conflict ends if lawlessness is to be curbed and strategic objectives achieved. Given that civilian police cannot operate in the early days, the choice appears to be that either combat troops continue to provide policing when there is no realistic alternative, or that they (or other troops) are organised with policing or peacekeeping duties in mind, or that some type of paramilitary force specialising in this work should be developed.

A number of options were discussed at the time. Tom Barnett, to name one prominent US proponent of change, believed that the US military should be split in two, with the first group responsible for fighting while the second (comprising older, married, more educated troops) rebuilt failed states (Barnett 2004). Another option entailed the creation of a designated paramilitary force that could carry out security missions, operating within the body of combat troops, rather than replace them. The multinational specialised units (MSUs) and special police units (SPUs) operating in the Balkans, and based on forces such as Italy's Carabinieri, and France's Gendarmerie, offered possible models.

In fact, a range of possibilities had been discussed in US defence circles over the years. Most sought to share the policing task, or to shift it to organisations other than the US Army (Beaumont 1995; Bronson 2002; Brown 2000; Cline 2003). Demarest, for example, argued that constabulary missions should include occupation duties and population control, as well as counterinsurgency and counternarcotics (Demarest 1993). A more developed proposal is that advocated by Field and Perito, who make a case for creating 'an intervention force for stability operations' consisting 'of four elements: military forces; police-constabulary units; civil police officers; and lawyers, judges, and penal system experts' (Field and Perito 2002–03: 80; see also Perito 2004). They note that such a package worked in Kosovo, where a combination of police, judges and prosecutors, supported by military forces, ensured a degree of security.

Yet even if such a force is realistic or politically desirable, the question of who should perform the role, and whether it should be subordinated to ground combat operations, remains controversial.

Standing paramilitary forces such as Carabinieri and Gendarmerie Nationale, which share the characteristics of military and police, seem a plausible model. They are equipped with armoured vehicles and mounted weapons, and can fight as light infantry, but also they are trained and equipped to maintain public order, conduct investigations, make arrests and direct traffic. They can deploy quickly and were used successfully in the Balkans.[7] However, their record elsewhere (in Iraq as in East Timor) is uneven. The record of Carabinieri in Nasiriyah, a city to the south of Baghdad, is a case in point.

The Carabinieri came to international attention in November 2003 when a suicide tanker bomb exploded outside their base, killing eighteen Carabinieri. Hard evidence is lacking – I have yet to find an open source assessment of their performance – but the ease with which the tanker reached the building calls into question their security precautions. They had been in Iraq for four months and were, according to their publicity, maintaining order less brutally than American forces. But their multinational colleagues were less flattering: anecdotal evidence suggests that they never left their base.

Since then Carabinieri helped to train SPUs at the regional police level in Nasiriyah in 2005, and in 2007 fronted a NATO training mission in Iraq, establishing (according to a spokesman) 'the Iraqi National Police as a professional military police force, filling the gap between the police and the armed forces' (MNF–Iraq 2007). The mission's goal was to ensure that at least one police battalion had paramilitary capacity. However, the notion that 'The national police can connect with the public in a way that armed forces cannot and the NATO Training Mission in Iraq considers that the training the Carabinieri provides will help build the Iraqi people's trust in the national police' is of dubious value. On the other hand, the successful if robust record of Portugal's Guarda Nacional Republicana (GNR) in riot control in Timor Leste suggests the utility of such forces. Whatever the case, the utility of Gendarmerie-style forces in an Iraq remains debatable.

An alternative source of police might be military police (MPs). They are trained and equipped for war-fighting and maintaining public order, and skills developed during garrison policing are directly transferable to civilian operations; in the summer of 2003, 48 armed British MPs, aided by 900 unarmed locals, policed Basra's 1.3 million inhabitants. But the roles and functions of national MPs vary considerably, as does their jurisdiction. And they are a scarce resource. Using MPs for policing would take them away from their traditional duties, which are policing military installations and directing traffic and handling prisoners on the battlefield.

The use of reserves to fill the perceived policing gap is another possibility. One-fifth of US troops in Iraq in February 2004 were reservists or part of the National Guard, and those most in demand worked as military police. Before the abuse of Iraqi prisoners at Abu Ghraib prison tarnished their reputation (all of the seven soldiers directly involved were members of the reserves or the National Guard) it was usual to claim that part-time soldiers brought a welcome degree of maturity to stabilisation operations; they are typically older than most troops, and most have civilian jobs to which they will return. Such arguments are no longer convincing.

Lastly, commercial companies, many of whom are willing to operate in the early weeks, could fill some gaps. Some (such as DynCorp) are notorious,[8] but the USA's domestic police structures mean that Washington has little alternative to their use. Its civilian police programme for post-conflict environments is run by the State Department and administered through a commercial contractor that recruits retired police officers from state and local agencies.

POLICE AND POLICING

My emphasis so far has been on policing by conventional militaries. This begins as control measures before shifting into preliminary or holding measures until policing can be handed over to a police force; it is policing by default.[9] The key to mapping the re-emergence of order is for this reason to be found in policing and, more importantly, the role played by public police.

There is no universal understanding of the purpose of the police as an institution. Indeed, today's international 'norm-derivative' definitions of police lack credibility in the regions in which they are imposed. It may be acknowledged by the subfield of police studies that the police must be understood in terms of the environment in which they operate, but the perspective of Western analysts, policymakers and practitioners invariably differs from those of indigenous officers. This is primarily because, to paraphrase Klockars, international assessments and understanding are based on beliefs about what police should do or are supposed to be.

Most definitions are based on Anglo-American practices. For Reiner, police 'refers to a particular kind of social institution, while policing implies a set of processes with specific social functions' (Reiner 2000a: 1). The police are, he suggests, commonly seen as a body of (often uniformed) officers who patrol public space, and are responsible for crime control and investigation, the maintenance of order and some social welfare functions (Reiner 2000a: 1).[10] He also describes the police as 'a specialised body of people given the primary formal responsibility for legitimate force to safeguard security' (Reiner 2000a: 7). In contrast, policing is 'an aspect of social control processes which occurs universally in all social situations in which there is at least the potential for conflict, deviance, or disorder' (Reiner 2000a: 7). Indeed, there is consensus that policing is a form of social control (Reiner 2000a; Jones and Newburn 2002; Johnston 2000), and that policing is what the police do (Waddington 1999: 1). Other interpretations based on Anglo-American policing argue that police are expected to deal with crime, or that policing is an aspect of public policy, or it is 'the exercise of the authority of the state over civil populations' (Waddington 1999: 30). Some scholars go so far as to state that policing is 'fundamentally about the establishment of security and peace' (Johnston 2000: 9), and that it typically involves activities (e.g. traffic regulation) which generate and maintain 'the conditions of general order under which the citizenry are most likely to be and to feel secure' (Loader and Walker 2007a: 97).

The picture is balanced by Bowling and Foster, who accept that 'there is a lot more to policing than just dealing with crime', and that 'policing is by definition ambiguous and complex in practice' (Bowling and Foster 2002: 982). They observe, too, the way in which the scope of Western policing has widened and diversified, and the number and type of roles and tasks undertaken by police expanded. This has meant that 'until recently, the police had themselves failed to understand that it is policing rather than police that is vital to social order' (Bowling and Foster 2002: 981). This understanding accommodates policing styles that range from covert policing to entrepreneurial, or consensual or negligent policing, but it remains rooted in Anglo-American policing.

Let us return to Riener, who argues that the police role 'is unique in that its core tasks require officers to face situations where the risk lies in the unpredictable outcome of encounters with other people' (Reiner 2000a: 88). He continues that, in order to deal with the situations they face, police have been given powers that are not available to the populace. Similarly, Jones and Newburn argue that the role is unique in that those who carry it out are authorised to legitimately use force or coercion (Jones and Newburn 1998: 7–67). This seems reasonable, and is consistent with Bittner's classic definition (Bittner 1970), yet it introduces a note of ambiguity into post-conflict and, indeed, comparative policing because the degree of acceptable coercion varies. There is no comparative, let alone systematic, analysis of police use of force even though the ability of police to use force symbolises or expresses the relationship between states and their inhabitants.[11]

More worryingly, such definitions are tied to Western and West-phalian notions. Hence police are said to exist 'within a remarkably uniform discourse. This may be due to the pre-eminent position of authority and power for policing agenda, or more directly it might demonstrate the commonality of policing functions' (Loader and Walker 2007a: 263). But this is misleading in the context of Southern conflict because while there are commonalities and a shared basis of understanding (otherwise Interpol and regional police organisations could not operate) there are major differences of emphasis and understanding on what is appropriate.

For this reason, definitions rooted in comparative studies, rather than in democratisation or security-sector reform, are more relevant and credible. Three alternative approaches are valuable. The first is that of Cain who, writing thirty years ago, noted that the term 'police' was rarely defined. She therefore argued that 'Police, then, *must be defined in terms of their key practice*. They are appointed with the task of maintaining the order which those who sustain them define as proper' (Cain 1979: 2).

Six years later Bayley offered an inclusive and comparative defini-tion whereby police means 'people authorized by a group to regulate interpersonal relations within the group through the application of physical force. This definition has three essential parts: physical force, internal usage, and collective authorization' (1985: 7). The group concerned may be a government or it may be customary with implicit, rather than explicit, authority implicit; Bayley refers to status, rather than behavioural attributes (1985: 9, 13). As a result the difference between police and a factional group may be a matter of judgement. The use of force is indeed probable in a post-conflict city, but even if it were not, the fact that police are authorised to use it shapes their interactions with its inhabitants.

From this Mawby concluded that 'we are left with a number of definitions which share some features in common but contain variations in emphasis and ... leave room for considerable differences in interpretation' (Mawby 1990: 3). For Mawby this means defining police in terms of an agency that can be distinguished in terms of its legitimacy, structure and function. Legitimacy implies that those with the power to do so, regardless of whether they are a political elite or an occupying force, grant police some degree of monopoly within a society. Structure implies that they are an organised force with a degree of specialisation and some form of code of practice. Function implies that their role focuses on the maintenance of some form of order and law, and the prevention and/or detection of offences against it.

This leads back to classic texts from the Cold War era such as that of Klockars, who argued that police cannot be defined in terms of its ends; definitions must rest on means, and the foundational means common to all police is coercive force (Klockars 1985: 9). In truth, such analyses have more in common with today's localised and fragmented urban policing than donors would wish. Enloe's work on the factors shaping the role of police in the Third World is a case in point. She noted that 'the notion of disorder within a political system has police connotations rather than military' (Enloe 1976: 25), and that whereas military modes of conflict tend to be regarded as structured, police operations are seen as more fragmented and local. They deal with actual or potential political dysfunction; riots, crime, corruption and banditry are regarded as policing matters.

Enloe's observations may be supplemented by Findlay and Zvekić's 1993 analysis of alternative policing styles. For they argue that policing is best approached as a process of interaction of interests and powers within a specific environment: 'the particular interactions of interest, power and authority which distinguish the structures and functions of police work should be viewed as constructed around expectations of policing within a given cultural, political and situational context' (Findlay and Zvekić 1993: 6). This emphasises the localised and specific nature of policing – and security – in the post-conflict city.[12]

Not enough is known of the informal groups operating in, say, Mogadishu to assess policing in terms of ideology, normative frameworks or, indeed, interactions. Nevertheless, this combination of approaches offers the most insight. I would add too that in most of the global South, police enforce decisions taken by the political or factional elites to whom they are accountable (Hills 2007). This conclusion matters because international forces, donors and organisations such as the OECD seek to impose non-negotiable structures and norms, whereas police models actually develop out of the political conflicts and negotiations that occur as patterns of order emerge. Also, the activities police perform usually result from contingencies, rather than rational and systematic planning. Tasks accrue because the police are there, or because they are representative of factions, or because it is thought appropriate. But regardless of the group authorised to provide policing, police powers are premised on a capacity to use force to ensure compliance. In other words, coercion lies at the root of policing and order.

It should be noted that the views of indigenous and international police often diverge sharply at this point, with the former arguing that coercion makes for effective policing because the application of substantial force usually gains compliance, while Western consultants hold that it cannot be justified and is counterproductive in the long term. More importantly, a consensus emerges that responsibility for social order is primarily the police's (Jackson and Wade 2005; Manning 1977; Neocleous 2000; Renauer 2007). It is therefore reasonable to assume that when there is no order there is no (or, at best, minimal) policing, but where there is order there will be some form of police, and that the re-emergence of both are linked. In other words, order may be measured by the activities of its police.

POLICE AND ORDER

Regardless of definitional issues, 'police' is more than a descriptive term. For it represents a broad analytical and empirical approach to addressing central questions of order and security, such as for whom and by whom. However, one of the factors complicating easy assessment is that police are vehicles for both specific and general order, which may emerge at different times and in different sequences. As Marenin has argued, police are implicated in the reproduction of specific order (defending the interests of those favoured by current patterns of domination) and also the general order guaranteeing wider order (Marenin 1982). They have the capacity to communicate social meanings as well as political intent (Manning 1997). The key point is that police reproduce, rather than manufacture, construct or produce order. For this reason, the re-emergence of police is indicative of the re-emergence of order. It also suggests that international programmes for police reform are indicative of the stages through which order is thought to emerge.

The situation becomes clearer in the medium to long term, though practice usually diverges from theory because theory is invariably based on the experience of mature democratic states.[13] We may agree that

> the conceptual building-blocks [of policing] take the form of a number of structural features or co-ordinates of the general policing role which shape the ways in which the police are implicated in the production of social meaning. These are the *singularity* of the police function, the tendency towards *uniformity* [and conservatism] in the pursuit of that function, its highly *permissive* character, its *time-bound* quality and its *societal locatedness*. (Loader and Walker 2006: 96)

But to suggest that the police act as an ideological unifier in that they are able to diagnose, classify and represent the world at moments of political crisis and social breakdown (Loader and Walker 2007a: 76) is misleading, especially when diagnoses are undertaken for factional reasons.

POLICE AND POWER RELATIONS

The police organisation and its activities are structured through power relations, as is the re-emergence of order. Three levels need to be addressed:

* power relations which designate a particular policing style;
* power as it is negotiated through policing practice;
* power struggles which result from policing.

The three often overlap or merge as a result of the social realities of power dynamics, but this is significant because the clearest insight into power relations in policing is gained when police and policing are seen as processes whereby conflicting interests are negotiated, managed or crushed (Loader and Walker 2007a).

In an ideal world this would be explored in terms of structural indicators such as sources of authority, regulatory frameworks and decision-making processes. Commonalities would then be identified. But such information is rarely available in post-conflict cities even when the institutions or frameworks exist, for choices are driven by powerful men, and by interests in, and claims over, police resources or power, rather than by commitment towards specific styles. When internal and external influences interact – as they often do in transitional environments – the resultant layering of institutions and practices is shaped by tactical considerations. Unavoidable political pressures are accommodated, manipulated or subverted, and policing interactions result in the creation, maintenance and termination of complicated or ambiguous relationships (Loader and Walker 2007a: 261). In other words, policing depends on power relations, and on the opportunities and structures associated with their expression; it represents the relationships existing between interests, needs, resources, structures and outcomes. Not only do such relationships adapt, accommodate or replace those that existed previously, but also links are retained with earlier forms, practices and personalities. The shifting alliances formed between local (and international) power players and moral authorities account for the ambiguities of emergent order.

This implies that police cannot be autonomous actors in the reconstruction of the state and society. We know that they can protect emerging state structures, constrain unwanted change, and assist in the reproduction of the state, society and the linkages between them. But, as Marenin notes, the lack of a theory of state change and reproduction incorporating the role of the police as actors in that reproduction is not accidental (Marenin 1996: 13). Governments may fear police, but this does not mean that senior officers are politically influential or wish to operate as agents of change, modernisation or development.

POLICING FIELD

Why, then, do indigenous police behave as they do in post-conflict cities? The extensive body of research into combatant behaviour in, for example, Africa offers relevant insights (e.g. Hoffman 2007b; Richards 2005; Bøås and Dunn 2007). It is probable, for example, that men join mainly because they need a job in order to support their families. Their behaviour is then shaped by peer pressure, personal psychology and concern for their own reputation and/or survival, rather than by ideology or political imperatives. Even so, there seems to be a differentiated domain of social practice (or field) that is specific to police. To paraphrase Bourdieu and Wacquant, police (like, say, religious, political or ethnic spheres of life) are endowed with their own rules and regulations and forms of authority, which form fields (Bourdieu and Wacquant 1992). By this is meant a structured space of positions that contains its own rules and regulations.

There is much to be said for this as a tool for understanding police. It is clear, for instance, that police know what their interests are and how to protect themselves (Marenin 1996). The institution is rarely reinvented when conflict stops, and police culture is notoriously resilient. And culture matters because it indicates the continuities underpinning security and order. According to Chan, who provides a compelling account of police culture and organisational change in settled democracies, the potential and limits of police reform and/or democratisation are to be found in the institution's deeply embedded organisational culture. She argues that it should be understood as shared cultural knowledge containing 'basic assumptions about descriptions, operations, perceptions and explanations about the social and physical world' (Chan 1999: 105). This informs the understanding and assessments of senior officers, and their choice of strategies and tactics, just as it explains the international emphasis on purging and retiring former officers whenever possible. On the other hand, it appears that new officers quickly adopt their colleagues' attitudes. They also reflect a specific but recognisable version of their society's norms.

What, then, do police do in post-conflict cities? The answer is that they do very little in the early days after conflict ends. One or two older career officers may try to direct traffic (this happened in Mogadishu and Baghdad), but routine policing is essentially irrelevant. Instead, police hide and, like their families and neighbours, look for personal or group security or gain. The individual has little value at such times, and security is primarily about groups achieving a symbolic presence and, where possible, securing territory. For sectarian groups and international forces this includes police stations, which are usually abandoned or looted. Indeed, securing territory is probably the key aspect of security provision in cities, for security is quickly ghettoised. And it is shaped by rumour, for officers as much as for their neighbours. Indeed, the importance of rumour or *radio trottoir* (pavement radio) in cities with low literacy rates or without electricity cannot be overestimated. It was the hate campaign launched by the pro-Hutu militia radio, Radio Mille Collines, that fuelled genocide in Rwanda, while many Sierra Leoneans owe their lives to the accurate and timely reports broadcast by radio stations during the rebel attack on Freetown on 6 January 1999.

In the short or medium term, indigenous police may supplement their low-visibility policing with revenge attacks, death squads and alliances, all of which enable them to manage or manipulate the emergent order. Take the case of alliances. When faced with the threat of an armed rebellion in February 2004, the Haitian government's response was to give a notorious gang leader and ex-army officer the uniform of the national police's (PNH) riot police and send him to the northern city of Saint Marc, where he helped the PNH and a local street gang besiege a neighbourhood. Such alliances can also turn sour. In the aftermath of President Aristide's flight in 2004, street gangs emerged in a series of violent and public murders of police officers, three of whom were beheaded.

In developed states (for example, Serbia), policing in this phase is about crowd control, static protection and rapid response to security threats, and it may involve patrolling by military and paramilitary forces. Elsewhere it may involve closing down localities, or removing squatters. In May 2007, several months after its December victory over insurgents, Somalia's interim government tried to strengthen its grip on Mogadishu by using police to destroy roadside kiosks selling tea, vegetables and other small goods. In the early morning, hundreds of police used sledgehammers and bulldozers to flatten unlicensed stalls and shops. All this requires coercive resources and appropriate training, but notions such as service and accountability are essentially irrelevant. Indeed, such policing often operates in tandem with alternative fields of security provision that offer (or deny) populations a sense of predictability and assurance. Guarantees often include security (or defence) based on cultural and personal identities as defined in terms of ethnicity, religion or sex.

LOCAL VERSUS INTERNATIONAL PERSPECTIVES

The playing of potentially contradictory roles by the police introduces an additional tension. On the one hand, the priority of indigenous officers is survival. They may be ineffective, untrained, corrupt and repressive (purged officers are often replaced by ex-fighters or un-employed youths), but they reflect the norms and values of their society. On the other hand, international officers may represent the UN, or their own country, or (for US officers) commercial compa-nies, but few know anything about the society they wish to reform. Some wish to promote what they believe to be 'good', 'modern' or 'professional' policing, whereas the skills of others, to say nothing of their motives, are questionable.

International policy statements and programmes quickly focus on police reform (though the effectiveness of reformed police is assumed, rather than proven), and there is little or no international interest in understanding the function, role and culture of indigenous police. There is even less interest in understanding the political economy of policing, even though it permeates every level of policing. It ranges from the constable who demands the equivalent of a few pence from the drivers of commercial vehicles, and the superintendent who skims his men's special allowances, up to the chief officer who diverts thousands of dollars into his own accounts or suitcases.

The prioritisation of reform is considered in more detail in Chapter 3, and here it is sufficient to note that the police and policing are seen as significant in so far as they support, obstruct or threaten wider international policy objectives and exit strategies. In Bosnia, for example, as Paddy Ashdown noted, 'We thought that democracy was the highest priority and we measured it by the number of elections we could organize' (CPRF 2003: 3). It was only with hindsight he concluded that 'we should have put establishing rule of law first. Everything else depends on it: a functioning economy, a free and fair political system, the development of civil society and public confidence in police and courts' (Smith et al. 2007: 5).[14]

The police role is indeed critical, though not necessarily for the reasons Ashdown assumed. Rather than ensuring crime prevention, accountability or diversity, the police play a key instrumental and symbolic role in reflecting and managing order, thereby potentially shaping identity, reconstruction and state formation. Policing is intimately associated with the social conflicts, political anomalies and cultural dilemmas associated with the re-emergence of order. It is about achieving a symbolic presence and, where possible, securing territory. Indeed, securing territory is probably a key aspect of how post-conflict cities and societies provide for the security of their inhabitants. Further, state police often operate in parallel with alternative forms of security provision. The guarantees of both are typically based on cultural and personal identities.

EMERGENT ORDER

Policing may reflect contextual historical processes (Marenin 1996: 9), or it may result from the dialectical or reciprocal networks of relations that exist between police and their state or societal context (Hills 2008), but certain key variables are evident. As noted earlier, they include the nature of the conflict and the manner of its ending, and whether or not there was a working government before it began; that is, whether there is a culture that recognises the importance of stability, public police and the centralised arrangements on which city-wide patterns of order depend. Intervention by multinational organisations influences the nature of recovery, too, though it is often more accurate to describe such arrangements as holding operations than as reconstruction.

This interpretation is reinforced by the way in which security developments tend to occur. The key characteristic is that order is fragile, and local violence may escalate even where a degree of order has been imposed by multinational troops. In 2006, for example, a year after the termination of UN operations in Timor Leste, the Timorese government was forced to declare a state of emergency and invite UN troops to return. And British forces retained a presence in Sierra Leone several years after their initial intervention because the UK government feared a potential coup by disaffected military. The situation is starker in Haiti where, despite an initial US intervention in 1994 and the 'restoration' of democracy in 2006, the infrastructure has collapsed and there is no functioning police. Despite this, the involvement of international agencies can make a critical difference in the short to medium term. They can supervise peace agreements, provide opportunities for belligerents to negotiate, impose basic security, monitor incidents, and offer credible and enforceable guarantees. On the other hand, peace processes usually involve disarmament and demobilisation, both of which may induce the insecurity that facilitates conflict.

Of the three potentially critical variables, the former existence of a central government is the least important, for corrupt or repressive governance often prompts conflict, and even juridical states claim to possess governance agents such as police, factional though they may be.

CONCLUSION

The city is to some extent the container or platform where the processes and relationships associated with order are organised and rearranged. It is not a fixed thing, or a closed institutional system, but it occupies a specific geographical territory in which the processes and activities associated with order and security can be examined.

No single factor dominates contemporary trends. Demographic change and globalisation may intensify the problems of managing cities, especially those requiring low-level policing operations by military forces, yet the impact of each is case-specific and the drivers are not necessarily mutually reinforcing; in some cases they work at cross-purposes, while in others reinforcement is characteristic. Even so, certain commonalities and trends are identifiable. For example, cities rarely experience a security vacuum or anarchy. The situation may be fragile or volatile, and the population may be numb, afraid or exultant, but the only real vacuum is that which exists between 'ordinary' political competition and armed conflict. And that distinction may not be great for a Charles Taylor or Mohammed Aideed. Again, although conflict takes its toll on officers and the police institution, the institution is not only resilient, but also retains political utility; it is a primary mechanism for international regimes and indigenous strongmen to augment their local power.

Above all, police are linked to order in its specific (rather than general) meaning. Further, police support, restore or reproduce order, rather than create it, and they do so in culturally specific ways. Contrary to Western commentary, their purpose in post-conflict cities is rarely if ever maintaining 'the conditions of general order under which the citizenry are most likely to be and to feel secure' (Loader and Walker 2007a: 97). Despite this, order has become unfashionable; Western analysts and policymakers refer instead to stability, rebuilding government capacity and legitimacy, or sustainable development (Jones et al. 2005:3; USAID 2005; World Bank 2002). Hence the UK's intra-governmental Stabilisation Unit (formerly the Post-Conflict Reconstruction Unit, or PCRU) regards the establishment of stability (not order) as an 'immediate priority' in post-conflict environments. By stability the unit means 'preventing a recurrence of violent conflict, buying time for a permanent peace settlement and demonstrating some form of peace dividend' (Stabilisation Unit 2007: 3). In reality, Western goals include the emergence or creation of a specific form of order. There is nothing new about this. But what is different is the debate surrounding who should provide security in the aftermath of international interventions, and the models on which policing should be based.

3

INTERNATIONAL POLICING

In 1966, F.S.V. Donnison, the UK's official historian of the Allies' civil affairs and military government programmes for occupied and liberated Europe during World War II, wrote that war consumes governments and administrations, leaving anarchy and chaos whenever minimal forms of order and administration are not at once re-established (Donnison 1966). Fifty years later, the successors of 1940s' military governors were of a similar mind. Sergio Vieira de Mello, interim governor of Kosovo and East Timor, stated that 'unless you can impose order, you cannot begin to rebuild. All else rests on that foundation' (*Newsweek* 2001: 37). This was the lesson Paddy Ashdown, the international community's high representative in Bosnia, wished had been observed in Bosnia.

It is now international orthodoxy that law is a prerequisite of order (Thakur 1982), and that the introduction of law and order cannot wait. Peace accords involving IGOs such as the OECD and World Bank include the introduction of liberal political institutions (such as elections between competing parties and the guarantee of minimum political rights) that are thought to require the rule of law, and police are widely regarded as the appropriate agent for managing them.

Little is known about the assessments made by illiberal regimes of the potential police contribution, but in democracies, at least, police are the security institution that most affects daily life, and 'democratic policing' is seen as a means for conflict prevention and stability. Democratic policing means 'the idea that the police are a service, not a force, with the primary focus on the security of the individual rather than the state. Its defining characteristics are "responsiveness" to the needs of individuals, and "accountability" for its actions to the public it serves' (Bayley 2001).[1] Increasingly, it serves as a guiding principle for the multilateral governance system associated with organisations such as the EU.

This seems reasonable, given the fear and contempt police commonly attract. Most people want merely a police force that keeps themselves and their property safe, does not demand bribes on every occasion, and does not routinely brutalise detainees. However, as Ashdown implied when he said that everything democracies value depends on the rule of law (Smith et al. 2007: 5), multinational organisations want more: they want to achieve sweeping social and political change. This is more than 'victor's justice'. Even when regime change is not a stated goal, it is usual for international authorities to state that they will reform a police force's principles and procedures, paying special attention to accountable civilian oversight, the monitoring of human rights, and the rebalancing of recruitment in favour of excluded minorities and women. In other words, multinationals assume that post-conflict societies ideally transition to democracy in three phases: order (stabilisation), law and order, and finally law and order with justice (Dziedzic 1998). Police are expected to move from offering miscellaneous low-level responses to the set of activities and procedures associated with democratic-style policing. This requires not only additional resources but also reform. Further, police reform is increasingly understood as forming but one (albeit significant) aspect of what is known as security sector reform.

In this chapter I outline liberal orthodoxy on the police's potential contribution to order, the principles and assumptions on which it rests, and the issues it covers, before considering its expression in UN operations. This offers a base from which to compare the realities of policing and police presented in the chapters that follow. The rest of the book explores the ways in which international and indigenous norms and practices collide, thus offering insight into the plurality of rationalities, power relations and structures affecting the post-conflict city.

I do not discuss the nature of liberal democracy as such, defining it simplistically as a system that values the rule of law, separation of powers, and the protection of liberties such as speech, assembly, religion and property. I have in mind the approaches of EU member states and Australia, but also the USA, where recent policy definitions have owed much to the Republican Party's vision of capitalism. I follow Duffield's understanding too, for he explicitly addresses the conflation of security and democracy and its consequences (Duffield 2000, 2007). This makes sense in this book because police reform is best placed in the context of the current conflation of security and democracy. Far from being neutral, police reform needs to be seen as an expression of donors and IGOs proposing simultaneously to re-create state structures, and to cultivate a pluralistic civil society while enforcing certain culturally specific values. The ideological imperatives driving such projects may be downplayed by the rich industrialised democracies that comprise the core of the international system (Paris 2002: 638), but this does not negate their significance. And, regardless of whether or not Duffield is correct in his conviction that a system of global governance has emerged, policing and security are politically manipulated and subordinated to political goals, and have much to do with the allocation of power and resources among elites. The resultant tangle of self-interest and idealism inevitably skews understanding of the dynamics of policing post-conflict cities. Add in differences between international and indigenous police and tension is inevitable. So, too, is disagreement about the rules ordering life in cities, with all that this implies for order.

APPROACHES TO POLICING

Western understanding of post-conflict policing is influenced by approaches that conceive of policing in terms of order maintenance, law enforcement, professionalism and community service. Four approaches are usual today.

First, police are the conventional means to manage order when levels of violence are low. They were, for example, incorporated into the civil-affairs organisations administering occupied and liberated territories during World War II. Their status was low vis-à-vis military forces, but it was clearly understood that 'without the re-establishment of order there could be no revival of economic life, no relief of distress and no medical services' (Donnison 1966: 274). Their role depended on the ally and theatre concerned, but usually involved vetting and deploying indigenous police, and establishing temporary rule of law. In north-west Europe police prevented refugees and DPs obstructing military operations, whereas the (London) Metropolitan Police in Naples supervised prisons and public prosecutors. They assumed direct command of new police forces in Italy's former African colonies, and of reconstituted pre-war forces in Far Eastern cities such as Hong Kong, Mandalay and Singapore (Harris 1957; Donnison 1961).

A second approach is associated with contemporary peacekeeping operations by UN police (UNPOL). Indeed, by the late 1990s, police reform was seen as an essential prerequisite for success in peace-building missions (Bosnia was seen as confirming this trend). Such operations were always a curious combination of altruism, firefighting, reform and opportunism. Some multinational police sought to sta-bilise a volatile situation, and enforce peace provisions, while others exploited the opportunities for more personal (usually sexual) forms of gratification. This was not surprising. For the difficulties of recruit-ing suitable officers from Western democracies means that UNPOL missions are usually filled by police from countries with records of brutal or corrupt policing. In August 2007, police pledged to UN operations in Darfur included Bangladeshis, Egyptians, Ethiopians, Indonesians, Jordanians and Nigerians. As this suggests, policing has for some countries become a preferred form of foreign-policy engagement (Goldsmith and Sheptycki 2007).

A third, more bureaucratic, approach to policing is common in the medium term. This is when donors focus on administrative mechanisms. For example, in Bujumbura, the capital of Burundi, UNPOL sought to consolidate the integration of the various police forces making up the new national force and increase its operational capacity by providing training facilities and equipment. The EU is particularly notorious for taking a technocratic approach in its sphere of influence. Its projects in Macedonia, for example, reduced reform to 'a technical process based on capabilities, limited to transposing EU legislation and meeting security concerns' (Ioannides 2007: 371).

A fourth approach blends realism and idealism. The EU's projects in the Balkans illustrate this, too. Although the focus on building institutional capacity was initially the result of member states needing to address the region's volatility and criminality, it then became a means to extend the European Security and Defence Policy (Berenskoetter 2006). Thus the EU wished to pacify and control, while humanising policing (Merlingen and Ostrauskaite 2006). Some member states combined the two, as when the UK government promoted community-based policing in Kosovo, even as it made use of intelligence gained from Uzbekistan's police (who, like many around the world, routinely use torture as an investigation technique) in the aftermath of 2003's war in Afghanistan.

In all such projects, policing is seen as a means to facilitate, embed or manage a new order:

> International support for police reforms is not simply aimed at creating or strengthening a rights-based, universal(ising) general order in recipient countries through the provision of basic security ... It is also about modifying or replacing one particular(ising) social order with another. (Merlingen and Ostrauskaite 2005: 219)[2]

Ambitious claims are regularly made on behalf of police reform. Just as security has broadened to include not only the state but also justice and the safety and well-being of its inhabitants, so too reform has 'become a central component of efforts to overcome fragility and conflict' (OECD DAC 2007: 3). Organisations such as the OECD (which consists of twenty-two bilateral donors and the Commission of the European Communities; the UNDP, the World Bank and the IMF have observer status) and its Development Assistance Committee (OECD DAC) increasingly regard 'bad policing' as a major obstacle in the way of poverty reduction and access to social and political processes (OECD DAC 2007: 13). The scope and potential of police assistance are as a result expanded from the provision of functional security into an act of overt reform that amounts to social engineering.

For such reasons, police effectiveness is judged appropriate in so far as it contributes to Western (rather than indigenous) notions of good policing. Human rights, conflict resolution, free markets, civil society and recruitment from minorities are valued. 'Local' ownership of policing is promoted too – but only in so far as it abides by liberal notions. It often seems that the repressive or corrupt nature of the police concerned matters less than the goal of reforming, restructuring and rebuilding indigenous police 'to an acceptable level of democratic policing' (UN DPKO Police Division 2007: xi).

On the other hand, consensus is often outweighed by a lack of agreement on what constitutes appropriate policing. Policing is always understood from national perspectives. Thus British advisers in the Balkans based their practice on notions such as police primacy, a sharp distinction between police and military remits, and England and Wales's common-law ideology of constables as citizens in uniform, though they accepted that the military should support police training in military-related tasks such as weapon-handling, patrolling and counterterrorism techniques (Joint Doctrine 2007: ch. 3 3–1). In contrast, French officers thought in terms of a military-based gendarmerie, while the USA's mix of federal, state, county, city and small-town forces meant that its contribution was outsourced to private security companies such as the Virginia-based DynCorp. Each officer regards the practices and norms of his home force as an appropriate standard. It could not be otherwise when, in 2007, British, Iranian, South African and North Korean police trained the Uganda force (*New Vision* 2007b), and Chinese riot police joined a Brazilian-led UN force in Haiti's capital, Port-au-Prince.

This raises questions about Sheptycki's claim that police from around the world share a common constabulary ethic that is driven 'by a genuine structural continuity between the dynamics of security-threatening situations across a broad range of national and transnational contexts and a real sense of the value of a common police-craft in repairing these situations' (Loader and Walker 2007a: 264).[3]

DEMOCRATIC POLICING

Despite national differences, the goal of most international post-conflict programmes is 'democratic policing'. The meaning of the term is controversial but it is usually defined in terms of key characteristics. These include ethnically representative officers serving the needs of the public in an unthreatening manner, working in partnership with 'communities' to solve crime, protecting human rights, and ensuring that police operations and procedures are transparent and accountable (Stromseth et al. 2006: 13–15).[4] The principles guiding democratic police are, it is usually said, accountability and responsiveness, and its officers are ethnically representative and non-partisan. Such police are described as a service, rather than a force, though the terms are political labels, rather than accurate descriptors.

The ideals (if not the practices) of democratic police dominate contemporary analysis of post-conflict policing, yet the term says more about Western values than absolute or non-Western functional standards, for it concentrates on what should be, rather than what is. For example, its advocates argue that 'international actors need to engage in ambitious agenda setting during peace negotiations to help the parties to conflicts envision new ways of policing that are rooted in unrestricted human rights, ethnic tolerance, and citizen service, and to help the parties incorporate such a vision into peace accords' (Call and Stanley 2001: 304–5). This is laudable, but advancing arguments of universalism in the face of clashing cultural values does not help us understand the dynamics of either the police or policing (Donnelly 2007; Goldsmith and Dineen 2007; cf. Sen 1999b; Chandler 2004: 60). In other words, the understanding promoted by international agents relies on what most needs justification.

The situation is further obscured by differences between democracies. Israel, for example, which over the decades has probably had a greater influence on more police than any other state, adopts a very different approach to that of the EU. Indeed, SSR has made no progress in the Middle East, where the emphasis is on national and internal security, and where reform is understood to mean greater functional effectiveness (Luethold 2004; Sayigh 2007). The enthusiasm with which some rich countries merge security and development introduces further ambiguities, though the OECD at least is aware of the dangers associated with this. As its *Handbook* notes, 'many capacity development interventions have failed because the wider governance constraints (e.g. systematic corruption) have not been understood' (OECD DAC 2007: 86).[5] But this does not stop organisations overestimating the value of change for the police concerned.

In the context of post-conflict cities I take democratic policing to mean policing that uses minimal force, is relatively incorrupt, and provides reasonably impartial assistance and redress within an accountable and known Western-style criminal justice framework. Such policing is skills-based, but it owes little to 'professionalism', especially when 'professionalism' is linked to moral or political choice, rather than status, education or employment.

STATE-CENTRED POLICING

Just as security has been redefined in recent years, so too has policing, leading some to conclude that the state is being displaced from its long-standing position of exclusive security provider. Security provision is now part of the liberal market economy in the UK and USA, but whether this means that security is no longer a state monopoly is less clear. If this is the case then it should surely affect liberal programmes in post-conflict cities. It would challenge Southern notions of order, too.

Three main perspectives are evident, each of which may be illustrated by reference to Wood and Dupont's edited volume *Democracy, Society and the Governance of Security*. Johnson represents the first, for he accepts the Hayekian proposition that the state's deficient knowledge and capacity to deliver security to local communities render it an 'idiot' (Wood and Dupont 2006: 48). Loader and Walker represent the second. They promote the role of the state on the basis that policing is a public good (Loader and Walker 2007); 'security cannot be enjoyed by a few in isolation from the rest of society without creating the conditions of more insecurity' (Wood and Dupont 2006: 242). Shearing then introduces a third possibility: nodal governance. This is when non-state entities operate 'not simply as providers of governance on behalf of state agencies but as auspices of governance in their own right' (Wood and Dupont 2006: 52, 2).

In reality, IGOs and donors continue to see the state and its agents as playing a foundational role in policing and reconstruction. Policing cannot be a public good in the sense that it is a universal good, or that there is equity in its distribution, provision and service; needs vary, and its distribution is rarely just or even (Wood and Dupont 2006: 5). But few politicians and officials would disagree with Marks and

TABLE 3.1 Police support in emerging nations: generic model of typical problems and international police responses

	CIVIL WAR		LAWLESSNESS		CORRUPTION		INSTITUTIONAL DYSFUNCTION	
CONDITION OF RECIPIENT STATE	The state has ceased functioning; there is open warfare or extreme violence between social groups.		The rule of law is weak and arbitrary, with widespread violent and other crime.		Endemic corruption debilitates state institutions; prevents establishment of necessary institutions by ombudsman.		All necessary state institutions exist, and function to various degrees, but require support	
LIMITING CASES	*Extreme*	*Acceptable*	*Extreme*	*Acceptable*	*Extreme*	*Acceptable*	*Extreme*	*Acceptable*
	Violent conflict	Monitored peace	Breakdown in rule of law	Rudimentary rule of law	Endemic corruption	Sporadic corruption	Institutional dysfunction	Effective public institutions
POLICE TASK	Peacemaking; principally a military task due to active warfare with possible police support	Peacekeeping; military and police supervision, including crime investigation	External provision of police services, lack of internal capacity; possible military support	Inline police to supplement local service	Inline police performing executive and advisory functions to corruption proof	Offline police act as advisers (no executive authority)	Offline police act as advisers, and targeted technical assistance (no executive authority)	Highly targeted technical assistance (no executive authority)

Source: Australian Federal Police 2006: 8. For the AFP's depiction of a development axis or continuum based on the severity of problems and their effects on state function, see Australian Federal Police 2006: 9.

Goldsmith's statement that 'the state is, philosophically and practically speaking, best placed to manage and deliver security in an equitable manner and in accordance with universal normative standards' (Wood and Dupont 2006). Indeed, Western-funded reconstruction usually involves not only making 'people' free, but also bringing the state back in; reasserting the state's rights and legitimacy in the face of multiple, overlapping and shared governance agents and points (Held 1995). Decoupling may be welcomed in Washington, which uses commercial companies to relieve its forces of policing tasks they cannot fulfil, but this is not the case in most Southern capitals. In much of the world it would be seen as the creation of alternative power bases.

Similar objections may be raised to the shift from state-focused security to what the OECD calls people-centred security. It is less ambiguous than human security, but both phrases are applied by internationals in terms of the physical security police are expected to manage, and both are essentially meaningless. Of course, to some extent both are reasonable. The safety and security of individuals matter, and, as Loader and Walker note, policing is oriented to answering the question, 'How well ordered is my immediate environment?', rather than towards all-encompassing notions of security in the broad sense (Loader and Walker 2007a: 205). But people-centred security makes no genuine difference to international assessments of police and policing: states remain responsible for alleviating insecurity and ensuring the well-being of their populace, even when they lack institutional capacity (Duffield 2007; Macfarlane and Khong 2006: 5–8; Matthews 1989; OECD 2001: 37; Ogata and Sen, 2003; Sen 1999a). Additionally, there are internal inconsistencies in the definition of people-centred security, such as the relative importance of threats emanating from violence in comparison to other threats to life or health (Paris 2001; *Security Dialogue* 2004). Paris, for example, argues that human security is merely 'the latest in a long line of neologisms – including common security, global security, cooperative security, and comprehensive security – that encourage policymakers and scholars to think about international security as something more than the military defense of state interests and territory' (Paris 2001: 87). He concludes that while not necessarily empty rhetoric, as a new conceptualisation of security, human security is so vague that it verges on meaninglessness (Paris 2001: 102).

Ironically, people-centred security fails to address the types of insecurity typical in post-conflict cities. It not only assumes that state-based policing is usually the most appropriate means, but also it assumes, rather than proves, that police can make a fundamental contribution to people's security. And it fails to acknowledge the influence exerted by powerful actors over subordinate groups living in specific localities. It is difficult to disagree with Macfarlane and Khong's argument that the normative value of human security may be stronger than its explanatory value. Not only is people-centred security difficult to operationalise, but also the benefits and costs of so redefining security have yet to be systematically assessed. Regardless of this, the creation of physical security through improved policing is commonly seen as a precondition for building civil society and improving economic development.

POLICE REFORM

As the weeks pass, multilateral and bilateral interventions place a premium on reforming police as an aspect of regime change and/or reconstruction. The usual approach is for multinational military or gendarmerie forces to identify, separate, vet, and disarm and/or demobilise indigenous paramilitary or politicised police. The authorities concerned usually wish to create an ethnically representative police, form a transitional government, hold elections for a new government, and then leave for the next crisis. The inadequacies of the local police's training and resources are recognised, and big promises are made, which are then only partially fulfilled (Stromseth et al. 2006: 8, 98). Each case is different, but a common pattern is imposed on all.

Technical assistance to police in post-conflict cities has been a consistent theme across the decades.[6] But a significant shift took place in the late 1990s when technical assistance was supplemented – and in some cases supplanted – by the broad notion of reform. Development agencies such as DFID promoted a politically influential approach to reforming not just police but the security sector as a whole. This included police, military, intelligence and, for some donors, penal systems and judiciaries. There is much to be said for placing policing within this broader context, for police cannot function without prisons and judiciaries. Also, 'police and law enforcement agencies' are themselves a broad group, incorporating (for the UN's Police Division at least) 'all national security agencies, such as the police, customs and border services and agencies with military status such as gendarmerie-like constabulary forces and stability police units, which exercise police powers, especially the powers of arrest and detention' (UN DPKO Police Division 2007: xi). The OECD DAC also includes intelligence and local security agents such as militia (2007: 22). The civil authorities responsible for control and oversight (such as parliament) are often included, too.

This approach emphasises the interrelated ('holistic') nature of security provision, thereby increasing its political attractiveness. It builds on the broader and refocused definitions of security that appeared in the 1990s and rapidly became standard among donors. It usually acknowledges the intensely political nature of police reform, the known problems (such as corruption and brutality), and also that police will not change their behaviour unless it is in their personal and professional interest to do so. It then reverts back to statements that 'the police must' reform (O'Neill 2005).

The resultant approach – 'programme' is too systematic a term – is known as SSR (Brzoska 2003). SSR is used here to refer to the broad range of policies, programmes and projects promoting democratic-style police reform in post-conflict cities. It is essentially a response to policy-relevant problems by a small group of rich democracies and intergovernmental organisations. It is driven (and funded) by countries such as Australia, the Netherlands, Scandinavia, the UK and the USA (though others such as Belgium, France and Israel are very active), by development agencies such as AusAID, the Clingendael Institute, the Swedish International Development Agency (SIDA), DFID and USAID, and by organisations such as the OECD and the UN. It is predicated on the broad belief that 'security from disorder, crime and violence is fundamental for reducing poverty ... and, more broadly, for sustainable economic, social and political development' (OECD DAC 2007: 20). Disorder and crime are in turn equated with conflict: according to the 2005 *Human Security Report*, 'violent conflict is one of the surest and fastest routes to the bottom of the HDI [Human Development Index] table.' It is not, the Report claims, coincidental that 'since the early 1990s, developing countries have accounted for over half of all armed conflicts – almost 40% of which occurred on the African continent' (Human Security Centre 2005).

SSR has become very influential in shaping the context and content of international notions of policing. As the weeks pass, police governance in post-conflict cities is increasingly analysed in terms of institutional capacity and technical proficiency, and is assessed in the light of equitable recruitment, transparent management practices, adherence to human rights legislation, and community service (OECD DAC 2005: 36). As a model of policing it has advantages and disadvantages. It offers criteria that can be used as indicators for measuring change. Unfortunately, it is also based on unsubstantiated assumptions, and is applied in societies where the prospects for long-term change are slim.

DEVELOPING A REFORM AGENDA

Although the greatest impact on current forms of post-conflict policing is arguably that of the Pentagon, liberal orthodoxy is heavily influenced by the work of development-oriented donors such as the OECD and DFID.

The OECD aims to transform specific security systems 'in a manner that is more consistent with democratic norms and sound principles of good governance' (OECD DAC 2005: 20). Publications such as 2001's *DAC Guidelines*, Part I of *Helping Prevent Violent Conflict* (OECD DAC 2001), and 2004's *Security Sector Reform and Governance* (OECD DAC 2004) consistently argue that SSR makes a major contribution to conflict prevention and peace-building. It argues that an accountable and efficient security system, operating under civilian control within a democratic context, helps to ensure and sustain the stability that is necessary for development to occur. Order is rarely referred to; at best it is alluded to in terms of its characteristics or objectives.

Like the OECD, DFID sees SSR as part of wider efforts to strengthen state capacity, prevent conflict, and promote human development. For example, the UK's November 1997 White Paper on International Development identified security as central to sustained development, conflict reduction and poverty alleviation (DFID 1997, 1999; Short 1998). Development assistance should therefore be used to engage in SSR (1999), while SSR can (as in Sierra Leone) become an expression or test case of new humanitarianism (Schümer 2007). In 2000, DFID further broadened its analysis by developing policies on safety, security and access to justice (SSAJ) (DFID 2000). None of this was specifically designed for post-conflict cities, but it shaped the allocation of UK resources in, for instance, Freetown. One reason for this was that the period saw the emergence of a relatively coherent policy agenda whereby the UK combined its approaches to SSR, SSAJ and small arms and light weapons under a broader Security and Justice Sector Reform (SJSR) framework. The UK also strongly supported the OECD's work on developing an SSR policy agenda that has at its core democratic security governance.

By 2003 the OECD DAC was sufficiently confident about the legitimacy of this project to identify three interrelated challenges:

> i) developing a clear institutional framework for providing security that integrates security and development policy and includes all relevant actors and focuses on the vulnerable, such as women, children, and minority groups; ii) strengthening the governance and oversight of security institutions; and iii) building capable and professional security forces that are accountable to civil authorities and open to dialogue with civil society organisations. For DAC donors, this policy agenda, therefore, focuses primarily on governance-related and democratic oversight dimensions. (OECD DAC 2004: 2)

There are several reasons why this shift occurred, but it was probably driven by developments in the Balkans, where it became clear that the indigenous police were undermining internationally sanctioned peace processes, and reinforcing the region's corruption and ethnic divisions. Also, there was analytical spare capacity. European countries, the USA and IGOs such as the OSCE had acquired expertise in reforming militaries in the former Warsaw Pact, and were arguably looking for ways in which to redeploy their skills. So, too, were academics in international studies and peace studies who previously had focused on peacekeeping by military forces. And once attention was redirected, the police were seen as more accessible than, say, intelligence agencies, less loathed than prisons, and less controversial than judiciaries.[7]

This was reinforced by an analytical trend favouring 'security govern-ance', and an increasing recognition of the part played by institutional capacity in ensuring state-based security and stability.

This was the context in which interest in police reform arose. It was increasingly recognised that 'police institutions fundamen-tally affect the character of political development' (Bayley 1995: 79); that they are the most visible coercive instrument available to governments; and that they shape city life by what they fail to do as much as what they do. There is, of course, nothing new about external agents trying to influence police, but this had previously been attempted using training and equipment, and much of it was supply driven: the aspect of policing that is easiest for external actors/donors to influence is technical capacity. Also, this approach sometimes worked in that Western policing's technological resources, organisation and skills meant it was seen as modern and desirable. What changed at the end of the 1990s was the way in which assistance and/or education shifted from being a technical issue to an ideologically specific set of objectives and activities: namely, police reform.

With organisations such as the OECD and DFID in the vanguard, the new agenda was justified in terms of 'People-centred security rather than state-centred security' (OECD 2001). Nevertheless, the resources allocated to reform, and the political value allocated to it, varied greatly – and usually inversely. Compare, for example, the millions of dollars allocated to police advisers and training projects in Iraq by the Bush administration to the situation in the Netherlands where in 2004 an SSR team of two people, without resources at their disposal, was located in the Ministry of Foreign Affairs (Krasner and Pascual 2005).

Police reform is only one aspect of SSR, but its guiding princi-ples are essentially those underpinning SSR. These are formalised in overlapping codes of conducts promulgated by organisations such as the Council of Europe, the OSCE, the OECD and the UN (Caparini and Marenin 2004: 7). Of these, the most accessible and authoritative is that offered by the OECD DAC. According to its *Handbook*, the overall objective of SSR processes is 'to increase the ability of partner countries to meet the range of security and justice challenges they face, "in a manner consistent with democratic norms, and sound principles of governance and the rule of law'" (OECD DAC 2007: 21). Four key objectives or principles are identified:

i) Establishment of effective governance, oversight and accountability in the security system.
ii) Improved delivery of security and justice services.
iii) Development of local leadership and ownership of the reform process.
iv) Sustainability of justice and security sector delivery. (OECD DAC 2007: 21)

Ironically, Donnison's official history of Allied plans for post-conflict Europe never identified general principles: 'The reason is that few of these emerge. Indeed, one of the chief lessons ... is the need for the utmost flexibility of thought and organization so that the endlessly varying tasks facing civil affairs and military government may be undertaken each on its merits' (Donnison 1966: ix).

Today's approach is more formulaic and less pragmatic than that of the 1940s – it can afford to be because most of the conflicts involving liberal democracies are wars of choice. Perhaps for this reason, certain policy strands are primarily rhetorical. 'Local ownership', for example, is both a paternalistic mantra and a lie. Democratic reform is to be locally 'owned', but no policymaker seriously suggests that the retributive policing commonly advocated by local people should be allowed. As the UNHCR diplomatically notes, where 'the population has had no experience with a police force that provides services and protection and observes human rights ... [then] the United Nations must be ready to help citizens formulate demands for respectful, responsive policing' (UNHCR 2006: 19). In other words, democratic policing is a matter of imposition, rather than understanding, and analysis of why and how its various expectations arose is rare. As Findlay and Zvekić note of non-state policing, 'All too often ... discussion ... revolves around the means adopted for achieving certain relational goals, at the cost of understanding how the expectations for policing arose, and what comes of their achievement' (258). SSR is in this way a mix of idealism, ideology, security imperatives and policy transfer.

ASSESSMENT

Four key features of SSR are evident. First, SSR is ambitious. The UNHCR states:

> Police reform will inevitably transform a society; it is a major exercise in State-building requiring the population to have confidence in the police and the police to serve the public regardless of political agendas and despite their recent experience. Such a dynamic represents a pivotal change in how society is governed in most post-conflict and crisis States. (UNHCR 2006: 16)

A corrupt, brutal or ineffective police force that is incapable of reforming itself is (in the words of the Sierra Leone police's mission statement) to be transformed into a force capable of winning 'public confidence by offering reliable, caring and accountable police services' (*Sierra Leone Police News* 2004: 4).

Second, SSR is about power. Policing does not take place in some abstract neoliberal – or neorealist – space, but through the mobilisation and mediation of cultural, political, sectarian and ethnic identities; it is a means for managing relationships. Consequently, SSR legitimises the exercise of specific forms of power. To paraphrase Neocleous, it is part of liberalism's recoding of the politics of order, which turns policing into a range of security measures consistent with liberal principles (Neocleous 2000: 43). In other words, SSR is a technique of liberal security. It is a tool for liberal governance, which is invariably regarded by its advocates in a positive light.

Its potential disadvantages are rarely noted. The imposition of democratic policing models may, for example, contribute to dependency and underdevelopment through imposing or advocating inappropriate or unsustainable schemes. Or it may constitute 'a new form of exploitative, entrepreneurial neo-colonialism' (Murphy 2005: 143), structuring change and assistance programmes in ways that are favourable to the geostrategic interests of key Western states such as the USA and EU members (Huggins 1998; Ioannides 2007). Such moves may benefit ruling elites in recipient cities, and the senior officers sent on study visits to the USA or UK, but they rarely improve the lot of ordinary officers, let alone that of inhabitants in the longer term.

Third, SSR's goal is ideological, and its perspective (perhaps bias) is largely that of the European centre-left (Williams 2000); it seeks to promote a specific philosophy or normative approach as much as techniques and procedures. As Brogden and Nijhar have shown for community-oriented policing, the transfer of policing models is heavily overlaid with political assumptions about the 'right' development trajectory, and the donor–recipient relationship is unequal (Brogden and Nijhar 2005). Police advisers may prioritise opening stations, and getting police on the streets, but donors from rich countries such as Canada and Scandinavia regard objectives such as demilitarisation, representative ethnic composition, the inclusion of women and the eradication of clientelism as equally important. Only when fair and accountable security is available for all, it is argued, will poor people report crimes, and democratisation and development – and order – be ensured.

SSR is not intended as a means of ensuring effective policing; it is not concerned with creating police capable of dealing with organised crime, trafficking and violence per se. Indeed, its ability to ensure effective policing in fragile environments has yet to be proved, as has its ability to deliver the social engineering necessary for its continuance (cf. Krause and Jütersonke 2005). Enhancing accountability and responsiveness may, of course, ensure that the police gain public support. Alternatively, it may be seen as weakness. In short, while the transfer of policing models may be 'conflict sensitive' (Saferworld 2007), in seeking to decrease corruption and alleviate poverty, SSR downplays the underlying causes of insecurity (Fayemi 2001), and assumes that international agents can manipulate political and social forces (Luckham 2003).

Fourth, SSR is based on ethnocentric assumptions. Global interdependence (and the less controversial process of internationalisation) encourages the West to understand policing in the South in Western political and cultural terms; it assumes that its structures and standards apply whereas they may not. Indeed it is most likely that they will not. Cities in developing regions may reflect rationalities and causalities that are different to those of Europe or North America. Not only may their politics be centrifugal or overtly shaped by religious fundamentalism, but corruption may be fundamental to their working by being disconnected from individual morality and the failure of state institutions (Chabal and Daloz 1999).

To paraphrase Carothers's assessment of the related field of rule-of-law assistance, police reform programmes operate from a worryingly thin base of knowledge (Carothers 2006: 27). Further, accumulating knowledge on the realities of reform faces serious obstacles that range from the institutional shortcomings of donors to deeper intellectual challenges about police culture, and the nature and purpose of police institutions in the South.

UN POLICING

Almost every problem associated with the rationale, recruitment, deployment, management and success of international police in post-conflict cities is evident in a UN context. Trends in UNPOL operations reflect changing expectations of international policing, the limits on what it can achieve, and the dominance of pragmatic and technical imperatives over ideology.

The potential contribution of UNPOL to managing cities once the situation has stabilised – and the absence of any internationally sanctioned alternative – is evident from the demands made on their services in response to Security Council mandates and calls from regional organisations: UNPOL numbers increased from 2 per cent of peacekeeping forces in 1995 to 12 per cent in 2007.[8] In the last six months of 2006, new operations took place in Nepal, Chad, the Central African Republic and Somalia, and the Security Council authorised the deployment of more than 15,000 UNPOL (at which point some 8,800 officers were in the field).

Until recently, UNPOL's role was administering what were seen as the prerequisites of order; officers were restricted to monitoring, advising and training local police. But the increase in UN operations and UNPOL's usefulness meant its remit soon expanded, reaching a peak in Kosovo and East Timor, where officers were given executive policing authority to make arrests and enforce law, and thus to regulate the emergent order. But Kosovo and East Timor were small territories with small populations, a majority of whom welcomed international intervention. This was not the case in Afghanistan or Iraq, where their role has been negligible. Even so, UNPOL's strategic mission is increasingly that of developing institutional police capacity in post-conflict environments, and its role is changing to supporting the reform, restructuring and rebuilding of local police. The mandates of eleven of the twelve missions authorised since 1999 refer to monitoring, reforming and rebuilding local police.

The first component of all new missions – reform – is understood in terms of democratic policing. This is followed by restructuring, which uses vetting and the introduction of new recruitment practices to depoliticise and demilitarise police, and by rebuilding, which involves UNPOL in assessing needs and advising on the use of donor funds. This makes UNPOL's role vis-à-vis order potentially significant. However, their contribution is uneven and temporary by virtue of their nature: UNPOL are the equivalent of temporary, miscellaneous, civilian (though increasingly paramilitary in nature) and comparatively cheap firefighters.

The two most pressing challenges confronting UNPOL throughout the 1990s and for the foreseeable future are the recruitment and training of officers, and their performance. Personnel contributions are usually based on time-sensitive political decisions, but officers are in demand at home, and (unlike the military) are normally not available for dispatch abroad. The solutions to recruitment proposed range from national rosters of officers placed on standby (as in Canada, Germany and Norway) and regular secondment and standby arrangements, to strategic initiatives such as 2007's 25-member standing police capacity (SPC). The use of formed police units (FPUs) has been especially popular, for they expand the number of countries providing police, and establish the equivalent of a standing cadre of experts for rapid deployment in relatively insecure conditions. Ironically, they also promote a style of paramilitary policing that is at odds with democratic policing's stated objective of demilitarising policing.

The UN traditionally recruits and deploys officers as individuals, but FPUs are cost-effective groups of 120–140 armed officers trained in skills such as crowd control and close protection. Heavily influenced by the paramilitary models of countries such as Argentina, France and Italy, FPUs were originally authorised for UN operations in Kosovo in 1999 where they were known as specialised police units. They became a regular feature of UN missions from Liberia in 2003 onwards, and by mid-2007, thirty-five FPUs (approximately 4,000 strong) were deployed in Côte d'Ivoire, DRC, Haiti, Kosovo, Liberia and Timor Leste.

FPUs make pragmatic sense. They are used for crowd control when local police are unprepared, unwilling or overwhelmed, and they have propaganda value; they can make it seem that local police can cope. Indeed, 'it is intended that FPUs will be a "role model" to the local police in the street' (UN DPKO Police Division 2006). They represent a module that facilitates planning and deployment, and they are cheaper than military or individual police officers. Traditionally, in non-FPU deployments, contributing countries pay their officers' salaries, and are not reinbursed by the UN, but UN service is attractive because officers also receive a mission subsistence allowance (MSA) of $80–150 a day ($2,400–4,500 a month). FPUs do not receive an MSA, but the UN provides a standard reinbursement to contributing governments of some $1,400 a month. Their cost-effectiveness thus makes them an attractive option for the Security Council. Further, the 2007 contribution of an all-female Indian FPU (albeit one with a reputation for repressive operations) to Liberia allowed UNPOL to be seen to conform to the UN's political proprieties, for Resolution 1325 called for the equal and full participation of women as active agents in peace and security. The British FCO has argued that FPUs reinforce the distinction between police and military, but this is disingenuous: FPUs have functional utility, but they are paramilitary and their composition and operations blur police/military boundaries.

The performance of UNPOL is as problematic as recruitment, for there are never enough competent officers. Poor-quality applicants, high turnover and rotation rates exacerbate the problems. A two-week pre-deployment training now exists, but there is no standardised training as such. Not only is criminal misconduct problematic in most operations (some national contingents are notorious for corruption and sexual predation), but also most UNPOL have little knowledge of the norms and standards associated with democratic policing. It could not be otherwise when the top contributing countries in August 2007 included Bangladesh, Benin, Cameroon, China, France, Ghana, India, Jordan, Malaysia, Nepal, Nigeria, Pakistan, Philippines,

Portugal, Romania, Senegal, Ukraine and the USA. Indeed, in some operations (Sierra Leone, for example) UNPOL have 'less professional experience and competence than the local police' they are supposedly advising (UN DPKO 2003: 53). Although UN officials refer to the ambiguous body of rules and precepts labelled 'international policing' as their guiding principles, national perspectives ensure that the parameters of policing, its transitional points, and rules of engagement differ according to national experience and special interests. Cultural attitudes to corruption, discipline and the application of force vary enormously, and the statement by Mark Kroeker, a former UN police adviser, that 'all UN police officers, no matter where they come from, play a vital role in assisting the UN to build institutional police capacity' is, given the liberal objectives of UN peacebuilding, misleading (Smith et al. 2007).

But it is easy to overstate the effects of this, because the gulf between international and domestic practice is one of the peculiarities of UNPOL. It matters here because it emphasises the artificiality of UN operations, and also the discrete and laboratory-like nature of their operations in cities such as Monrovia and Kinshasa. Take the case of Nigerian officers and men in Liberia and the DRC. Nigeria publicly adheres to UN standards. As UNMIL police commissioner Mohammed Alhassan said in 2006, the Nigerian contingent in Liberia 'served in a multinational environment with courage, tolerance, understanding and respect for others to fulfill the mandate of the mission' (UNMIL 2006). In turn, Nigeria's police contingent commander said that 'his officers were proud to be part of the UN efforts in Liberia "to restore peace, maintain law and order and to support the elections which ushered in a democratically elected government".' In fact, complicity, accommodation and sexual exploitation were stronger themes in Nigerian operations. Indeed, in September 2005 Nigeria had withdrawn its 120-strong police contingent from Kinshasa after the UN launched an investigation into allegations of sexual harassment against ten members of its unit; the operation had been plagued by allegations of sexual abuse, with peacekeepers being accused of rape and giving food or money in exchange for sex.

To Nigeria's credit, the unit was sent home on the basis that its actions contaminated all Nigerians. A spokesman said: 'We have contingents in about 19 countries right now and we want to send a message to all other contingents that if one finger collects oil, the whole hand is stained.' But corruption probably went right to the top. Towards the end of their time in Liberia, some senior military officers were accused of dubious business dealings with Liberian leaders, and this was presumably true of police also (BBC 4 August 2003). What is more, it is alleged that senior officers (including then inspector-general Ehindero) extracted the UN duty allowances of officers and men in Liberia (*Daily Trust* 2007).

The difference between Nigeria's international and domestic standards are, however, most evident from the number of people killed by police in Nigeria. Dozens of badly trained and poorly paid Nigerian officers die at the hands of armed robbers every year, and some instances of abuse are a response to this. Others result from public and political pressure on the police to address Nigeria's high levels of violent crime. Hence the language used by the officials who announced that between January 2000 and March 2004, police killed 7,198 'armed robbers' in 'combat' (HRW 2005: 15). Some officers extract confessions through torture, or kill suspects in their custody whom they believe to be guilty, precisely because they lack the skills or resources to carry out effective investigation. A lawyer told New York-based advocacy group Human Rights Watch (HRW) that members of the Mobile Police Force publicly admit that torture is the only way they can get suspects to confess (HRW 2005: 36). Suspects held in the custody of agencies such as the Economic and Financial Crimes Commission (EFCC) and the National Drug Law Enforcement Agency (NDLEA) receive similar treatment (HRW 2005: 3)

Whatever the reason, official statistics from 2007 indicated that police had shot and killed more than 8,000 Nigerians over the preceding five years. Indeed, as HRW notes, the true number of people killed probably exceeded 10,000, given that the police killed half as many armed robbers as they arrested during the first three months of the then inspector general's tenure alone (casualties are usually described as armed robbers) (HRW 2005: 15). In the words of the UN Special Rapporteur on Torture, torture and extrajudicial killings by police appear to be 'an intrinsic part of how law enforcement services operate' (HRW 2007c). But none of this prevents Nigeria making a useful contribution to UNPOL missions. The domestic record of Zimbabwe's police does not bar them from UNPOL either.

POLICING OPERATIONS

Assuming a relatively benign environment, UNPOL operations illustrate the policing methods typically used to manage street-level order.[9] However, UNPOL cannot operate without the protection of military forces, especially in the early weeks. Just as the police civil-affairs officers of World War II depended on Allied forces for protection, logistics, and petrol, oil and lubricants, so the International Police Task Force (IPTF) in Sarajevo required logistical and medical assistance from NATO's Implementation Force (IFOR). But support for police is always peripheral to the military role. IFOR's main task was collecting intelligence regarding the location of mines, damage assessment, and locating prisoners being held by Muslims, rather than supporting IPTF. Any policing activity was incidental, and the teams concerned never investigated organised crime or the activities of the Serb police. The same will apply in future operations.

Assuming a degree of 'peace' prevails, the immediate policing challenges are, from a UN/multinational perspective:

- clarification of the relationship between police and military forces;
- the establishment of a command unit;
- putting police on the streets for functional and reassurance purposes;
- organising registration processes;
- developing rapid response units.

Thought must also be given to legacy issues such as:

- racial/ethnic split divisions in the police;
- distrust between officers, and between officers and the populace;
- the consequences of serial/systematic underfunding;
- literacy levels.

In practice, the usual pattern of UNPOL/multinational tactical response to security threats involves transitioning down from:

- calling in military forces;
- using firearms;
- employing physical contact (pushing crowds apart with shields);
- rubber bullets (non-lethal weapons);
- physical presence (with armoured vehicles and the equivalent of a fanfare);
- community policing.

The means usually employed include curfews, mass arrests and paramilitary raids. Curfews or states of emergency are applied by UNPOL or governments to prevent retaliatory attacks in the aftermath of multiple deaths or the murder of significant individuals such as politicians or police chiefs. They are typically imposed in the aftermath of bombings targeting specific sectarian groups, or when insurgent gunmen set up roadblocks in order to carry out attacks. Raids by troops supported by armed and masked international and/or indigenous paramilitary police are another feature. So too are mass arrests, which are used to exert pressure on specific parties or groups, or to punish. In fact, curfews and mass arrests are typical of state-based security operations in post-conflict cities. Thus the Iraqi government declared a daylight curfew in Baghdad on 13 June 2007. It was intended to prevent revenge attacks after a Shia shrine was attacked in the Sunni city of Samarra, 60 miles north of Baghdad. A bombing in Samarra in 2006, for instance, had resulted in 140 deaths over the following twenty-four hours as clerics and mosques were targeted. In the Palestinian territories thousands have been arrested at night, at checkpoints, or after demonstrations and riots. Those arrested are usually accused of throwing stones, assaulting officers, damaging property, or with public order offences such as participating in an unlawful assembly or rioting.

CONCLUSION

The preceding discussion warrants five general conclusions.

First, post-conflict policing is understood by liberal democracies primarily in terms of the opportunities it presents for promoting reforms that will, it is argued, enhance stability and security. While not fundamentally different to reform in other settings, post-conflict

reform is thought to offer opportunities for wide-ranging organisational change. For example, costs can be cut by the integration of
several forces into one, and recruitment patterns radically changed
(Brzoska 2003: 32; OECD DAC 2007). Yet ideas about the nature,
purpose and potential of police and policing in post-conflict cities
are based on research conducted by American, European and Australian scholars in their own countries or areas of influence, and the
transferability of Western norms, practices and policies to Southern
police is assumed, rather than proven. Yet there is no reason why
recruits to a new police force will behave or think differently to
their predecessors, especially when recruitment is treated as a job-
creation scheme for ex-combatants (Liberia), as an enticement for
minority buy-in to a peace process (Bosnia), or as a political indicator
(Iraq). Similarly, it is assumed that conflict and violence are prompted
by misunderstanding (Bosnia or Macedonia) and can therefore be
managed by police, whereas revenge may be the motivating factor
(Celador 2005: 366).

Second, we know that policing, like security itself, is defined
situationally and contextually, and that police are notoriously resist-
ant to change, yet Western policymakers and advisers consistently
seek to impose the values, norms and practices of democratic-style
policing on indigenous police, and to reflect their own national practices. Commentators speak of developing 'a rational structure that
encourages standard responses and enables delegation of authority
and accountability'. This, it is said, 'is a necessary foundation for a
police organization' (Murray 2007: 117). In other words – and here
I extend Fatton's observation about governance – 'in the name of a
common social purpose, proponents of the [SSR] governance model
display a cavalier disregard for material realities, class interests, and
the predatory relations nurturing the structures of power, affluence,
and status' (Fatton 1992: 142).

Third, models of state building assume that police can play a
significant role in restoring state legitimacy and stability; that is,
that insecurity can be avoided with aid and advice. Multilateral and
bilateral interventions accordingly place a premium on reforming and
educating police. Yet, as the following chapters will show, there are
few success stories. For SSR cannot reform the social matrix and/or

power networks that use or abuse policing. As Goverde observes in relation to power, 'as soon as the mechanisms of dominance and suppression, of insecurity and violence, of influence and power, of competencies and reluctance, etc., are undervalued, the theoretical construction seems to be unrealistic, or at least artificial' (Goverde and van Tatenhove 2000: 102).

Fourth, the problems confronting liberal democracies in multinational operations are not fundamentally different to those confronting contingents from illiberal countries. The functional problems of resources, training and recruitment are similar, even if the significance attached to them, and the resources and solutions, are different. Most UN operations share common aims, norms and guidelines, and police behave much as peacekeepers behave: no one police force has a monopoly on incompetence, corruption or virtue. Some national contingents are ineffective, unqualified and corrupt. Some are armed and some unarmed, with all that implies for their working styles, responses and responsibilities; some are paramilitary and work closely with the military, and some do not. Some leave the safety of their headquarters and others do not. Some behave much the same whether they are in their own country or on the other side of the world. The Norwegian police training officers at the Nigeria Police staff college at Jos for deployment in Darfur value consensus and cooperation, and their standards are consistent across a range of environments. But this is not the case for their Nigerian students whose international and domestic practices are often dramatically different. But in practice, Western publics only distinguish between contingents when there are scandals or casualties. The involvement of DynCorp officers in sex scandals in Bosnia in 1998 made the headlines (UN police, NATO troops and international humanitarian employees were involved too),[10] as did the death of nineteen Italian Carabinieri in Nasiriya.

Fifth, international forces and advisers are themselves actors and nodes in the network of interests and power bases underpinning the post-conflict city. Further, they exacerbate tension. Thus police conventionally support the status quo and restore order, rather than create it, yet Western authorities demand otherwise. To restate the words of Klockars, donors' assessments and understanding are 'based on beliefs about what police should do or are supposed to be, about the purposes or ends of policing' (Findlay and Zvekić 1993: 17). The result is 'norm-derivative' definitions of police and order that are associated with specific forms of order, and are achievable only in a culturally partial manner (Loader and Walker 2007a: 105).

The last two chapters have provided an overview of cities, their problems, and the solutions promoted by IGOs and donors. But in order to understand the interface between local and international objectives and practices, we need to look in more detail at what indigenous police do in post-conflict cities, why they do it and how their actions reflect or influence the re-emergence of order and the creation of security. We need more information about the situations they typically confront and their responses to them. Only then can democratic goals be meaningfully compared with the realities of post-conflict cityscapes. This is the task of the next four chapters, beginning with US- and UK-led operations in Iraq after the war of 2003. Two main themes run throughout. First, order, security and policing are best understood as aspects of power relations, and second, the key to power relations is to be found in manipulation, negotiation and accommodation.

4

GHETTO SECURITY

Power relations mould the post-war urban environment. Pragmatic modes of manipulation, negotiation and accommodation among and between factional leaders, international agents and the populace soon develop into patterns of domination and exclusion. This usually leads to a ghettoisation of security whereby specific groups are secure only in specific areas; citywide security is rare. Security is localised, superficial and often temporary, and order is essentially the sum of myriad local arrangements. It is usually decided not by international politics but by mutually suspicious interactions between indigenous strongmen, external agents and influential sections of the populace. The ways in which this situation develops shed light on the consolidation of local order, and its interaction with national and international order. Further, the role of police in facilitating or obstructing citywide order consistently offers a more accurate indicator of order than the protestations and statistics of international spokesmen, indigenous politicians and factional leaders.

Baghdad, Iraq's capital, and Basra, its strategically important second city, provide paradigmatic cases of these trends from several perspectives. First, security in both cities was ghettoised. Just as the Coalition authorities were walled off in Baghdad's so-called Green Zone, so Baghdad's districts were purged, divided into isolated neighbourhoods by concrete walls, barriers and checkpoints, and guarded by factional militias and gunmen. Similar trends are identifiable in Basra. Second, in both cities security was a symbol, a sign and a signal that had sense at many levels and referred to different things; it had multiple meanings. Of special interest is that Baghdad and Basra provide pragmatic illustrations of the issues signified by theoretical debates concerning the nature of order and, above all, security. They answer classic questions such as, security for whom, and from what? They provide a base point from which to judge claims that the concept of security must be refocused from an external enemy or a state, to irregular or non-state actors. They engage with arguments, such as those offered by Booth, that security implies not only the absence of violence but also the gaining of specific types of emancipation (Booth 1991: 318). Above all, they emphasise that security needs to be understood as a functional process or means, as much as a concept or ideal.

This chapter focuses on developments in Baghdad and in Basra, and the time frame used runs from April 2003, when US forces took Baghdad and Basra was occupied by UK forces, to 2007. The emphasis is on the early months of the occupation when the Coalition Provisional Authority (CPA) sought to impose its vision of order. But Iraq's chronic insecurity makes it impossible to tell whether the post-conflict period ended in June 2004, when the US formally handed sovereignty to an interim government, or in May 2005 when the first democratically elected Iraqi government was sworn in, or in late 2007, when a surge in US troop numbers dramatically reduced insurgent attacks. There were improvements throughout this period, but they tended to be local; the presence of US troops damped down violence, which then migrated to areas with fewer troops. Damningly, Johns Hopkins Bloomberg School of Public Health estimated that some 655,000 people died between 2003 and 2005 (Johns Hopkins 2006).

Iraq is both paradigmatic and extreme. After four years of insurgency and civil conflict, a national government existed in name only, 3 million Iraqis were internally displaced, some 3,000 were murdered each month, and many more were subject to kidnapping, rape, extortion and robbery. The police were little more than a sectarian militia, many of whose members were responsible for torture and extrajudicial killings (McCaffrey 2007).[1] This, despite receiving significant aid and support in kind from members of the US-led coalition. The USA alone spent $194 million on rebuilding the police and military during its year of occupation (*Financial Times*, 27 August 2007), and most of the UK Ministry of Defence's gift aid (including guns, ammunition, and public-order equipment such as protective vests and armoured Land Rovers) went to the police (*Observer* 2005). By July 2006, the UK (which made support to the police a priority) had disbursed £533 million to projects that included police training and mentoring (Hansard 2006). Meanwhile Japan had given about $1.5 billion in grant aid for comparable programmes (*Japan Times*, 13 October 2005). None of this made a genuine difference to order or security. Rather, it underscored the gulf between democratic ideals and Iraqi realities.

IRAQ'S SIGNIFICANCE

Iraq raises a number of important questions about the relationship between order and security. These include whether security is essential for order, whether the concerns of states should be prioritised over those of individuals or associational groups, and what they should be protected against. For security dominated everyone's calculations. Force protection shaped US military tactics, though Washington had no taste for the nation-building (that is, conventional order) that might have mitigated urban insecurity. The UN, meanwhile, played no part in managing Iraq once its chief envoy, Sergio Vieira de Mello, was killed in August 2003. Five years on, international attempts to create an effective and reliable police force had yet to succeed, and street-level security remains the province of sectarian militias. Iraq suggests that, while an inclusive or broadened sense of security has value, security has multiple meanings but remains primarily a matter of physical safety.

Iraq shows how the Coalition's neoliberal ideals of cooperation, democratisation and police reform collided with Iraqi requirements: Baghdad's inhabitants understood security to mean the physical safety and protection of themselves and their property. The two understandings are symbolised by the American troops who drove around 'announcing in a loudspeaker "security for us in return for electricity for you"' (BBC 6 July 2003).[2] They also collided with the USA's own security imperatives, for Iraqi police were recruited as part of the USA's counterinsurgency campaign and exit strategy, and the US troops charged with recruiting and training police could not think beyond the short term because they were regularly rotated in and out of areas. None of the lessons from Iraq is new, but they emphasise our incomplete understanding of security.

Also, Iraq tests the extent to which policing models that respect the rights of all 'citizens' and are responsive to their needs can maintain order. In particular, it tests whether democratic policing based on a close relationship between respectfulness, responsiveness and effectiveness has meaning in violent cities. For in Iraq, as in most of the world, the police's primary purpose is not crime-fighting, reassurance or protection. Indeed, anecdotal evidence suggests that many Iraqis believe that police must be allowed to violate rights if they are to ensure security. This belief is reinforced by the widespread conviction among police that there are certain criminal or dangerous classes that represent a threat to the broader social order, and that therefore deserve fewer rights.

But Iraq's significance here is primarily threefold. First, it provides an empirically verifiable case for assessing the part played by police in emergent order. Second, it throws light on the ways in which the meaning and purpose of security are determined, and on the processes by which security and, by extension, order are represented. Third, it indicates the fundamental importance of power relations in determining order, security and policing. For the only certainty is that security (both for those who provide it, and often for those who want it) means whatever powerful actors make of it.

IRAQ'S RE-EMERGENT ORDER

Baghdad was burning from fires set by looters when, a month after the 2003 Iraq War ended, Paul Bremer arrived as head of the Coalition Provisional Authority (CPA). The first question he asked was, Where are the police? (Bremer and McConnell 2006). There were no police because officers had destroyed or hidden their uniforms during the war, while the bureaucracy, buildings, procedures and political relationships on which the police institution was based were destroyed. Nevertheless, many officers responded to US appeals that they return to work, and by mid-April some manned joint patrols with US soldiers. In May a former Interior Ministry official and Ba'athist loyalist was appointed as Baghdad's police chief, though he was forced to resign a week later for refusing to implement procedures required by US authorities (Rai 2003).

The re-emergence of police in Baghdad was, as in Basra, Iraq's strategically important second city, facilitated by several linked traits. First, police occupy a residual position that is symbolically different from other forms of security provision. Although the police were widely despised as brutally ineffective, they represented a valuable prize once groups began jockeying for access to Iraq's resources. Second, the police institution is inherently strong; it is a primary mechanism for political groups to augment their power, impose a particular morality, entrench factional or sectarian practices, and secure funds and weapons (Herring and Rangwala 2006: 268). Third, the police, in Iraq as elsewhere in the world, are content to be used. Regardless of rhetoric, regime and resources, senior officers rarely build power bases comparable to those of the military. Some seek to preserve a minimal degree of operational and professional autonomy, but most appear unable or unwilling to operate as independent political actors; they are typically adjuncts to groups that control resources more directly. And most identify with the state; when wearing their uniform they see themselves as state representatives. At the same time, most have personal patrons with whom reciprocal exchanges of favour are made. This applies at all levels, emphasising the analytical significance of power relations. Thus political or sectarian sponsorship is important for initial recruitment because police are one of the few sources of employment. Similarly, Nasiriyya's city council, which was nominated by the Supreme Council for the Islamic Revolution in Iraq (SCIRI – a Shi'a political party now known as the Supreme Iraqi Islamic Council), established a new police battalion by giving each council member the right to appoint seven members (Herring and Rangwala 2006: 133). SCIRI later used the Ministry of the Interior (which by April 2005 it controlled) to integrate its militia into the police.

POLICING IRAQ

Little was known about Iraqi policing before 2003. Publications such as al-Khalil's *Republic of Fear* presented a picture of low-status police operating in an ordered and stable society whose inhabitants were secure from the criminality common elsewhere (al-Khalil 1989). An interlocking network of security organisations with overlapping functions guaranteed the Ba'athist order, with the 60,000-strong Iraqi National Police at the bottom of the hierarchy. Since then multiple accounts or policy-relevant analyses have been written that touch on the police (e.g. Chandrasekaran 2007: 93–101; Deflem and Sutphin 2006; Jones et al. 2005; Perito 2003, 2004, 2005), supplemented by the memoirs of those who dealt with them (Etherington 2005; Stewart 2007). Yet there are no known English-language analyses of policing from a comparative perspective.

Under the direction of Paul Bremer, an Iraqi Police Service (IPS) was established and placed under the authority of the Ministry of the Interior. The remit of the new police was crime control, order maintenance and assisting coalition forces (though the latter retained responsibility for investigations involving terrorism and military crimes). Vetting ensured that Ba'ath Party members were purged, and international attention focused on 'professionalising' the new police (Perito 2004, 2005). But little changed. Former senior and mid-level officers were removed, but most officers stayed in their stations, beating suspects and extorting bribes just as before the war. By 2007, sectarian militia groups infiltrated every level of policing; the Interior Ministry reputedly supplied militiamen with police uniforms and vehicles.

Police reform was a failure even by the Coalition's politicised standards. The CPA measured progress quantitatively. In the first year of operations, 32,000 recruits aged 18–24 received an eight-week training package, and by late 2005, 67,500 had been trained in Jordan and other regional centres. By May 2004, some 90,000 officers were supposedly active, though the number of operational police was probably less than half this figure. Again, by 2007, twelve police academies were supposedly producing 26,000 new police a year (McCaffrey 2007: 142). But the reality was, as General Martin Dempsey (who led the Multi-National Security Transition Command) admitted to a congressional hearing in 2007, that more than 32,000 of the 180,000 newly trained and equipped police generated under Coalition schemes were no longer in the police. Approximately 8,000 had been killed in action, 6–8,000 were seriously wounded, 5,000 had deserted, and 7–8,000 were unaccounted for (*JDW* 20 June 2007). The Interior Ministry's payroll exceeded 10,000 officers, but numbers were impossible to determine since local chiefs inflated numbers to get funding, and individuals drifted in and out of service.

In fact, recruitment was never a problem. Unemployment rates of 40 per cent meant that men applied regardless of the dangers of the job. And the dangers were real. The Iraq Body Count database found police casualties to be higher than those of any other occupation, including politicians and religious leaders (Deflem and Sutphin 2006). Suicide bombings and roadside explosive devices aimed at recruiting stations, police convoys or military convoys escorting police account for many of the casualties, especially once the insurgency emerged in the summer of 2003. Most officers were unarmed and patrolling was suicidal, but men joined because the starting salary of an IPS officer in 2003 was 90,000ID ($60) per month, plus 130,000ID ($87) per month in hazardous duty pay (Chandrasekaran 2007: 328; Herring and Rangwala 2006: 197). Chief officers were targeted too. On 8 June 2007, carloads of attackers descended on a chief's house in Baquba, 35 miles north-east of Baghdad, killing his wife, two brothers and eleven guards, and kidnapping three of his children (*Guardian* 9 June 2007).

MAPPING ORDER

It is difficult to map the re-emergence of order because so much is unknown. Despite their sophisticated technologies, American forces knew little about developments in the localities in which their adversaries were based. And although the CPA's policy decisions can be seen as marking significant moments or shifts, its vision of order was developed in isolation from Iraq's existing patterns of domination and subjugation. The CPA was rarely seen to address the concerns of most of the population. When it did, the result was often incoherence and more insecurity.

Crime is a case in point. There had been low-level non-organised crime in the 1990s as sanctions and economic stagnation reduced living standards and encouraged the middle classes to emigrate, but this could not be compared to the situation in 2003. The disappearance of regime authority, the emptying of prisons, and the failure to control looting encouraged criminal violence. Home invasions, muggings and murders increased dramatically, together with carjacking, kidnappings, rapes, revenge killings, drugs trafficking and prostitution. From being almost non-existent in pre-war Iraq, street crime became the primary concern of most Iraqis. Murder and kidnapping were especially problematic, not least because victims included more children, females and the elderly than is usual in non-war environments. Additionally, kidnapping was about economics as well as retribution or sectarian hatred. As a Shia man later said: 'They kidnap 10 Sunnis, they get ransoms on five, and kill them all, in each big kidnap operation they make at least $50,000, it's the best business in Baghdad' (*Guardian* 27 January 2007). Many crimes went unreported because there was no one to report them to. Militias and groups subcontracting protection required payment.

Bremer thought that it would be unacceptable to use police agencies associated with Saddam's regime, so one of the CPA's first acts was to dissolve the Ba'ath Party and purge Ba'athists from government positions. This left the police leaderless. In particular, Bremer underestimated the degree to which effective police depend on institutional structures. The Ba'ath Party permeated every level of Iraq's administration, and public and private life, so the policy of killing or detaining even local leaders deepened the security vacuum. Insecurity was made worse by the policy of dismissing the many civil servants needed to support the police. Insecurity appeared to deepen and widen, religious vigilantes soon created alternative local security systems, and looting and street crime were subsumed into a more pervasive security crisis.

At a press conference on 30 April 2004, General John Abizaid (commander of US forces in the Middle East) showed a diagram categorising the threat in cities such as Kirkuk and Mosul (both of which had seen major disturbances). Crime represented a major factor driving violence in such cities, compounding the problems caused by former regime elements, terrorists and extremists. When asked what were his immediate military tasks for the sixty days left before the handover of sovereignty to an Iraqi government, Abizaid said that the immediate military task was the rebuilding of Iraqi security capacity, followed by counterterrorist operations, both of which demanded policing operations: 'we've got an awful lot of conventional forces tied up conducting patrols and maintaining the normal day-to-day security environment' (US Department of Defense 2004).

Crime was in this way indicative of the order that prevailed. Even so, the use of crime and levels of violence to measure order is complicated by the difficulty of distinguishing between criminal violence, gang violence, political violence, and violence as a response to coalition violence. Also, crime may be characteristic of, or an expression of, order, as order may be based on chronic insecurity. Crime did not of itself mean that order was missing, any more than de-Ba'athification and the US authorities' toleration of looting did. Rather, it signified that alternative forms of order were present, though they were not those the Coalition favoured.

There was a short window of opportunity in the first days of the occupation when the CPA, as the temporary but lawful government, could have facilitated or imposed (symbolically or genuinely) a framework conducive to, or reflecting, some form of 'democratic' control. But the Bush administration's ideological approach to regime change and reconstruction obstructed this. The moment was lost, and each passing week created more spoilers. Groups vying for political resources, turf control or profits quickly exploited potential security gaps. And the US forces allowed them to gain the initiative. This was most evident in the Coalition's approach to looting. Its troops concentrated on defending selected public buildings, and they looked the other way as Iraqis engaged in wholesale looting in Coalition-controlled areas. Many Iraqis profited, but many more saw the looting as a symbol of the insecurity characterising Coalition-style order.

The omission or failure by Coalition forces to control looting or ensure public safety reinforced the conviction of Iraqis that their security was not a Coalition priority. Coalition authorities sometimes allowed looting because it was thought to send a powerful message that the Coalition was in control. But this ignored the fact that disorder and insecurity primarily affected ordinary Iraqis who were already angry about water and electricity shortages, angry about civilian deaths from Coalition bombing, and resentful of foreign invasion. Many workers lost their source of livelihood because factories and shops were looted.

The situation was admittedly different when seen from the perspective of Coalition forces, who, as the de facto occupying power, were obliged by international humanitarian law and convention to restore public order and safety. When questioned as to why forces stood by, senior officers usually argued that they lacked sufficient troops to protect cities and therefore focused on protecting vital infrastructure such as oil facilities and food warehouses. Other (low-ranking) troops thought looting was tolerated or encouraged as a cathartic reaction to the fall of Saddam's government. What was clear was that the combat troops in Iraq's cities at the end of the war were not trained to ensure civilian security; they were untrained for policing duties and by their actions often increased the sense of insecurity.

In this way, order re-emerged in the first weeks of the occupation, but, like the forms of security it reflected and depended on, it was a hybrid: it contained elements of both a free-market economy and sectarian imperatives. The balance between the elements varied, and order, like security, was fragmented, localised and temporary, rather than coherent or comprehensive. But both existed and there was no vacuum.

NEGOTIATING ORDER

The key to understanding this situation is to be found in power relations. This interpretation is supported by developments in the year that followed the CPA's dissolution, for by 2004 Iraq was divided into fiefdoms and factions, of which the US-led coalition was only one, albeit the best resourced in material terms. The dominant security themes were those of coercion, negotiation and accommodation. Thus in the summer of 2004, Iraq's new prime minister, Iyad Allawi, tried to take a hard line by claiming personal control of the security forces while refusing to negotiate with militias loyal to the radical Shia leader Moqtada al-Sadr. On other occasions, accommodation was more typical. July saw former fighters paid to collect rubbish, plant trees, direct traffic and help the police (*The Economist* 24 July 2004: 50–51), and the lifting of a controversial ban on al-Sadr's newspaper *al-Hawza*. Al-Sadr was seemingly co-opted by the authorities, but in fact agreeing to a truce spared him from intrusive American raids while allowing his militiamen to act as roughly as ever in the suburbs.

Or take the case of Ramadi, a city of some 450,000 people, which US troops normally entered mid-morning, when police were on the streets. However, the police disappeared at 14:00, and police stations closed, as did governorate buildings and shops. The reason was that insurgents had announced (by loudhailer) that fighting would begin after 14:00. Which it did. At 14:00, up to twenty Daewoo cars and Nissan trucks armed with RPGs and Kalashnikovs emerged from side streets, remaining in control until daybreak when police arrived for their eight-hour shift, and shopping for the day began (*Financial Times* 30 July 2004). Some of the insurgents wished to impose Islamic law in place of Allawi's American-backed law: 'We have two missions in the city. One is to defend Ramadi against the Americans who enter and the other is to kill anyone who sells alcohol or sex CDs.' But the colonel commanding Ramadi's 2,880-strong National Guard claimed to have no particular loyalty to either side.

Security was localised. It was then fragmented by Coalition authorities who subcontracted its provision to organisations and groups ranging from private security companies (PSCs, such as Control Risks, DynCorp and MPRI) to sheiks or Sunni groups capable of securing their own areas against insurgents. This allowed the authorities to define security broadly or narrowly, according to context. Coalition authorities publicly defined security broadly in the sense of it being developed for 'the Iraqi people', but security was really about force protection and the safety of Coalition officials, just as order was about imposing the CPA's ideological model. The resultant ambiguities offered space for security to become a relative and politically flexible notion. Accordingly, PSCs were used to provide security for the head of the CPA, escort supply convoys, defend key locations in Baghdad's Green Zone, and (most controversially) interrogate prisoners.[3] Twenty-seven of the thirty-seven interrogators involved in the abuse of prisoners at Abu Ghraib prison belonged to CACI International, a Virginia-based private contractor, and twenty-two of the linguists who assisted them were from the California-based Titan International.

Such civilian employers were effectively unaccountable, for they were not subject to military law or the Geneva Conventions, and Bremer had issued an order protecting them from local prosecution.

OVERVIEW OF ORDER AND INSECURITY IN IRAQ

Iraqi order operated at a number of levels, most of which were inaccessible to outsiders. Furthermore, within weeks of the occupation, swathes of Baghdad (which was strategically the critical city) were out of international control. Much of the burden of policing fell to US troops, but they were neither trained nor equipped for it. Infantry complained they had not been trained in arrest procedures, tank crews were not equipped for foot patrols, M-1 tanks and Bradley fighting vehicles were too large to move through Baghdad's streets, and the imperatives of force protection meant troops could not engage with Iraqis even if they wanted to. Some 4,000 US military police were eventually deployed in June, but there was little they could achieve; a force smaller than many US metropolitan police departments was responsible for a looted city of 4.5 million inhabitants (Perito 2003). Also, while security often improved when troop numbers increased, it declined when they left.

Four years later US control remained incomplete. Indeed, according to a review of a security operations in Baghdad in February 2007, US and Iraqi forces controlled 146 of Baghdad's 457 districts; that is, fewer than one-third of its neighbourhoods (BBC 5 June 2007). The review vividly illustrates the results of four years of Coalition operations: Iraqi police and army units failed to provide the forces necessary to carry out basic security tasks, including manning checkpoints and conducting patrols; almost daily bombings caused misery in flashpoint districts; sectarian violence remained serious in west Baghdad, and Shi'ite death squads continued to operate. In February 2007, for instance, most of the 100 bodies found dumped on rubbish dumps and street corners were Sunni, who had been tortured before being shot. The deployment of more than 20,000 US reinforcements temporarily halted the murders, but by May 2007 dozens of bodies were found in Baghdad every day. May also saw the third highest death toll of American soldiers (127) since the invasion. As ever, police melted away before incidents occurred.

Insecurity was partly caused by many Iraqis being heavily armed, and partly by the stores of weapons and ammunition (including RPGs, mortars and Katyusha rockets) left behind by the Ba'athist government. But it was worsened by the Coalition's inconsistent policies, which failed to control the deteriorating situation. One reason for the inconsistencies was that security had different meanings for the various actors involved. Coalition forces defined it in terms of their own physical safety, military objectives and operational success; security was about force protection and minimal own casualties, and Iraqi regulars, irregulars, and the urban terrain threatened it. To paraphrase Ayoob, security was defined in relation to the vulnerabilities that threatened danger and disorder (Ayoob 1997: 130). But Iraqis had a different understanding based on their functional needs; Baghdad's inhabitants understood security to mean the physical safety and protection of themselves and their possessions.

Shaping and managing this environment so as to achieve the Coalition's (that is, Washington's) strategic objectives called for robust but consistent and non-inflammatory forms of policing. In theory the Coalition recognised its need to persuade Iraqis to do what it wanted but in practice its approach to policing failed to achieve this. Despite the rhetoric of freedom and liberty, its vision of order and its set of control practices were given public meaning and enabled by a specific and assertive rationality expressed in terms invoking punishment and pacification, or by appeals to democracy or the 'Iraqi people', which failed to achieve its objectives. Perhaps as a result the Coalition measured success in metrics. These were easy to manipulate but essentially meaningless.

POWER RELATIONS

The order that existed in Iraq's cities 2003–07 reflected the power relations underpinning Iraqi politics and society, rather than international ideals. It was a web composed of myriad groups, some of which understood the cultural rules guiding behaviour and outcomes, and some of which did not. The location of power within this environment is impossible to determine, but by 2004 there was no doubt that the police were a faction in need of allies. They were not only brutal, ineffective and unreliable, but were also a symbol of pro-government forces and as such were targeted by sectarian militias and insurgents. In Baghdad, as in cities such as Maysan in the south-east of the country, 'no one was frightened of the police and the police were frightened of almost everyone' (Stewart 2006: 83).

Police stations were frequently attacked. When this happened, some police shed their uniforms and joined the rebels while others put themselves under the protection of pro-rebel clergy; in late 2004, almost all of Mosul's police fled when insurgents attacked their stations, while Shia police in Najaf joined rebels from the Mahdi Army and handed over their weapons. Despite this, state resources such as the police remained desirable to most if not all of the actors operating in Baghdad. Consequently, sectarian infiltration of the police began early on, though charges that the police were becoming creatures of the Ministry of the Interior grew after Bayan Jabr, a SCIRI leader, became interior minister in April 2005.[4] According to ICG, Jabr worked with the commander of the Badr organisation (SCIRI's armed wing) and its intelligence chief to politicise the police and paramilitary forces. He in turn claimed that criminals used police uniforms to hide their identity. Whatever the case, factional fighting increased as local powerbrokers forged or broke political and economic alliances. An additional factor was that, while some officers may have claimed to represent the state, all shared the personal, tribal or sectarian loyalties of their peers. This was notably so in the special units of the Iraqi National Police (INP), which were unvetted, given military weapons and counterinsurgency training, and quickly infiltrated by Shi'ite militias. Provided with embedded US advisers and logistic support, the units proved effective in COIN, but without them they resorted to torture, secret prisons and extrajudicial killings.

The police's perspective was counterbalanced (though not outweighed) by that of the US authorities. The key characteristics of the US-led occupation and its associated form of order were ideological certainties, incoherent policies, chronic insecurity and brutal pragmatism. The CPA treated democracy and capitalism as integrated concepts, and while the CPA's philosophy was that the IPS would be democratically accountable, run according to modern principles of managerial efficiency and contemporary methods and technologies, and would ensure democratic forms of public order, policing was actually seen as secondary to economic development and a free market. Also, Washington assumed that conventional security could be provided independently of the relationship in which it was to be exercised (Iraqi concerns focused on security at the level of the individual or group). Thus police were recruited regionally on the basis that this would match the ethnic and religious balance of a region, rather than allegiance to local political leaders.

Incoherence was deepened by differences of opinion between military advisers from US forces and civilian advisers from the State Department and Department of Justice (DoJ), and by assumptions about the transferability of training programmes. Military advisers wanted to create a force capable of counterinsurgency, whereas civilian trainers wanted a lightly armed civilian police service that used Western investigative standards and community-policing techniques to remove terrorists and criminals. Indeed, the curriculum at the DoJ-run training school in Amman was based on a programme developed for the radically different case of Kosovo. But proposals for democratic-style policing were unrealistic, not least because Iraqi police faced car bombs, insurgents and gunmen with heavy weapons.

At the empirical level Washington's misunderstanding of the nature and potential role of policing and security governance as a strategic tool for managing its relations with Iraqis contributed to its use of provocative policies that increased the insecurity it sought to manage. Admittedly Washington repeatedly emphasised its need to develop formal and informal partnerships with Iraqis so as to manage the prevailing insecurity (only then could the handover of sovereignty to Iraqi authorities in June 2004 be permitted), but it consistently misunderstood the relationships it wished to control. So did its troops, especially in the early days. That they misunderstood the situation is not in itself surprising. They were war-fighters who were neither trained nor equipped to perform police functions or to manage order. However, Baghdad was not the first time US forces were confronted by a breakdown in public order. Similar outbreaks had occurred in the aftermath of US interventions in Panama, Haiti, Bosnia and Kosovo; troops stood by while mobs looted the commercial district of Panama City, while Haitian police beat to death demonstrators celebrating the US intervention, while Sarajevo's buildings were destroyed, and while ethnic cleansing took place. American responses then swung to being heavy-handed.

US spokesmen referred to troops acting in self-defence, but many international commentators took a less charitable view of the response pattern that continued throughout the summer of 2003 and beyond. A representative case concerned the ten Iraqi police who were killed in Falluja in July 2003, when the cars in which they were chasing robbers ran into American soldiers who opened fire in a gun battle that lasted forty-five minutes. This came at a time when the USA was emphasising the value of Iraqi police cooperation in improving security. US forces were widely perceived to have adopted a provocative approach that led to a cycle of Iraqi revenge attacks, retaliatory searches and mutual recrimination. In this way, US actions had a corrosive effect on Iraqi order, as troops were perceived to have killed or injured bystanders, accidentally or intentionally, while inadvertently or deliberately destroying property. Also, they exacerbated already strained relations between Coalition members.

Order was in this way underpinned by myriad unresolved tensions, which were further deepened by the USA's approach to policing and the police. Troops treated policing with a mix of ideology and brutal pragmatism, especially once insurgency developed. The creation of a new police force was part of a strategy to bring democracy to the Iraqi people (and thereby allow troops to depart), but, as Etherington notes, the impassive and taciturn troops concerned combined casual acceptance of US military power with inexperience (Etherington 2005: 196, 208, 219). His impression of lapses of discipline regarding shoot-to-kill was that they were the result of inexperience in handling civil populations and were exacerbated by procedural failures, reliance on raw reservists, and a lack of interest in the region and its people. This dehumanised Iraqis in their eyes, with all that this implied for US forces' construction and assessment of order.

But it is easy to overstate the significance of this, for (as Etherington notes) one thing US troops shared with Iraqis was a brutally practical understanding of security and policing. Inevitably, many Iraqis failed to see advantages in democracy, especially when it failed to provide protection, for their assessments were governed by 'economic, social and local considerations, rather than national ones' (Etherington 2005: 85). Almost all Iraqis thought that the biggest economic problem – and a major source of insecurity in that addressing it required Iraqis to venture out into unsafe streets – was unemployment; at least half of working-age men were out of work. Iraqis were, however, unfazed by the Abu Ghraib scandal because that is how they thought the West always behaved.

BAGHDAD

What, then, was the situation from which order re-emerged? Baghdad offers a key, and journalists such as *The New Yorker*'s Jon Lee Anderson provide the best overview of Baghdad in the days immediately after 9 April 2003. No soldiers or police were visible, no one observed traffic regulations, and everyone seemed in a great hurry (Anderson 2006: 294, 315). Buildings burned, and bombs and gunshot could be heard as gangs staked out their turf. By the following morning most of the eastern side of central Baghdad had been looted. Indeed, the weeks of looting that followed arguably caused more damage to Iraq's infrastructure than the bombing campaign (Chandrasekaran 2007: 49).

Iraqis (who were already deeply suspicious of the US's motives) saw this as symptomatic of the breakdown of law and order, though it is arguably more accurate to see it as reflecting the new order's ambigui-ties. Coalition forces looked the other way, seeing looting as a way for Iraqis to vent anger, while Defence Secretary Rumsfeld dismissed it with the comment that 'freedom is untidy' (CNN 2003). General Tommy Franks, commander of US forces, said that 'people just go wild' when autocratic regimes fall, and that the true measure was how quickly the lawlessness was controlled (*Financial Times* 14 April 2003). In truth, lawlessness (which was never managed, let alone controlled) was symptomatic of the emergent and opportunistic order.

There were pockets of heavy fighting and it 'was not entirely clear which parts of Baghdad were in American hands and which were not' (Anderson 2006: 311), but ghettoisation began early on, with armed vigilantes aggressively stopping cars, and residential streets barricaded and guarded. Anderson records how he passed through a checkpoint manned by marines on the outskirts of Saddam City, a slum of 2.5 million, before driving into to the area where 'almost immediately, the paved road fell apart into a badly patched track with large potholes and huge puddles of standing water. We passed hundreds of people on foot heading to the slum, burdened with stolen goods' (Anderson 2006: 317; *Financial Times* 2006). Roadblocks of zigzagged oil drums, furniture and cement blocks were guarded by 'rough-looking youths ... holding iron bars'. In the alleyways Anderson saw armed men, a stolen fire engine and a red double-decker passenger bus. Elsewhere locals and US forces passively watched looting and vandalism.[5]

Anderson thought there was no one single defining moment when Baghdad moved from its immediate post-conflict state. If anything, Baghdad spent several weeks 'suspended in a bizarre limbo between its past and its future' (Anderson 2006: 367). Also, Saddam remained free. Even so, when Anderson left at the end of April it looked as if US forces were gradually asserting control. This proved to be a veneer overlaying an increasingly localised and fragmented order, for when he returned in the third week of July:

> There were fewer overturned tanks and burned-out vehicles ... than there had been two months earlier, but great heaps of rubble still spilled out from bombed buildings, and tin cans and plastic bags were strewn everywhere. Traffic was dense, and most of the major intersections were gridlocked, but there were no traffic cops in sight. Driving into the city, we passed an armoured convoy of American soldiers in full combat gear, their guns at the ready. (Anderson 2006: 373)

A curfew lasting from 22:00 till 04:00 was in place, during which time Baghdad became eerily dark and silent except for the occasional dog barking, automatic weapons fire and helicopters clattering above the river. Temperatures were over 120°F, but the city had been without electricity (and therefore without running water, sewerage, refrigeration and air conditioning) for days, and there were long queues at petrol stations. It was no longer safe to walk around.

What happened in the intervening weeks? How soon was order visible? What were its indicators? Despite the unintended consequences of looting, the situation looked initially hopeful. By 14 April Baghdad was divided into 55 to 60 zones, of which some 40 were under Coalition control. The US officers in charge of civil administration met Iraqi police chiefs at the Palestine Hotel to discuss the 'restoration' of law and order, and, according to US calculations, Iraqi police were due to start patrolling on 14 April. By this time US Humvees and armoured vehicle were on guard outside most of the main hospitals. But tensions were always evident. The US resisted calls to re-employ most police because it suspected their loyalties, while the police gathering near the hotel who wished to return to work distanced themselves from the occupiers: 'We came to protect the people, not to work with America' (*Financial Times* 14 April 2003). Meanwhile, localised order re-emerged, as when neighbourhoods, acting on the instructions of the Shia religious leader Ayatollah Ali Sistani, set up armed roadblocks to stop looters and retrieve stolen property.

Anderson thought the watershed occurred at the end of April in Falluja, fifty miles west of Baghdad, where a 'dismal, refuse-strewn welter of auto repair shops, metal scrap yards, and factories ... gradually gave way to a low-slung jumble of mud-colored squares and rectangles overhung with a skyline of television aerials and the minarets and domes of a dozen mosques' (Anderson 2006: 395). American forces had fired into a crowd of demonstrators, killing seventeen, and, when Iraqis retaliated by killing two Americans, the violence spread to towns to the north and west of Baghdad. Sectarian, factional and nationalist discontent then combined to challenge the order associated with the occupiers.

SECURITY IN BAGHDAD AFTER JUNE 2004

Iraqi order was based on a web of tensions, insecurities and violence. In the first month after the handover of sovereignty, the new government was under pressure to ensure order and security. But its claim to do so was rapidly undermined by innumerable incidents of violence, assassinations, kidnappings and explosions, many of which targeted the police. On 28 July 2004, for example, a massive car bomb exploded near a line of would-be police recruits in a centre of anti-government opposition north of Baghdad, killing sixty-eight. The government increased police patrols and checkpoints and mounted crime crackdowns, but internal politics meant that it failed to activate the emergency powers it had assumed after the transfer. The war may have finished some fifteen months previously, but jihadists and nationalists fought an escalating battle for local control. Streets in Baghdad (as elsewhere) were under the control of rival militias competing to control territory and revenue sources such as oil and weapons smuggling. In this way, the situation in Baghdad illustrates important aspects of Iraq's order and security.

Three linked elements or expressions of Baghdad's order deserve note. First, crime played a significant role in everyday life. Control of the black market and access to protection money helped to finance turf wars (*Financial Times* 22 August 2004). For example, petrol stations were a desirable prize because they made money, were symbols of territorial control, and acted as recruiting stations, as they were gathering points for unemployed youths.

Second, the boundaries between criminality and sectarianism became increasingly blurred. By 2006 most killings were done by a handful of armed bands, vying for turf control or kidnapping members of other sects for profit (*The Economist* 2 September 2006: 51). Some groups were not members of the Mahdi Army or Sunni insurgency groups so much as street gangs. Iraqi officers said that in the suburb of Adhamiya, for instance, the most dangerous were teenagers or in their early twenties, often drug addicts in it for thrills and prestige. The gangs were safe in their own districts, and had powerful protectors outside. This was evident from the way in which local Sunnis avoided using Baghdad's largest hospital complex a few kilometres to the south even though their own district had few resources. The reason was that the health minister was a radical Sadrist, and the medical complex used hundreds of Mahdi Army militants as security guards. In other areas, children banded together in fifty-strong gangs to throw stones at US troops, or they collaborated with Sunni kidnappers and robbers. One 13-year-old told the UN that his family were unemployed, so 'I decided to help a gang specialised in kidnapping. For each kidnap I get US$100 and it is enough to help my family with food for the whole month' (IRIN 2007a: 51).

Third, the role played by the growing and politically active group of young, bored and urban slum dwellers was significant (40 per cent of Iraqis were under 15). Of these groups, the 10,000-strong Mahdi Army was the most noteworthy, not least because it policed its own version of order. Created by the Shi'ite cleric Moqtada al-Sadr, the Mahdi Army originated as a small group in Sadr City where it provided security and welfare services, dispensing aid and preventing looting; Mahdi fighters patrolled on foot and in commandeered police vehicles. Formalised in June 2003, in some areas it amounted to a shadow government. Inspired by Sadrist themes of political marginalisation, unequal suffering and exploitation, members claimed that the militia was a group of pious youths supporting their religion and clergy, rather than a military structure. In fact it repeatedly clashed with Coalition forces. Armed with assault rifles, rocket-propelled grenades, mortars, Strela anti-air missiles, and other light weapons, and using IEDs (improvised explosive devices), it seized control of public buildings and police stations. The Mahdi Army's later activities also illustrated the state-based understanding on which Iraqi order was based. For, in June, al-Sadr declared an end to operations in Sadr City, and sought to turn it into a political party capable of contesting the 2005 election, having gained a good deal of public support. Security was a means to an end.

BASRA

Similar dynamics to those in Baghdad and other US-controlled areas accompanied the re-emergence of order in cities such as Basra, 250 miles south-east of Baghdad, where the UK was the responsible power. Coalition authorities adopted a different approach in Basra, yet the results were equally unsatisfactory from their perspective. As in Baghdad, active combat operations lasted for approximately three weeks, with the operational balance shifting from conventional war-fighting to internal security operations drawing on counter-insurgency tactics. Days of intense looting were followed by weeks of low-level looting, rising crime, and the collapse of Basra's remaining infra-structure. The result was, as far as most Basrawis were concerned, a security vacuum. As in Baghdad, security was ghettoised.

Three aspects of Basra's experience are addressed here, each of which illustrates different aspects of post-conflict order: the multiple meanings of security, sectarian infiltration of the police, and the inability of British forces to shape the city's order.

SECURITY

Events in Basra are significant for a number of reasons.[6] They suggest that while an inclusive or broadened sense of security has real value, security remains primarily a matter of physical safety, and achieving it on a citywide scale depends on the actions of statist agents. In the weeks after the war individual or localised security was provided or withheld by agents sanctioned by governments. Individuals may or may not be 'the ultimate referent' of security, and 'true security' may or may not be the product of '[e]mancipation, not power or order' (Booth 1991: 318), but security initially depended, for most Basrawis, on the actions or inaction of coalition forces. Basra emphasises that notions of self, identity or otherness are permissible in societies such as Iraq's only when the dominant order permits their reality.

Basra suggests that the meaning of security depends on the specifications made about the notion, and that the lines of demarcation between the various interpretations of security are themselves indeterminate. Significantly, there was as little agreement in Basra as to what constituted security as there was in Baghdad. Coalition forces defined security in terms of their own safety and operational success, whereas Basrawis were primarily concerned about bullying by militiamen or police (who were often the same) at checkpoints, the corpses found near police stations, the prevalence of violent crime, and the authorities' unwillingness or inability to stop it. A third perspective might be that provided by local mosques, for clerics organised groups of men to act as unarmed guards for the hospitals that could not deter looters. A fourth view could be that of the displaced and impoverished people that most of Basra thought responsible for the scavenging and looting dominating the early weeks.

Events during the week of 7 April 2003 show the complexity of the security picture, and the lack of a common understanding of what security entailed. As in Baghdad, the problem presented itself in terms of the looting that began immediately after the British occupation, and, as in Baghdad, the authorities' failure to respond convinced many Iraqis that their security was not a Coalition priority.[7] Much looting was opportunistic, but much was organised. Thousands of criminals had been released from prisons in late 2002, and many eyewitnesses told Human Rights Watch that they recognised known criminals in the gangs targeting banks, hospitals, government institutions, shops and houses belonging to ordinary people (HRW 2003). But British forces failed to respond. Troops reportedly left the university, for example, once militias attacked them and mobs of looters arrived on the scene, and even when things quietened down the provision of security at hospitals and other significant sites was sporadic.

This situation came about partly because the number of Coalition troops available in the city was relatively small (the 48 British military police available in April 2003 could not replace the 16,000 Iraqi officers who had formerly policed Basra's 1.5 million inhabitants), and partly because the authorities were making a political point. As a UK officer at Central Command headquarters in Qatar said, 'Normally we would stop looting because it's a sign that things have got out of control and law and order have broken down. ... But in this case we decided that to allow it would send a powerful message – that we're in control now, not the Ba'ath party' (*Financial Times* 7 April 2003). Unfortunately the officer did not notice that insecurity primarily affected ordinary Iraqis, who were already angry about water shortages and the lack of electricity, resentful of foreign invasion, and angry about civilian deaths from coalition bombing.

Although security was the preserve of British forces, their indifference to local politics, and toleration of looting meant that security could never be more than partial so far as Basrawis were concerned. The prevalence of rumours (mostly about violence and crime) increased the sense of palpable insecurity; Basra's communications systems had been destroyed, so British authorities had difficulty in communicating with the population, making hearts-and-minds operations difficult to conduct. In other words, there was no common understanding of what security meant and there were pragmatic limits as to how it was interpreted. Human Rights Watch recorded an extreme example: a Christian woman begged British soldiers for protection after religious militias threatened to kill her: 'Tell her it's not our jurisdiction', they said (*The Economist* 7 June 2003: 56).

SECTARIAN INFILTRATION

By early 2006, the British approach to managing Basra's policing was to combine the prospect of improved training for the police with the threat of arrest in an attempt to create a more professional non-sectarian police. Enhancing the police's status was seen as a key factor in transferring security responsibility to Iraqis, and thereby allowing British withdrawal. According to Lt Gen. Sir Robert Fry, based in Baghdad and the most senior officer in Iraq, the process of handing over more control to Iraqis would provide an incentive to depoliticise the police.

This was an unrealistic aspiration, for by then Basra belonged to militias, death squads and organised crime. By October 2006, some twenty security and police groups operated with impunity; they ranged from a dozen religious militias, and the governor's 200 armed guards, to the directorate of education police and the justice police (*Guardian* 19 May 2007). Indeed, the appearance of a functioning state was illusory because the police comprised militiamen, and in any confrontation between political parties officers splintered according to party lines and fought one another. By May 2007 no one could be appointed to the police or any official job without a letter of support from a militia or political party. There was a rule of law, but it was militia law (*Guardian* 19 May 2007). In practice, the main characteristics of policing were sectarian division and brutality. Basra's order reflected its power relations.

The extent of sectarian brutality is most evident in the activities of the so-called Jameat, a group of officers drawn from police intelligence departments and representing all the major factions. It was named after the police station its members were alleged to use as a base. When 1,000 British forces demolished the station in December 2006, they discovered 127 prisoners in the basement. Some had had their kneecaps shot off, while others had electrical or cigarette burns, or crushed hands or feet. But most Iraqi police thought that torture was justified as a way of obtaining confessions and deterring retribution (*Financial Times* 25 January 2005).

By then, the police were the equivalent of a sectarian militia. The ability of the 24-strong team of British police advisers who, supported by 70 civilian private security staff employed by Armor Holdings (under contract to the Foreign Office), sought to influence them was minimal. Nominally British-trained, the police were out of the control of both British and Iraqi authorities. As a senior general in the Interior Ministry said, 'Most of the police force is divided between Fadhila which controls the TSU [the tactical support unit, its best trained unit] and Moqtada which controls the regular police'. (*Guardian* 19 May 2007).[8] This meant that 'Fadhila control the oil terminals, so they control the oil protection force ... Moqtada controls the ports and customs, so they control the customs, police and its intelligence. Commandos are under the control of Badr Brigade.' Inevitably, officers who were not part of a militia joined in order to protect themselves. As a commander told a British journalist, once a policeman 'affiliated with a militia then as a commander you can't change him ... because then you are confronting a political party' (*Guardian* 19 May 2007). A further complication arose from militiamen associating with different groups, switching identities according to whoever paid the most. The relationship between militias and the units they infiltrated was fluid and difficult to pin down.

The realities of policing are evident from journalists' accounts from April 2005. When, for instance, a man loyal to the Fadhila Party replaced an official in the directorate of electricity loyal to al-Sadr, the units affected fought. Whenever there was a clash between militias, the police split and units fought other units. As General Hassan al-Sade, the secular-minded chief of police in Basra admitted on 30 May, he had lost control of most of his 13,750 officers, and trusted only a quarter of them. Sectarian militias had infiltrated the force, using their posts to assassinate their opponents (*Guardian* 31 May 2005), and police cars openly carried pictures showing their factional allegiance. Other officers were politically neutral but had no interest in policing. The provincial council soon sacked al-Sade, but he was probably correct to claim that Basra was peaceful because authority had been ceded to conservative Islamic parties who ignored the corruption and violence of their militia squads.

If Basra experienced this form of order it was because the militias preferred it that way. In fact, militias had seized the initiative in April 2003. Immediately after the invasion, Sadrist mosques organised lorries to bring in water and used vigilantes to patrol the streets against looters. They then used 2004's efforts to increase police numbers to embed militiamen into the police. The result was a web of security agents and interests, many of which the Coalition authorities tried to avoid provoking. Police stations such as Jameat were known to be bases for death squads and organised crime, but British military authorities usually avoided confronting powerful Shia militias like the Badr Brigade and the Mahdi Army (which had close ties to the government). Not only were the occupation authorities merely one faction among many, but also the temporary nature of their stay made them one of the weakest. This undermined British attempts to mould order.

Operation Sinbad, launched in September 2006 as a joint UK–Iraq multiphased operation lasting six months, illustrates the weakness of the British approach, and the resilience of Basra's indigenous forms of order.

Working with about 2,300 Iraqi troops, 1,000 soldiers took part in what was seen as a crucial test of the ability of the Coalition forces to rehabilitate Basra's police by removing death squads and militias, and extending civilian control (*Independent* 8 October 2006). Some aspects of the operation were relatively uncontroversial; contractors were brought in to boost public confidence by quick measures such as repairing streetlights and clearing rubbish. Others, such as the insertion of Royal Military Police teams, were controversial. But the operation neither cleansed the police, nor was sustainable beyond the end of October when British forces changed. Its overall result was to demonstrate the weakness of the British position and the freedom of militias to act as they wished. The UK MoD claimed that it helped cut the murder rate from a high of 139 in June 2006 to 29 in December, and halved the number of kidnappings, but most Basrawis probably shared the opinion of the British journalist who thought that Sinbad's combination of politics and lack of manpower cast doubt on the British project for policing Basra and on the British presence in Iraq (*Independent* 8 October 2006).

Operations such as Sinbad emphasised that policing in Basra was a matter of British soldiers patrolling while sectarian police enforced their own rules. Patrols were favoured because they allowed troops to become familiar with neighbourhoods, determine immediate security threats, identify key leaders and where they lived, determine/ understand public sentiments, and develop intelligence sources in the city. 'Snap' traffic-control positions in the city acted as a filter, while joint patrols with police allowed troops to intercept weapons trafficking, though public safety played little part in determining military objectives (Sickle 2005: 28; Strachan 2007). In contrast, the police were a means for factions to augment their local power, and, as Coalition forces discovered, democratic-style policing was tolerated only when it suited factional leaders. Above all, patron–client relations structured the policing field, which was maintained by reciprocal exchanges of favour. By November 2007 the Sadr office was the real centre of power in Basra (*Guardian* 17 November 2007).

ACCOMMODATION

The UK reduced troop numbers immediately after the invasion, and British commentators congratulated them on their 'soft' approach to policing Basra. However, an alternative assessment is that this was only possible because the authorities had ceded power to militias. In Herring and Rangwala's opinion, the relative calmness of Basra resulted from the British 'failure to bridge the state–society gap at national level', which led them to abandon efforts to control the political process locally (Herring and Ranwala 2006: 163). The British stayed for as long as they did because they were tolerated, and they were tolerated because they did not interfere in the competition between local political forces. As soon as they did their position became precarious.

The development of pragmatic working relationships with power-brokers was in some respects reasonable: British forces were out-numbered. Also, it was consistent with UK practice in other theatres of operation, most notably Northern Ireland, where Whitehall was prepared to do deals, granting concessions to Sinn Féin as part of the effort to broker a peace deal, or (according to Peter Mandelson, one of the then prime minister Blair's closest political allies) 'conceding and capitulating to republican demands' (*Guardian* 13 March 2007).

The conclusion of the Washington-based analyst Anthony Cordes-man is more damning. He argues that the British lost any opportunity to shape a secular and nationalist Basra in the summer of 2003 (Cordesman 2007: 2). Islamists not only controlled neighbourhoods whenever British troops were not present, but local politics fractured into factions that were not loyal even to their national parties. The police, like the other Iraqi forces that Britain helped create, were little more than an extension of Shi'ite Islamist control by other means. Consequently, Basra's police became part of the problem, rather than the solution. British efforts to deal with this led to local attacks on forces, which in turn meant that forces were confronted by no-go areas and could only operate elsewhere as armoured patrols. He concludes that British strategy to impose internationally acceptable policing failed; its authorities lost at the political level in early 2005, and were defeated at the military level from the autumn of 2005 onwards. British claims to transfer responsibility to Iraqi security forces in 2006 were little more than political cover.

COMPARATIVE PICTURES

This chapter's overview can be supplemented by the detailed accounts of two British officials, Mark Etherington and Rory Stewart, of contemporaneous developments in al-Kut and Maysan, provincial capitals to the south-east of Baghdad and north-west of Basra, respectively.

AL-KUT

Etherington became head of a small CPA team in al-Kut in October 2003. When he arrived,

> Police clustered in small groups on the steps of their stations and nearby fences like crows. There appeared to be thousands of them, in almost comical disarray. The police had no infrastructure, rules, leadership or staff worth the name; most had no weapons and few officers appeared to do any work though it was clear that many were directly implicated in widespread and systematic corruption if not criminal activity. (Etherington 2005: 27)

The fundamental problem arose from the police's inability to carry out their tasks; most could not run their own stations, let alone carry out security tasks (Etherington 2005: 137, 155). Indeed, 'stability in a district or sub-district hinged almost entirely on the competence of the local mayor and his police chief' (Etherington 2005: 217). Poor leadership resulted in low morale that made the lower ranks lethargic and easily intimidated. Arms, transport, flak jackets, batons, radios and winter clothes were distributed according to status and hierarchy.

And when fuel shortages meant that police were sent to keep order in petrol stations, the officers concerned confined themselves to taking bribes from the queuing motorists in return for offering preferential treatment. They were then beaten up by motorists and fled (Etherington 2005: 136). Their unreliability was particularly dangerous, as Etherington noted when a group of emergency police attacked his compound alongside Sadr's militia.

Etherington's vivid description of the office of the province's chief of police, Brigadier Abdul Men'em, and the challenges confronting him (2005: 80–82) emphasises the gulf between Iraqi and Western ideas about the relationship between appointments and performance. Democratic accountability meant little because Iraqis valued appointments for the opportunities for patronage they offered; the primary task of individual clan members was to ensure the ascendancy of their group (tribe, family or friends). Similarly, the principle preoccupation of senior officers appeared to be promoting one another (Etherington 2005: 137). This made dismissal (especially of a chief officer) significant, for it meant dismissing a host of other individuals. Also, the officer concerned would have his own patron in the Ministry of the Interior whose job it was to protect him and block attempts to move him. The problems presented by incompetent or corrupt police were thus social, political and institutional, with the police being not only a problem in their own right, but also one that exacerbated others (Etherington 2005: 113). Despite this (or perhaps because of it) Etherington notes that the Iraqi governing council feared the police (2005: 139).

Etherington emphasises the centrality of insecurity, but he also argues that the Coalition's military response to public order crises suggested an institutional inability to grasp the nature of the problem (Etherington 2005: 153–5). The difficulties were compounded by the Coalition's inability to mount appropriate public-order operations; military forces lacked the surgical capability required to support public-order objectives, and Caucasians could not mount successful intelligence operations. Meanwhile, the police had no experience in crowd control, and were weakened by fears of retribution, the assassination of chief officers, and mutiny (Etherington 2005: 288).

MAYSAN

Stewart's experience is similarly informative. Sent to Maysan to represent the US administrator in Baghdad, and tasked with rebuilding public administration, restoring services and building local democracy, Stewart exercised executive, legislative and judicial authority in the province and was well placed to observe the police. Perhaps his most significant conclusion is that developments in Maysan were not decided by grand politics but by difficult interactions between individual Iraqis and foreigners; mutual suspicion was decisive.

Everyone was preoccupied with security, but the administration had no Iraqi executive on which to rely, no middle classes and no judges, while the remaining police were unarmed against the Badr militia's Iranian Kalashnikovs and RPGs. Accordingly, their 'procedures were based on legalistic paperwork and illegal brutality'. Many police did not work because they were injured, idle or dead, but their salaries continued to be paid – and collected – by relatives, widows or senior officers; families survived on the 200,000 dinar (about £73 or $140) monthly salary paid posthumously (Stewart 2007: 83). It was not long before militia became incorporated into the police. Emergency Brigades (which were heavily armed and often illiterate militia groups) and other militias acting as Islamist vigilantes had established their own security organisations as the war ended, and were the only effective security presence in the province (Stewart 2007: 63).

Coalition authorities consistently misunderstood the populace's concerns. Under Saddam security had been enforced by special units, heavy armour and checkpoints, arbitrary mass arrests, blackmail, torture and execution by brutal and unpopular security forces. In contrast, the CPA implemented programmes on human rights, free markets, feminism and constitutional reform (Stewart 2007: 82). But people in Maysan talked only of security. And insecurity was made worse by the CPA's inability to control carjackings, kidnappings and the gangs smuggling diesel. Traditional means of social control crumbled as the young urban elites rejected sheiks who tried to reassert themselves (Stewart 2007: 7).

Stewart noted the Iraqis' standard response to insecurity: 'Employ five times as many new policemen. Get heavier weapons. Impose curfews. Set up checkpoints ... Establish secret services ... Be more brutal' (Stewart 2007: 87). In contrast the Coalition's police advisers thought that crowds could be controlled effectively but humanely by a small, well-trained, lightly armed and citizen-friendly police service. British police trainers refused to allow the police to set up secret units or carry heavy weapons. They insisted that training was the answer, but were unable to produce 'the light intelligent police service they dreamed of' (Stewart 2007: 83; 335). Too many international police advisers consistently failed to question the transferability of their usual practices. Ignoring Iraqi realities they discussed instead the prospects of psychometric testing and gender-awareness workshops for all. A Committee of Public Safety was established to provide oversight, but its members saw themselves as super police; all wanted to carry weapons and permits and give orders to policemen at will (Stewart 2007: 324)

Stewart tells how by the time the Coalition authorities left, the police had quadrupled in size, acquired heavier weapons, and, by establishing checkpoints every 500 yards up the highway, had brought some form of security. Some large tribal gangs had lost power, and there were fewer carjackings, kidnappings and protection rackets, and less smuggling. To that extent the state functioned. Only two forces – the Iranian-linked Badr militia and the Sadrists – remained outside the law. But 'they were now the elected government. And the leadership controlled its followers' (Stewart 2007: 423).

CONCLUSION

Order re-emerged after a brief period of limbo. But it was an order characterised by chronic insecurity, barricaded neighbourhoods, and a web of shifting power relations. It offered a dramatic contrast to the Coalition's vision, which was expressed in an assertive rhetoric appealing to freedom, democracy and the 'Iraqi people'. On the other hand, the control practices of all concerned were enabled by an aggressive rationality invoking punishment and pacification.

Four general trends are identifiable. First, security was the central point around which discourse and competition took place, and it was present as that which was absent (Laclau 1996: 53). At the same time, security was a means to an end, rather than an end in itself, not least because it expressed the power relations structuring politics and society.

Second, in the absence of citywide security, factional groups provided localised arrangements. But there is little evidence to suggest that institutional structures could have provided security for all.

Third, although it is impossible for outsiders to assess accurately the nature of Iraq's emergent order, it was resilient yet unstable. Neither Etherington nor Stewart, for example, had a coherent picture of developments in their cities, but Iraqi powerbrokers did. Iraqi strongmen not only shared a common understanding that challenged international ideals, but also they exploited or subverted them. By the time British forces withdrew from Basra in late 2007, the main factions had reached an understanding about sharing out Basra's resources; that is, running the police, controlling the revenues from oil smuggling, and the distribution of political power in the city.

Fourth, policing was a matter of coercion and negotiation. Because police operated according to sectarian or political imperatives (as they do in most of the world), reconstruction became a matter of skill, 'hazard and chance' (Etherington 2006: 239).

Baghdad and Basra emphasise that power relations represent a key to understanding the re-emergence of order; that order is malleable by external forces only in the early days; and that its management (that is, policing) cannot be understood in isolation from the political context in which it is to be employed. Finally, both show how order and security make sense at many levels and refer to different things, and that the optimum point at which international and Iraqi definitions of order and security become meaningful has yet to be identified. That there was tension between the various meanings was not a fundamental problem per se – military and/or individual security, for instance, often have separate dimensions – but it was politically and practically significant. In other words, the notion of security can accommodate multiple interpretations, but in practice a dominant discourse usually controls its meaning. Security is a means and a process within order.

5

SOCIAL CONTINUITIES AND THE
PRODUCTION OF ORDER

Parallel forms of order emerge as local powerbrokers fight turf wars and international officials apply Western institutional templates. But there is never doubt as to which is the most resilient, for order is founded on agreement and predictability, which are primarily influenced by indigenous norms, cultural undercurrents and legacy issues. This is especially noticeable in fragile or juridical states, such as Bosnia and Afghanistan, where international authorities attempt to establish a new police force in the face of entrenched ethnic or sectarian pressures. In such cases, the most accurate indicator of order is to be found in the continued existence of ineffective, corrupt and ethnically unmixed police.

Bosnia-Herzegovina (hereafter Bosnia) and Afghanistan have been subject to intense international pressure to remake their political order and reform their police in accordance with international best practice. Both are strategically important – Bosnia is on the edge of the European Union (EU), while Afghanistan is between the Middle East, central Asia and the Indian subcontinent – but they are in separate geopolitical regions, with different policing styles, legacy issues and cultures. The EU has played a key role in Bosnia's security governance since the signing of the Dayton Peace Accords in 1995, whereas Afghanistan is widely regarded as a lawless place where Islamic militants find sanctuary and warlords profit from the drugs trade that is the country's largest and most profitable business. Even so, both police forces were expected to become professional and accountable organisations capable of managing a democratic order.

Much of today's post-conflict orthodoxy is based on the experience the EU and USA gained after the Balkan wars of the 1990s, so this chapter identifies the factors shaping developments in the Bosnian cities of Sarajevo and Mostar, and, for comparison, in Kosovo's Podujevo. Kabul is then used to illustrate the limits of generalisations based on European experience. In both cases, indigenous forms of order soon re-emerged. But other possibilities must be acknowledged too, so the chapter concludes with a discussion of policing in a city – Rwanda's Kigali – where order was distorted, rather than submerged or lost.

BOSNIA

Bosnia is a fragile new state built on compromise in an unstable region with a violent past. Approximately 100,000 Bosnians died and 2 million were displaced during the three-year war between the former Yugoslavia's Bosniak, Serb and Croat entities. The new order was, according to international organisations, designed to facilitate the creation of a democratically accountable police institution conforming to international standards and human rights legislation.[1] But this was soon subverted by legacy issues and the rapid institutionalisation of corruption, economic underdevelopment and social exclusion, and by collusion between government officials, members of the ruling nationalist parties, security agencies and organised crime (Johnson 2000). The regional criminal networks which developed as a result of the region's need to circumvent international sanctions on the import of weapons and oil during the wars easily adapted to trafficking women, drugs and cigarettes; an estimated 90 per cent of the Afghan heroin in Europe is distributed through such networks (Andreas 2005). Also, smuggling, like the social exclusion that undermined liberal ideals, reflected decades of governmental neglect, and population displacement during the wars. Bosnia's nationalistic political parties continued to control the government, security agencies and the economy, using corruption to maintain their personal and financial powers.

The picture is different from a Bosnian perspective. Bosnia's economy may be stagnant, the average monthly wage about €250, and more than 20 per cent of the working-age population unemployed, but the EU is only a few hours' drive away, and Bosnia lies across traditional smuggling routes. As a result the informal economy is thriving, trafficking of illegal migrants and women is big business, local police are easily persuaded to look the other way – and corruption is a survival mechanism to supplement inadequate income, as well as the exploitation of public office for private gain. Further, the most lucrative forms of corruption, like economic power itself, remain concentrated in the hands of what Donais calls Bosnia's 'three ethnically divided and geographically separated cartels': the nationalist political parties, organised criminals, and remnants of the socialist-era *nomenklatura* (2005: 10). Curbing corruption (that is, effective EU-style policing) would have reduced the cartels' ability to maintain their control. The consequences for Bosnian policing were predictable.

SARAJEVO

During the war, urban areas were destroyed because of their ethnic identification. This phenomenon, which became known as urbicide (Coward 2004), led to certain cities, of which Sarajevo is a prime example, becoming a symbol of both destruction and hopes for reconstruction. For this reason, Sarajevo, situated on the frontier between Bosnia's two opposing autonomous entities of the Dayton-created Muslim–Croat Federation and Republika Srpska (RS), became a test case for a new democratic order. In reality, it provides an illustration of the local and regional strategies used to facilitate the re-emergence, rather than emergence, of order.

The formal emergence of order was programmed by the Paris Agreement of December 1995, which outlined the framework (and priorities) on which a new order would be built. These included regional stabilisation, elections, human rights, the preservation of national monuments, the establishment of public corporations, and the introduction of an International Police Task Force (IPTF). Additionally, the strategic interests of the EU and NATO meant that there was a coherent and consistent commitment on the part of the EU, especially to offer long-term support; Bosnia was small enough to be manageable; and, more importantly, Bosnia wanted to become part of 'Europe'. The EU was prepared to pay for reform so Bosnia's elite paid attention to the norms and processes associated with being European.[2]

Sarjevo's post-war order was in some respects markedly different from what had gone before, for shelling had destroyed streets, and the city was ethnically cleansed. In 1991, Sarajevo's mixed population of 540,000 was 40 per cent Bosnian Muslim, whereas its post-war population of approximately 400,000 was 80 per cent Muslim. Fearing retribution, many Serbs fled after the Dayton Accords, while Muslim refugees from the former eastern Bosnia (now Republika Srpska) moved into Sarajevo's shelled and burned-out flats. Most males of fighting age had fled or become casualties. Consequently, although Sarajevo was not strictly a divided city (checkpoints were absent), the emergent order was built on issues of ethnic, nationalist and religious identity.

At the same time, it was shaped by organised crime based on prostitution, pirated goods, and the trafficking of drugs, weapons, vehicles and people. Sarajevo's markets were not as big as the notoriously unregulated Arizona Market on the outskirts of the town of Brčko, where women could be bought as easily as cars or cigarettes, but corruption and a lack of training and resources ensured that its policing was ineffective. In truth, it was never likely that policing would be other than ineffective, for the networks on which organised crime depended were robust, having survived the siege. Many of the gangs concerned had links to extremist political factions and the police, all of which were facilitated by poverty, unemployment and corruption, and by the animosity that existed between the entities' police and criminal justice systems. A combination of weak state controls, demobilisation, border disputes and criminal activity ensured that small arms and light weapons (including man-portable air defence systems, MANPADS) were easily available.

MOSTAR

The role of social continuities and institutional changes in Sarajevo can be cross-checked by reference to Mostar, a small city of about 126,000 people in 1991 and 127,000 in 2005. Mostar, like many Bosnian cities, was besieged and partially destroyed during 1993–94, before being further transformed by post-war settlements. Indeed, reinforcing the wartime divisions appears to have been a post-war priority for the city authorities. The post-war nationalist leadership sought to consolidate its grip symbolically and demographically, resettling as refugees people from their own community so as to secure their post-war claims (Bieber 2005). Mostar was further subject to social engineering by the EU, which defined order in the broadest possible sense.

Mostar's new order was formally inaugurated when the EU took over the city administration in 1994, imposing a policy of ethnic equality and spatial segregation as Croats and Bosniaks (Muslins) squabbled over the peace negotiations. The EU's aim was to overcome Mostar's ethnic division through a process of reconstruction, thereby providing a model of cooperation for the new Muslim–Croat Federation. Repairing the city's infrastructure was part of this overall plan, as was municipal reorganisation. In the two years of its administration, the EU spent about US$50 million repairing and rebuilding schools, hospitals, courts, government offices, hotels, rail and bus stations, water and electricity distribution, and bridges (cf. Bollens 2006). However, the EU was far less successful in its political project to reconstruct Mostar's cultural institutions and associational life. For the affiliating element of Mostar's post-conflict population was 'solely a relationship to a particular ethnic group' (Herscher 1998). Further, the 'new' order was shaped by exploitation and the growth of alternative forms of power. Just as reconstruction allowed some to entrench or legitimise the profitable businesses they had started during the war, so corruption, political connections, and ethnic and demographic manipulation undermined EU ideals as soon as they were announced. Far from being unified and reconciled, the two sides were intent on exploiting EU resources and increasing their group's political influence and territorial claims. This was reflected in the city's policing.

POLICING SARAJEVO AND MOSTAR

The order that characterised the new Bosnia was fragile and resilient, not least because of tensions between the ideological peace agenda supervised by the international community's high representative and the realities of Bosnian politics and policing.

The defining ideal of the democratic policing paradigm is the creation of multiparty or multi-ethnic police forces that represent the society they serve in an impartial and professional manner. In Bosnia this meant that reforming and restructuring the police was an essential element in the social engineering necessary for democratic-style policing. It would, it was thought, lead to toleration (if not reconciliation) among minority and majority groups, lessening inter-group violence. Restructuring the police would, it was argued, restructure society, with minorities returning to pre-war areas. As Graham Day put it, 'minority recruitment [is] an essential first step in breaking down structural barriers to a professional non-ethnically prejudiced local police service' (Celador 2005: 18).

However, as Celador notes, such policies were based on a number of unsubstantiated assumptions. The EU and UN assumed that making officers from the different groups undergo the same training would result in the development of a common police culture that would mean that all Bosnians were treated equitably.[3] They assumed that the police, as representatives of the state and the rule of law, could (and would) facilitate the public confidence required for successfully implementing the Dayton Accords. In fact, the Bosnian state was widely regarded as an artificial construct that imposed laws and structures running parallel to those structuring Bosnia's real life. What could not be avoided was accommodated or manipulated.

The new political order was held in place by international forces backed up by military capabilities. The UN's IPTF, headquartered in Sarajevo, was the most ambitious civilian police operation to date, with 1,700 monitors deployed in Bosnia in 1996. However, the bitter nature of the war, and the closeness of Bosnia to EU member states, ensured that the international actors shaping the policing environment combined paramilitary capabilities with a softer more community-oriented philosophy, with the balance between the two styles varying according to operational phases and contingencies. In theory this should have resulted in effective and appropriate operations, but in practice it meant inconsistency and ineffectiveness. For instance, the initial task of the international police in Sarajevo was to support the

NATO-led international Stabilisation Force in Bosnia in enforcing law and order and to assist with the formation of a reformed civilian police. Dealing with disorder was, however, problematic. SFOR could deploy rapidly in unit strength but was reluctant to engage in confrontations with civilians, whereas IPTF, many of whom were unarmed, was incapable of dealing with serious disorder. Also, its culture was undisciplined – IPTF was slow to arrive in Bosnia (as in Kosovo and Cambodia) because of the holiday season.[4]

The precarious nature of the new order was evident in a multitude of ways. A major flaw concerned the unrealistic nature of the IPTF's remit (HRW 1998). The IPTF's ambitious mandate – to screen all police applicants, and to ensure that anyone who had committed war crimes or serious human rights abuses was prevented from holding any police post – was unrealistic. After the first year, the Security Council gave IPTF authority to investigate human rights abuses by local police law enforcement, but in reality ITPF left most investigations to local police. According to HRW, the IPTF was unable or unwilling to assist victims of human rights abuses, let alone hold accountable the local police guilty of the abuses against the 'citizens' whom international standards held they were obliged to protect (they commonly intimidated, harassed and abused sections of the city's population). IPTF's interpretation of their oversight responsibilities in police restructuring was similarly minimal. Some local police were investigated but few were dismissed. This situation is significant because Sarajevo's position was in many respects exceptional. The IPTF's accessibility in Sarajevo made it easy for complaints to be made, and the heavy presence of international police and media ensured that its police were subject to scrutiny.

IMPLEMENTING A NEW ORDER

A primary purpose of the IPTF was to facilitate the creation of a democratic police force capable of creating a sense of security and democratic order. The so-called Bonn–Petersburg agreement of April 1996, which structured the process, referred to Bosnia's commitment to developing policing structures 'which will support the democratic system and protect internationally accepted human rights and fundamental freedoms of all persons' (HRW 1998). This would, it was thought, encourage toleration and encourage minorities to return to their pre-war homes.

Achieving this required significant restructuring and re-education. A key requirement was reducing the size of the existing forces. This meant reducing the Bosniak-Croat Federation's 20,000 officers to 11,500, and the RS's estimated 50,000 regular and special police to 8,500. Agreement was reached in April 1996 following negotiations between the IPTF, the Federation and the more intransigent RS authorities, which repeatedly obstructed implementation of the Dayton agreement, and sheltered indicted persons, some of whom were working as police. In the event, the Federation accepted the so-called Bonn–Petersburg agreement, but the RS did not formally accept the need for restructuring until late 1997, and did not begin the process until 1998. It seems that agreement was reached only because IPTF acted under the protection of SFOR, an organisation backed by US military resources.

Restructuring was essentially a procedural matter of vetting. Under the terms of the agreement and subsequent instructions issued by the IPTF commissioner, all police were required to reapply for their jobs and pass several tests. The names of successful eligible officers were then published in newspapers so that anyone questioning their inclusion could put their case. Candidates who survived this procedure received IPTF-provided identification and new uniforms, and began a twelve-month probation period, during which they could lose their job if found guilty of abuse or of non-compliance with the peace agreement. The process of testing and readmission was carried out canton by canton over two years. There were, however, differences between the two schemes. The RS agreement provided for a police force reflecting the ethnic divisions of the post-war population, whereas the Bonn–Petersburg agreement required ethnic percentages in the police to reflect pre-war divisions. The certification system was similar.

In practice, the restructuring programme confirmed that the tensions underpinning the old and the new forms of order remained, and that group pressure offset any advantages of using police as a tool for social engineering. Mandatory minority quotas were not met, though ethnic recruitment was rebalanced. However, many of the new recruits did not live in the locality they policed, while others resigned as a result of group pressure or because of poor living conditions. Also, it was clear that the use of ethnic quotas was incompatible with the development of a meritocratic police force, especially at the level of senior officers (Celador 2005).

The IPTF was able to impose its agenda partly because it was under the umbrella of US military power and partly because of the uniquely comprehensive, coherent and well-resourced commitment made by NATO (that is, the US) and EU. For the EU, commitment to police reform was only one dimension of a broader programme for political engagement, assistance and monitoring. Long-term support was in the EU's own interests.

PARAMILITARIES

The precarious nature of the new order was evident from the need for international paramilitary forces throughout the period under discussion. In 1998, NATO created a multinational specialised unit reporting directly to military headquarters out of forces provided by Argentina, Italy, Romania and Slovenia. The MSU's mission was to maintain public order and safety by providing a constant presence. If prevention failed it was to deploy using force, if necessary reverting to a light infantry role. Its remit was to deal with public-order issues on the basis that neither the military nor the police were equipped and trained to handle the type and range of tasks presenting. Located next door to SFOR HQ at Camp Butmir, it was a stand-alone facility, and by 2004 was built around Italian Carabinieri and gendarmerie-style forces from Austria, Hungary, Romania and Slovenia, all of whom constituted a regiment-sized unit, described by MSU as 'light infantry' (*JDW* 4 August 2004: 25). An integrated police unit (IPU) later replaced it within the EU mandate.

The nature of the order the MSU policed is evident from the 221 public-order missions carried out between October 2003 and June 2004. Like its successor, the IPU, the MSU's tasks ranged from seizing small caches of weapons and munitions, to assisting with the arrest of locally indicted war criminals, to single firearm incidents. This complemented SFOR's approach, for by then SFOR tactics were relatively low key, involving interacting with the local population, rather than aggressively collecting intelligence, and using soft-skinned vehicles

otection. Later, just as the IPTF relied on
ㅡFOR (the EU's 7,000-strong military force in
,oo-strong paramilitary IPU. By 2006, the IPU's
.sisting local police to deal with organised crime,
a͜   ɪfficking of illegal weapons (often in Sarajevo itself)
and c͜   g smuggling operations along the border with Serbia.

The Iɴ ⟋ was not designed for urban policing as such, but its
personnel and equipment made its purpose clear. Its headquarters at
Camp Butmir on the outskirts of Sarajevo were supported by four
company-sized mobile units that carried out normal framework operations, public-order and rapid-reaction operations, and by specialised
investigative teams and a logistics element. Its mobile units were
equipped with protective weaponry and equipment that included
shields, tear-gas launchers, bulletproof helmets, bulletproof/flak
jackets, automatic rifles, heavy machine guns and armoured cars.
Significantly, it was often referred to as the IPU regiment or as
'troops'.

TYPICAL PROBLEMS

Policing problems varied according to whether the police concerned
were Bosniak Croats, Bosnian Serbs or internationals. The concerns
of indigenous officers were probably those of protecting their own
group, watching their own back, and cultivating connections. For
internationals, concerns varied from professional issues relating to
restructuring and reforming the local police, crime prevention and
personal safety, to personal imperatives such as avarice and sex (*Central
Europe Review* 2001).[5] But this is perhaps only to be expected of the
10,000 police from forty-six countries who served with the IPTF
between 1996 and 2001.

At the day-to-day level, policing problems ranged from handling
teenage males looking for a fight to investigating war crimes. Land
and property disputes were a feature, as they are in most post-conflict
cities; the war meant that Bosnia had not been able to develop the
institutional mandates needed to restore the publicly owned buildings of socialist Yugoslavia to their former private owners. Riots
were not a major problem. Most riots in post-conflict cities are big,
coordinated and vicious, with rioters obeying no obvious rules or

behavioural constraints. On such occasions control ʊ,
methods becomes difficult; as a senior French officer comnᵢ
if rioters know that troops will only employ tear gas 'then you are
in trouble' (*JIDR* 2000: 49). However, Bosnia saw few instances of
wide-scale disorder inspired by religious and/or ethnic nationalism.

Police were not used for demobilising military or militias since they
lacked the necessary training and equipment, but there were some
3,000 armed UN civilian police (CIVPOL), with arrest powers, who
could act if the emergent political order was openly challenged.

WEBS OF CORRUPTION

The various strands in Bosnian order are not easily disentangled, and
it is difficult to separate criminal activities from the funding of the
nationalist or ethnic survival strategies that were legitimate in the
eyes of Bosnians. For example, millions of dollars of international
aid were sent to Bosnia to finance reconstruction in the mid-1990s,
only to be channelled into the bank accounts of Bosnia's political
and security elite. In 1997, it was reported that Muslim authorities
had diverted as much as $30 million dollars of the World Bank's
$150 million transitional assistance credits to finance their own ethnic
structures (*Sunday Times* 27 July 1997).

In reality, crime, corruption and (in international eyes) disorder are
interwoven in cities such as Sarajevo because criminal organisations
have political protection; many criminals enjoy excellent working
relationships with politicians, businessmen and security officials.
One reason why trafficking, for instance, is big business is because
successful traffickers are well connected and are rarely prosecuted.
Collusion is difficult to prove, but two high-profile criminal cases
illustrate the intricacy of the security environment. One year after
the Dayton Agreement, Nedzad Ugljen, who was second in command
of Bosnia's secret intelligence services in Sarajevo (the Agency for
Investigation and Documentation, AID) and liaison officer with the
CIA, was killed in a gangland-style execution. But it was never clear
whether Ugljen was killed by war criminals, gangsters, gunrunners, the
Bosnian government, the Iranian government (which was suspected
of using Bosnia as a means to spread Islamic radicalism in Europe),
or by his own agency (*Sunday Times* 10 November 1996).

As a result, Bosnia's alignment with democratic values remains flawed. The order that re-emerged was characterised by 'the saturation of political structures with enthno-centric provisions, the strength of ethnically-based patronage, the weakness of central authority and the illogic of internal borders [that make Bosnia] both ungovernable and economically unsustainable' (ICG quoted in Donais 2005: 373). As the British officer in command of EUFOR noted in November 2005, 30–40 per cent of Bosnian police were unreliable (*Sunday Times* 10 November 1996). More damningly, despite an October 2005 agreement on police reform, fifteen separate – and uncooperative – police forces operated in a country of 3.8 million (ICG 2005).

KOSOVO

The situation in Sarajevo and Mostar may be compared with that in Kosovan towns such as Priština or Mitrovica, where parallel forms of order were similarly identifiable. In Kosovo criminal networks and intimidation resurfaced openly even before the war stopped. However, the collapse of the criminal justice system in the aftermath of NATO's 1999 bombing campaign forced NATO's Force (KFOR) to take the lead in enforcing basic levels of public order and creating a new police force. Indeed, KFOR effectively took over the administration of the province – the presence of 40,000 troops and 10,000 civilians was the equivalent of 1 for every 36 Kosovars. Even with this, thuggery and organised crime flourished, moulding the new order.

A typical urban situation confronting British troops entering Kosovo in 1999 – and of the order evident in such towns – is found in a newsletter, written for their families, by men of the King's Royal Hussars Battle Group (Hills 2002: 105). In it they describe their entry into the town of Podujevo, 25 km due north of Priština. The town smelt of sewage, death and neglect; the main streets were full of rubbish, rubble and feral dogs; broken glass from shop windows and household debris covered the pavements. Other than the blue and black Serbian Ministry of Internal Affairs (MUP) uniforms and flags, the only colours to be seen in the town centre were those of clay, red bricks and blackened wood. Yet within a week street vendors were selling cigarettes, chocolate and a few vegetables. Tractors, buses, cars and the occasional horse and cart moved through the streets.

The dominant smells became those of Bond cigarettes, grilled meat, chai and exhaust fumes.

In the immediate post-intervention period, policing (which often concerned localised violence and intimidation) was provided by NATO soldiers, by UN police using their home-country procedures and standards for apprehending, questioning and detaining suspects, and by Kosovars, who patrolled after completing a basic training course at a UN police school. Occasionally the three groups shared responsibilities, but each used different methods and standards. KFOR's approach, for example, was miscellaneous and arbitrary, reflecting its multinational nature, whereas British forces policed in terms of law, which meant that they lacked credibility; criminals went free because there were no means to maintain the necessary continuity of evidence. Also, KFOR made mass arrests, but most detainees were released because there were no courts to try them or prisons to hold them (Stromseth et al. 2006: 320).

The types of crime confronted varied. In the summer of 1999, for example, Provost Marshall Lt Col. Carlucci, senior KFOR adviser, saw more serious revenge and arson attacks than petty crime. But twelve months later the balance was reversed because the arrival of KFOR and the UN brought money to Kosovo, with a direct increase in ordinary criminality the result. According to US force headquarters, patterns of crime soon became those common to most urban areas, with murder, robbery, shootings, forgery and prostitution to the fore. The problems were even more challenging for international officers stationed in Mitrovica, a town of approximately 95,000 Albanians and 15,000 Serbs, twenty-five miles north of Priština. The town's administration was as divided as its population, and the 60 international and 40 Kosovo Police Service (KPS) officers operating there in 2004 (five years after the war) were confined to the southern, Albanian side of the heavily fortified bridge that divided the city. Police time was spent on responding to calls, stopping traffic, or conducting formulaic and highly visible mobile and foot patrols. Property crime was a major problem, as were smuggling, trafficking and theft involving cash, portable electricity generators and vehicles (*The Economist* 17 February 2001: 52; Peake 2004: 24–5). But the biggest policing problem was dealing with the customary laws and traditions governing dispute resolution among the Albanian population.

GROUP DYNAMICS

In summary, it is not always clear why Bosnia's police – or Kosovo's – behaved as they did, but political calculations and personal and/or group concerns doubtless dominated their decision-making. After all, each group had to ensure its own survival while accommodating, subverting or exploiting the demands of international, regional and domestic regional interests. Further, the police were only one of a number of actors seeking to manage Bosnia's security and broader state-building programme, and such programmes are invariably associated with struggles for the control of security organisations. In other words, parallel and contradictory forms of order emerged. This assessment is supported by the continuing presence of international organisations and the fact that the main policing challenges so far as such organisations were concerned were, in 2007 as in 1996, organised crime, corruption and ethnic bias. Organised crime could, theoretically, be treated as a professional or technical issue, but in Bosnia and Kosovo corruption represented social and cultural factors that international police were unable to influence, let alone reduce. For such reasons the record of the international policing project in the Balkans is mixed. Nevertheless, the models developed there have been influential in shaping reform projects in other regions, the most extreme example of this being in Afghanistan.

KABUL

On 7 October 2001, Kabul, the capital of Afghanistan, was bombed as US forces prepared to invade the country in retaliation for the September 2001 suicide attacks on New York and Washington DC. The Bush administration's goal was to capture Osama bin Laden, destroy al-Qaeda, and remove the Taliban regime that had supported al-Qaeda. The war was militarily successful and on 13 November truckloads of troops from the Western-backed Northern Alliance[6] flooded into Kabul as the Taliban retreated. Kabul's physical and social structures had been substantially destroyed (parts of the sprawling areas of mud-brick had not been rebuilt since the factional fighting of the early 1990s), but within days the Alliance conducted security patrols in the city centre, traders and markets reopened for business, women and children went about their daily business. The re-emergence of political order was more problematic and potentially dangerous.

Afghanistan had by 2001 been subject to several decades of war that had destroyed its infrastructure and economy. The Taliban had brought a measure of stability to the country, but a major consequence of their fall was infighting between local commanders over power and territory. Although Kabul in November 2001 was relatively calm, it was an exception. Other cities experienced brutal forms of victor's justice, with several hundred Pakistani supporters of the Taliban killed following the fall of Mazar-i Sharif in the north.

The fall of the Taliban left a power vacuum that guaranteed Kabul would experience a power struggle between rival warlords and ethnic groups. Moreover, just as the Northern Alliance sought to ensure that its vision of political order dominated (it announced an interim administration, and took over key ministries) so, too, the US and UK, working closely with the UN and its special envoy to Afghanistan, Lakhdar Brahimi, determined to ensure that the emergent order reflected their vision of a multi-ethnic representative regime. The 'international community' promised to rebuild the country and introduce social changes that would, for example, improve the opportunities open to women. A UN envoy and a Russian delegation arrived in Kabul to coordinate talks on forming an interim broad-based government, to be immediately joined by the leaders of factional militias, each of whom demanded a share in any administration.

The rapid resurgence of local warlords ensured that, by January 2002, security rather than reconstruction was the new government's priority. Not only were looting, intimidation and road tolls crippling movement and undermining international goals, but also scores died as warlords fought for power in the provinces. By early 2002 it was clear that neither Washington nor London planned to extend peacekeeping beyond Kabul, and even in Kabul the emergent forms of power-based order were those negotiated and contested by Afghan's powerbrokers, rather than by Washington or the UN. Warlords permitted President Karzai to 'control' Kabul precisely because his weak government could not, for instance, limit the production of opium. In this way, the order that emerged operated at several levels. At the macro-level it reflected ethnic, religious, regional and personal rivalries reinforced by the influence of al-Qaeda and the Taliban, the opium trade, banditry, land disputes, tribalism, external influences (Pakistan and Iran), the presence of foreign forces, and the legacy of decades of war and repressive and inefficient systems of governance. At the micro-level order resulted from warlord rivalries, and the exclusionary variables shaping the lives of most Afghans, such as political exclusion, food insecurity and economic marginalisation.

Afghanistan is significant here because the weakness of the Afghan state challenged international assumptions on the nature and management of order. A national police force requires a tax base, which requires some form of development or stability, while government structures are required if human rights are to mean anything in a culturally unsympathetic environment, but these were missing in Afghanistan. In particular, the strength of indigenous illiberal norms and values clashed with the beliefs of the international officials promoting a normative agenda designed not only to facilitate regional and international stability, but also to create social justice. As Brahimi observed in 2004, 'we want to bring about some form of sustainable economic development, we want to change the way people do things, we want to improve the way they run their courts, the way they police themselves, the way they uphold human rights, the way their women are treated, etc.' (Brahimi quoted in Freeman 2007: 7).

POLICE IN 2002

In January 2002 the interim interior minister, Younis Qanooni, estimated that order could be maintained throughout Afghanistan by a 70,000-strong police force, but a German fact-finding mission to Kabul that month found that approximately half of the city's police stations were unstaffed, and the remaining police had no equipment, few weapons, and only ten (privately loaned) vehicles.

An international donor conference in Berlin in February sought to address the problem. A senior German official stressed that the aim was to build a national police force that reflected Afghanistan's ethnic composition, included women, and was committed to human rights and democratic principles, but delegates quickly agreed that work should focus on Kabul.[7] Fifteen new police stations were to be built, the police academy was to be reopened, a standardised training programme (including packages for training trainers) developed, and links between the variables underpinning order (such as disarmament, crime and drugs) simultaneously addressed. Germany pledged €10 million to rebuild the police as part of its commitment to act as lead nation in coordinating international efforts.[8]

The twenty-eight donor nations and eleven multinational organisations present approved the proposals, not least because they feared that security would deteriorate rapidly once the initial deployment phase of the International Security Assistance Force (ISAF) ended in June. The order they wished to see emerge in Afghanistan is clear from the EU's programme of police reform, which aimed to establish 'sustainable and effective civilian policing arrangements under Afghan ownership and in accordance with international standards' (European Union 2007). As the second largest donor for 2002–06, the EU contributed €3.7 billion. Also, it was a major contributor to the Law and Order Trust Fund (LOTFA) that supported the Afghan National Police (ANP), channelling some €135 million into LOTFA between 2002 and 2007, so its vision was politically influential.[9] Its programme emphasised the need for a comprehensive and long-term approach of monitoring, mentoring, advising and training covering the whole of Afghanistan; 160 police and justice experts were to be deployed in Kabul, regional police commands, and provincial reconstruction teams.

KANDAHAR

Kabul was atypical in that it received favoured treatment by internationals; it was the seat of Karzai, their protégé. Elsewhere order had little to do with security, stability or development. Rather, it depended on personalities, local politics and drug production. This was the case in Kandahar, the second largest city and the main city of ethnic Pashtuns, Afghanistan's largest ethnic group.

Despite almost thirty years of destruction, Kandahar, with a population of approximately 450,300, was a major trading centre, with an international airport, and roads to Kabul and important cities such as Herat and Quetta (in Pakistan). It received large sums of American money for construction purposes; new buildings replaced old ones, sewerage systems and schools were built, and major roads were repaired or completed. There was potable water and electricity (summer temperatures reach 55°C) even if 30 kilometres away in Panjwai, Taliban fighters fought running battles with Canadian forces, which could do little more than hold the centre of the town (*Independent* 21 August 2006). However, although the Americans brought money, projects and jobs, they left intact the drugs mafia and warlords, who included a former governor and Karzai's brother, who also headed the Provincial Council. In fact, Kandahar's order and prosperity were based on drugs. But this stable state was undermined when NATO replaced US forces, because NATO sought to eradicate poppy cultivation, and the first casualty of the destruction of poppy fields was the power supply. Electricity failed when NATO took over because without drug profits Kandahar's inhabitants could no longer afford the oil required to run the American-donated generators. (The average bill for a month was approximately $40 whereas the average government employee made about $50 a month.)

Police played little part in managing Kandahar's order. Small stations were often located in alleyways in run-down areas at risk of infiltration by insurgents (Wright 2006: 41). Most officers were unable or unwilling to leave their stations, especially at night, and relied on low-level extortion or intimidation to make up their salaries. In theory patrolmen received about US$65–70 a month, but salaries were unpaid when funds failed to filter down, commanders demanded a stipend from their men, and money available for registered police was also used to fund unregistered officers. A policeman at a substation in Kandahar told Wright that some of his men were paid $15 a month, adding: 'For the ordinary police to be satisfied with their work and not make links with [crime] they would need USD120.' As a result most supplemented their salaries or lived off bribes from anyone who wanted them to look the other way.

ORDER AND DYSFUNCTIONAL REFORM

It is clear that order existed at several levels, the most fundamental of which incorporated (or instrumentalised) insecurity and localised disorder. In contrast, international-style order was as superficial, localised and temporary as its attempts to create an effective and accountable national police force. One reason for this situation was that police reform was split between a numbers of donors, resulting in contradictory or unrealistic policies. Germany, for instance, acted as lead donor and re-established the National Police Academy for training officers and NCOs on European lines, while the US developed a US-style constabulary programme for lower ranks, and UK advisers taught common-law policing principles.[10] The five-year plan that these programmes represented cost US$160 million and was intended to train 50,000 regular police (and 12,000 border guards) by the end of 2006 (US GAO 2005).

Reform was also obstructed by the fragmented nature of the country's political order. There was no central control, and the weakness of the Karzai government (which was further undermined by corrupt local politicians) ensured that policing remained dysfunctional from a Western perspective. In 2002, most of the 30,000–50,000 'police' were untrained, ill-equipped, poorly paid and illiterate former fighters, who, after receiving a basic training from international advisers, either returned to stations that were effectively militia outposts, or were loyal to local warlords (Hodes and Sedra 2007). Reform was further undermined by the political value to warlords of an unreformed police force. Despite its low status, policing offered factional leaders attractive opportunities; this is why in March 2003 five senior officials claimed responsibility for police leadership. Similarly, many former militia commanders used the police as a means to retain power and resources. They avoided the constraints imposed by the demobilisation, disarmament and reintegration (DDR) process by taking up positions in the Ministry of the Interior, and moving their militias with them in an official capacity (Tajik Afghans held most senior posts). This partly explains the divided loyalties and top-heavy nature of the police hierarchy. Finally, reform was undermined by chronic corruption and poor discipline. For example, the end of 2005 saw the number of police generals (many of whom were illiterate) cut from 286 to 120 and colonels from 2,790 to 2,350 while the National Highway Patrol increased from 39,600 60 to 48,000 (Wright 2006). However, the patrolmen's involvement in smuggling was so blatant that the Patrol was disbanded in 2006, its members moving to border areas, where, rather than disrupt smuggling networks, they targeted residents as a source of revenue. Few if any Afghan police shared Murray's assumption that 'the civil security required for social stability and security is founded on the rule of law and encompasses law enforcement, the prevention of crime, the protection of human rights in homes and public places, and the creation and maintenance of orderly communities' (Murray 2007: 108).

The superficial veneer of international-style order was evident when the police failed to contain riots in Kabul in May 2006 after a US military vehicle crashed into an early-morning traffic jam (Murray 2007: 122–3). Before then police reform had appeared to achieve some success in Kabul, with traffic control (one of the visible signs of order) improving as traffic police displayed competence and traffic signs appeared (Murray 2007: 116–17). However, police not only failed to contain the rioting, but also some ran away, while others allegedly shed their uniforms and joined in. The rioters took two hours to reach the centre of Kabul, yet no efforts were made to close streets or divert the mob.

Murray notes that the riots highlighted other reform failures too, including poor leadership. The government therefore announced changes to command posts immediately afterwards. These had in fact been planned for some time, but international advisers were dismayed to discover that the list of eighty-six names they had helped compile using a merit-based screening process had been revised by the President's Office in favour of men with minimal educational qualifications or unacceptable records. The new police chief of Kabul was one such case. In this way, five years of reform ended in failure.

POWER RELATIONS

Most international police advisers and consultants understood the creation and reform of the ANP as a technical or institutional exercise, albeit one shaped by a distinctive philosophy and ideology. All knew that the country was a juridical rather than an empirical state emerging from decades of conflict, but few questioned the desirability or practicality of developing international-style policing arrangements under local ownership, and fewer still appreciated the implications of Afghanistan's social realities. Few appreciated that social continuities mattered most. Of course, order manifested itself differently after the fall of the Taliban. Some men cut their beards, some boys played football, some women appeared on the streets, and some schools were opened, but the fundamentals of the Pashtun honour code and the role of warlords were unchanged.

If, as is suggested here, order is about predictability and the resilience of certain norms, values and processes, its institutional expression may be of secondary importance. This was evidently the case in Afghanistan, where order (re-emergent or otherwise) and its policing depended primarily on relationships of power built on ethnic, cultural and coercive factors. It meant too that resilient indigenous forms of order existed in parallel with weak international impositions. In particular, traditional local systems ran alongside state institutions such as police, and traditional groups contributed to social order through informal processes and the exercise of traditional authority, rather than through bureaucratic institutions. Indigenous order was then reinforced by the Pushtunwali, which is the main tribal legal code and dispute-settlement mechanism, and by the traditional local assemblies (jirga/shura) that are the real enforcement bodies in the provinces at least. Capital punishment is a feature (and indicator of the nature) of the resultant order. Karzai's decision in 2007 to order the execution of fifteen prisoners regardless of legal requirements may have appalled international officials, but it boosted his reputation in Kabul (*Financial Times* 23 October 2007).

Governments and occupiers have always encountered resistance in imposing alien practices on Afghan order, and there was no reason why this should have changed in 2002. That so much effort was expended on imposing alien values and practices merely emphasises the extent to which order and security governance were seen by international authorities through an ideological lens. Moreover, international police programmes reflected power relations within and between donors, as is shown by the parallel reform projects developed by Germany and the USA.

KIGALI

In Bosnia and Afghanistan social continuities ensured that order re-emerged when conflict ended. But in other cases, existing forms of order were distorted, rather than lost. An extreme example of this effect is to be found in the case of Rwanda's economic, cultural and transport hub, Kigali.

April 1994 saw the start of a coordinated and premeditated attempt by the majority Hutus to kill the dominant Tutsi minority. Hutu militias (Interahamwe), Rwandan troops and ordinary Hutus massacred approximately 1 million Tutsi and moderate Hutu before an informal ceasefire was agreed in August. But this did not mean that order had fragmented, let alone collapsed. Rather, Kigali's order, genocidal or otherwise, was efficiently managed. Post-genocide Kigali was different to pre-war of Kigali, yet order never collapsed.[11] The order that existed before, during and after the genocide was such that it tolerated a range of violent activities, from the genocide itself to the extrajudicial killings that continue today; between November 2006 and July 2007, twenty detainees are known to have died in police custody (Reyntjens 2006; HRW 2007b). Rwandan order was also volatile and often difficult to manage, being marked by high levels of grievance, frustration and aggression (caused by population growth, structural adjustment and decreased food production), and by political crisis and the manipulation of ethnic identity by elite groups. Not only was Rwanda's highly stratified society expressed in (and ensured by) structural violence (Galtung 1996), but also the then government was unable or unwilling to manage Rwanda's transition from authoritarian to democratic rule in the face of external pressures for political concessions.

One reason for this may have been the elite's insecurity about their place in the broader order. But order was always closely controlled in Rwanda. For example, the Belgian colonial authorities had issued every Rwandan with an ethnic identity card, and when Gen. Habyarimana seized power at independence in 1973, he banned moving house without permission, and insisted that all Rwandans join his ruling party. After his death in 1993, his associates (led by Col. Bagosora) harnessed the state apparatus (the expression of, and tool for managing, order) for their cause. This enabled local officials to call meetings where peasants were ordered to act in 'self-defence' against the rebels' accomplices.

The killing was made possible by the authoritarian nature of Rwandan order. It started when the presidential guard in Kigali began a systematic campaign of retribution after the airplane of Hutu president Habyarimana was shot down above airport. That its organisers included military, politicians and businessmen is indicative of the importance assigned to a specific form of order. So, too, was the encouragement soldiers and police gave Hutus to kill known or suspected Tutus: they were to kill to purify order. And all were able to exploit the highly centralised nature of the Rwandan state. As Prunier noted: 'The genocide happened not because the state was weak, but on the contrary because it was so totalitarian and strong that it had the capacity to make its subjects obey absolutely any order, including one of mass slaughter' (Prunier 1997: 353–4). The representatives of the democratic governments and intergovernmental organisations, which had been monitoring the situation since October 1993, accepted this. And, just as in Afghanistan, international agencies followed their own agendas. The United Nations Assistance Mission for Rwanda, UNAMIR, for example, which was based in Kigali, had 120 civilian police among its 5,500 military personnel. But according to Dallaire, UNAMIR's commander, the head of the UN Civilian Police Division wished to build an independent UN police unit, rather than develop a good working relationship with the Rwandan Gendarmerie and communal police (Dallaire 2004: 159).

UNAMIR's own mandate included assisting in ensuring Kigali's security (or order in this case). The reason was that all roads led to Kigali, and whoever controlled the city controlled Rwanda (Dallaire 2004: 113). However, internationals did not have strategic interests in Rwanda, and their commitment to enforcing their vision of order was correspondingly weak. Most withdrew after the murder of ten Belgian paratroopers in April 1993, leaving the killings to continue until July, when the Tutsi-led Rwandan Patriotic Front (RPF) captured Kigali. At that point the government collapsed, the RPF declared a ceasefire, and an estimated 2 million Hutus fled to Zaire (now the Democratic Republic of Congo). It was only then that UN troops and aid workers returned to Kigali to 'help' establish and maintain order, and restore basic services. UNAMIR finally left in August 1996, by which time it had cost more than $400 million.

The UN evidently saw the re-establishment of order primarily in terms of an end to the killing. In the aftermath of April's events,

UNAMIR's mandate was adjusted so that it could act as an intermediary between the belligerents in an attempt to secure their agreement to a ceasefire, monitor developments, and facilitate the resumption of humanitarian relief operations. When the situation deteriorated further, UNAMIR's mandate was expanded to include the provision of security for civilians and relief operations to the degree possible, but in practice this meant little. Even so, following the August ceasefire and the installation of a new government, UNAMIR was specifically tasked with assisting in the establishment and training of a national police force, which was seen as a key instrument for achieving and managing an internationally accepted form of order.

In the event, the political and functional readjustment required for this occurred relatively smoothly. It happened at a number of levels, which cumulatively illustrated the nature of the new order, and the place of security within it. Kigali's physical infrastructure (built across four high ridges and valleys) was damaged, but recovered relatively quickly once the Kagame government was established. But many of the elements that are understood to manifest order were missing. There was a marked absence of roads, bridges and telephone lines, and in the longer term a shortage of schools, educational materials and teachers, many of whom had been killed. More fundamentally, the massacres resulted in a demographic imbalance that affected Rwanda culturally and structurally. For example, children were both victims and perpetrators of the killings, while in parts of central Rwanda there were few adult males left alive, and HIV/AIDS was prevalent throughout the country.

Three additional factors deserve note. First, the resilience and compliance of Kigali's populace played a part in shaping order, as did the surveillance and coercion that had long characterised everyday life. Second, the order that prevailed in the early post-genocide years was not dissimilar to what had gone before. For example, there was a real risk of further killings, as when the extremist government in Kigali was on the edge of collapse in mid-June 1994, and fled (together with its radio station, and the majority of the Rwandan armed forces and militias) to Goma in south-west Rwanda, where the French government had carved out a 'safe zone' managed by 2,500 troops. Fighting in Kigali and the RPF's advance kept the extremists in exile for a year, during which time they rebuilt their military infrastructure in preparation for imposing a new order on Rwanda. Their intent was (in the words of Col. Bagasora, the former government official reputed to have led the killings) to 'wage a war that will be long and full of dead people until the minority Tutsi are finished and completely out of the country' (HRW 1995). Third, the political skills of the new government in Kigali (and of Paul Kagame in particular) ensured that both discontent and order were managed in an effective (conventional but authoritarian) manner. Security was a key feature of this, as the Rwanda National Police website makes explicit:

> The Government of National Unity set up after the Genocide has had an uphill task of rebuilding the country's infrastructure, revitalising the economy, promoting unity and reconciliation generally creating an environment conducive to sustainable development ... these plans cannot be realised in the absence of security.[12]

The order that exists today is in this way different but not dissimilar to what went before. Poverty was – and is – widespread, but living conditions gradually improved over the first two years of the new government, especially in Kigali, which was treated by the government as a special case. Although some 43,000 people benefited from food-for-work programmes, by 1996 the UN's Food and Agriculture Organization estimated that conditions had improved sufficiently in Kigali city for assistance to be reduced (UN FAO 1996). Ten years later, the roads between Kigali and the major towns are good, and crime is low. Regardless of whether this improvement was the result of specific government policies, or the legacy of an authoritarian state or a combination of both, it was significant.

Despite the trauma of genocide, a new model of order, adapted to the changed political circumstances, and expressing the RPF's total control (Reyntjens 2006: 26), appeared within a short space of time. The reason for this appears to have been the strength of the transitional government's intent and societal acquiescence. The resultant order was not aligned with liberal ideals (though it is clear from, say, French operations in Operation Turquoise that those ideals were always interpreted from a national perspective), but it was nonetheless resilient and appropriate for many Rwandans. Thus it soon became clear that the RPF would tolerate neither criticism nor any challenge to its authority. Once Paul Kagame was selected by MPs as president in 2000 (he won a landslide victory in the first presidential election in 2003), the police cracked down on the opposition press, and by 2002 individuals suspected of supporting the political opposition, and journalists reporting on them, were detained. According to Amnesty International, the authorities were determined to stifle peaceful political dissent, using unlawful detentions (Amnesty International 2002). On the other hand, from 1997 onwards this trend was balanced by attempts to establish a socially cohesive form of order. For instance, children allegedly responsible for crimes during the genocide received special treatment. This was supported by the UN, which spoke of offering 'international assistance to Rwanda for the reintegration of returning refugees, the restoration of total peace, reconstruction and socio-economic development' (UN 1997). The United Nations Children's Fund (UNICEF) funded a task force of forty police officers to work exclusively on cases of children and adolescents, with priority given to the identification of non-responsible children and their transfer to a re-education centre.

Such moves were consistent with the regime's conception of order, and were enabled by its control of state institutions. Kagame is a skilful tactician, and his abilities, combined with the new government's determination to survive, ensured that it pragmatically adopted strategies that accommodated certain international pressures while ignoring others. Thus the regime permitted UNICEF to operate while crushing what it regarded as dangerous political movements promoting alternative loyalties and identifications (Job 1992: 27). It consistently used the language donors wanted to hear (in 2007 the donors most directly engaged with assistance to the police were Belgium, Sweden and South Africa), and provided training courses on subjects such as stress management, trauma counselling and gender-based violence, while tolerating extrajudicial killings by government soldiers, the deaths of thousands of unarmed civilians, the disappearance of scores of people, and, no doubt, police involvement in the arrest, harassment and sometimes killing of government critics. The order it promulgated included the detention in cruel, inhuman or degrading conditions of some 130,000 genocide suspects without trial (Amnesty International 1998).

TRENDS IN POLICING

It is difficult to assess accurately the impact of events on the policing of Kigali, but the role of the police was symbolically and functionally critical for managing order. They were less tainted than the army and gendarmerie, and their use emphasised the adjustment that had occurred. Also, justice had to be seen to be addressed, and police were widely regarded as an appropriate instrument for this.

Before 1994, a 6,000-strong Gendarmerie Nationale, Rwanda's third structured force, the bulk of which was in Kigali and the heavily militarised northern region of Ruhengeri, enforced order. Its chief of staff reported to the minister of defence for operational issues, support and logistics, and to the minister of the interior for day-to-day policing. Additionally, a Communal Police force reported to the Ministry of Internal Affairs, and a Judicial Police force to the Ministry of Justice. But by the early 1990s, the Gendarmerie had tripled in size, and in the process lost cohesion, discipline, training, experience and credibility. According to Dallaire, it included criminals as well as professional policemen. French and Belgian officers advised it, though their precise role was difficult to assess, and they were rarely seen; Dallaire saw French soldiers only at the airport or at night when they operated patrols and roadblocks around the capital (2004: 71). Policing was also brutal. For example, after an attack by the RPF on Northern Rwanda in 1990, more than 8,000 were detained, and interrogated (often using torture) by the security police, Gendarmerie and Central Intelligence Service (Service central de renseignements, SCR) (Amnesty International 1992: 70).

In the aftermath of the genocide, the police kept a low profile, but once the coalition Government of National Unity was firmly established in 2000, it announced that a new national police would be recruited to replace the Gendarmerie, and communal and judicial police forces. The Rwanda News Agency (RNA) reported that the new national police force would consist of 3,500 policemen, to be selected from 'the existing soldiers of the national gendarmerie, local defence and the public'. RNA quoted the Gendarmerie commander responsible for the force as saying, 'Those gendarmerie who were not ... taken on in the new force would have the option of joining the Rwandan Patriotic Army (RPA)' (IRIN–CEA 2000). The rationale was that merging forces with a policing remit would enhance coordination, uniformity in training and administrative and operational procedures, more efficient use of resources, and a more effective and efficient management of 'stability and social order' (*Daily Monitor* 2007). Significantly, the merger's stated guiding principles and core values were those advocated by donors: justice, respect for human rights, professionalism and accountability. Also, the force's vision linked security and order. Its mission was 'to deliver high quality service, accountability, and transparency, safeguard the rule of law, provide safe and crime free environment for all' so as to make people 'feel safe, involved and reassured'. In this way, the new national police were seen to play a critical role; they were a 'cornerstone in implementing the programs that promote reconciliation and social behavior in the country.' In other words, security was necessary for order, and order was critical because the government's objective was to make Rwanda stable and progressive.

This line was reinforced by interviews given by senior officers such as Deputy Police Commissioner Mary Gahonzire, who stated that 'Police is a law enforcement organ charged with the security of the people and their property' (*Daily Monitor* 2007). Further, 'Our mission is to make the people feel safe, involved and reassured.' She said that the previous year 139 police officers guilty of offences ranging from theft to bribe-taking had been paraded in public before being dismissed. This was seen as ensuring 'the peace of the people and their property'; that is, as key factors in attracting development and investment. The ratio of police to inhabitants then stood at 1 : 2,500, though the government's aim was to improve this to 1 : 1,0000.

ORDERLY SOCIETY

The result was an orderly society. The RPF abolished ethnic identity cards, and forbade the breakdown of statistics by tribe, but it tolerated no criticism or challenges to its authority, and a rigidly hierarchical system of organisation was imposed. Kagame's austere leadership style ensured that ministers were not ostentatiously corrupt, and the police did not routinely demand money, but there was no press freedom or freedom of association.

Ten years of RPF government has left Kigali an ordered, secure and stable city. Order means that street hawkers and prostitutes are cleared off the streets, gutters are swept by thousands of women every day, shopkeepers plant (and water) trees outside their premises, street children are rounded up and taken to an institution outside Kigali, and untidy buildings are demolished (Private communication 2007f; Baker 2007c). Order means that not only do police not take bribes, but also that they move noisy markets and bus stations out of town, and monitor the sound levels of popular churches, threatening to remove their amplifiers. Approved candidates win local government elections even when local candidates are more popular. Order is underpinned by ruthlessness – witness the deaths of a number of genocide witnesses in recent years (HRW 2007a) – but this is arguably what most of Kigali wants. The educated approve since it ensures that the masses are not allowed to tarnish Kigali for potential businessmen or tourists, and the poor like it because it provides security (Private communication 2007f).

CONCLUSION

It is not clear from the examples discussed here whether there is a causal sequence of factors commonly facilitating or obstructing order. But developments in cities such as Sarejevo, Kabul and Kigali emphasise that order submerges before or during conflict, only to re-emerge because of the social continuities involved in its reproduction, and that this is reflected in policing. The violence that obstructs or rechannels order is part of a social and political phenomenon that emerges through (and, indeed, consists of) social and cultural practices that make violence or coercion acceptable means of change and enforcement. Thus the nature and expression of Rwandan policing changed after the RPF's victory in Kigali, just as policing in Sarajevo and Kabul adjusted to international demands, even as the agents concerned drew on the structural features of the social and cultural systems they represented. In consequence, order and insecurity share certain features. Both are about inclusion and exclusion, and both may serve as instruments of policy.

At the empirical level, the trends identified here suggest that policies promoting accountable democratic policing styles are influential only where there are cultural resonances and, more importantly, compelling political reasons, and even then police reform may be an essentially tactical accommodation to unavoidable political pressures. War weariness alone is insufficient. The attractions of closer relations with the EU combined with pressure from Brussels and Washington to ensure that Sarajevo's policing was aligned with that promoted by the EU, but there were no such incentives in Kabul, so there was no reason for the ANP to adopt the values of Canada or Germany. As Chapter 6 will show, in such circumstances people make their own rules.

Lastly, developments in the Balkans, Afghanistan and Rwanda demonstrate that order does not necessarily require security. Specific forms of liberal order may require the stability associated with established democracies, but order may also be based on the instrumentalisation of insecurity. In reality, both forms may exist simultaneously. Further, order may either disappear during conflict, especially when cities are physically destroyed, besieged or occupied, only to re-emerge in a different political guise, or it may be manipulated to achieve specific ends: order is rarely lost. More importantly, all the cities discussed here suggest that cultural forms of order are more significant in determining a city's development than the political and coercive institutions on which understanding is currently built. For these reasons, police represent an accurate indicator of the true nature of order, and the relationships of power on which it is founded.

6

MAKING THEIR OWN RULES

Western ideas about how Southern cities function are often inaccurate. In the absence of Western-style infrastructure and governance, donors and international financial institutions champion their own versions of security governance, while treating urban residents as if they are the passive victims of contingencies or structural processes beyond their control (Murray and Myers 2006: 17). Research focuses on the pathological aspects of post-conflict cities, emphasising organised crime, sectarian or communal violence, overcrowding, poverty, unemployment, exclusion and pollution. Yet there is considerable variation in response patterns, and developments in Mogadishu, Monrovia and Kinshasa show how informal patterns of order and organisation can offer alternatives to state dysfunction. They show how people make their own rules, especially where the influence of international policing is minimal.

Mogadishu, Monrovia and Kinshasa differ in location, size and history, but each saw the complete or partial destruction of its physical and cultural infrastructure, followed by the re-emergence of policing systems that reflected its political and social order: fragmented and factionalised in Mogadishu, uncertain and ineffective in Monrovia, and dysfunctional in Kinshasa. Each shows that, even where governments are unable or unwilling to exercise authority, cities are structured around a variety of localised, personalised, fluid and illiberal security arrangements that frequently provide predictability, enforcement and order. And each shows that war and peace are not easily distinguished, for significant aspects of everyday life are organised around the remnants of violence (Hoffman 2007b). They provide partial answers to perennial questions such as:

- What happens to the organisation and activity of state policing when the institutions and processes on which it is predicated for existence and opportunity fragment for long periods of time?
- How self-sustaining is the acquisition and maintenance of policing (i.e. coercive) powers in the absence of state institutions?

Of the three, Mogadishu offers the most extreme response to the preceding questions, Monrovia the most ineffective, and Kinshasa the most innovative. All three testify to the continuing relevance of Bienen's observation from 1968:

> In the power realm, nation-wide political structures [in conflict-ridden countries] are either non-existent or too weak to enforce the will of ruling national elites, no matter whether they are of traditional lineage groups, civilian bureaucracy, or the military. … Highly localized determination of political life need not be synonymous with disorder, anarchy, and chaos. In fact, it may be the only way to avoid these conditions in certain circumstances. (Bienen 1968: 36)

This situation has been taken to its logical extent in Kinshasa, where the populace has reinvented order in the face of a crisis that is exceptional in terms of its degree and longevity. Yet it is the Mogadishu scenario that haunts international policymakers, for the Somali police disintegrated as political power fragmented in the early 1990s, only to be replaced by alternative forms of localised policing in a juridical state that threatens to become a terrorist sanctuary and source of regional instability. Nevertheless, while Somalia is the most notorious example of a failed state, governments and state institutions often disintegrate during conflict. Compare the collapse of Samuel Doe's government in the face of several hundred Liberian fighters with the disappearance of Sierra Leone's government when its military joined the rebels, or the fragmentation of Afghanistan's government when challenged by the Taliban.

MOGADISHU

Somalia challenges accepted wisdom on the state, order, police, policing and the sharp distinctions usually made between conflict and post-conflict environments. It is a state in name only and, with a few exceptions (mainly in the self-proclaimed republic of Somaliland), there are none of the institutions associated with statehood, little security and even less development. Small factions proliferate, and leaders spend more time plundering than leading; banditry is common, as are no-go areas. There have been some fifteen attempts to establish governments since 1991, but the latest is no more meaningful than its predecessors. More than half of Mogadishu's population fled the city as conflict intensified during 2007.

Yet Somalia is not anarchic. Centrifugal forces dominate at the expense of centralising ones, but there are agreed rules for settling disputes, and the development of a domestic economy free of regulation, prices and exchange controls, together with localised policing arrangements, offsets the disadvantages of Somalia's lack of conventional regulatory policing. Islam (as an identity and way of life) provides security, mainly in urban centres and small towns (Little 2003: 153). In some places sharia law and courts perform a judicial function, while in others neighbourhood watch groups serve as rudimentary police, elders are occasionally able to manage local and inter-clan disputes by drawing on customary law and social contracts, and committees manage assets such as ports and airstrips. Such groups are better at providing law and order than minimal social services and institutions (Little 2003: 85), but they are also significantly cheaper than formal police.

URBAN CONFLICT

This situation has lasted for more than seventeen years, thus offering a laboratory in which to explore the relationship between policing and order in a seemingly dysfunctional city. Further, Mogadishu offers a key to Somali order because conflict centred on Somalia's urban areas, and developments in Mogadishu dominated political life. UN Operations in Somalia (UNOSOM) allowed the special problems of Mogadishu to dictate its agenda for the entire region, and so did warlords. Also, the bulk of Somalia's economic resources, infrastructure and flows of development aid were concentrated in Mogadishu and the southern city of Kismayo (where the port had been modernised by the USA), so their control was worth fighting for (Little 2003: 47).[1] Indeed, President Siad Barre and his followers fled to Kismayo in 1991 when he lost control of Mogadishu itself.

Heavily armed militias controlled Mogadishu, and banditry and looting exacerbated the destruction, hunger and displacement that followed the overthrow of Barre in 1991. After a climactic firefight between US forces and clan militias on 3–4 October 1993, which resulted in the humiliation and withdrawal of US forces, Mogadishu, like most of the country, was divided between rival warlords. They redefined order to suit their own interests and shifting alliances, and used their militiamen to enforce it. And would-be militiamen were plentiful, for the collapse of public provision for health, welfare, food, emergencies and security resulted in a generation of uneducated youths who begged on Mogadishu's streets, shone shoes, and engaged in petty theft: Somalia was at the bottom of the HDI's 1998 ranking (at 175; Sierra Leone was at 174). Kalashnikovs and small arms were easily available in Mogadishu's markets, certain streets became no-go areas, and there was a sharp rise in factional street fighting and armed banditry, and in attacks on minorities and vulnerable or weak clans. At the same time the informal economy thrived, and foreign exchange bureaux, with brightly coloured paintings of $100 notes on their walls, proliferated, as did the telephone, fax and Internet exchanges that facilitated the movement of goods and money throughout the region.[2] Some of the largest Mogadishu-based enterprises operated on a global scale (Little 2003: 143–4).

The best way to gain some idea of what Mogadishu was like in 1991 is from journalists such as Aidan Hartley, who described Mogadishu as a city of roofless districts shrouded in dust and smoke, with the streets full of debris, smashed cars and corpses. When Hartley and his colleagues landed in the city, the first thing they saw

> Speeding towards us were battlewagons bristling with militias in aviators goggles, long synthetic wigs, youths peering into the spider websights of multibarrelled anti-aircraft guns. The vehicles were decorated with antelope horns, festival tinsel and plastic flowers, the cabins were sliced

away, and the paint jobs had been blowtorched off and sprayed over with militia graffiti. (Hartley 2004: 182)

Everything – hospital equipment, museum artefacts and telephone exchanges – had been smashed or looted, but, at the same time, everyday life continued. Some streets were rubble but others were full of fleets of pick-ups carrying qat-chewing and heavily armed militiamen. Bakaara market (Mogadishu's main market) continued to sell everything from alarm clocks and guns to gold bangles, and aid staff raced about in 4x4s with their armed guards in the back. Hartley and his colleagues swam or strolled around the narrow alleys of the old port, and ships unloaded at the seaport even as it crackled with gunfire. Rival clans fought to control the port's perimeter, while inside the docks freelance gangs comprising militias, the private armies of grain and sugar merchants, stevedores, gangs of armed cripples in wheelchairs, and 'unemployed members of the defunct police forces in tattered uniforms' killed one another (Hartley 2004: 212, 219, 217).

Little is one of the few analysts to address why the Somali conflict focused on the control of urban centres (2003: 46). He argues that urbanism has shaped the Horn's economic relations and patterns, as businessmen and civil servants traverse clan lines. In contrast, pastoralists had never benefited from the state (Little 2003: 123). Also, he emphasises the role played by power relations. For he understands many of the issues underpinning conflict (including ethnicity) as historically constructed and as subject to interpretation, manipulation and negotiation. He argues that Western models of social structure (and this may be extended to Western categorisations of war and peace), with their distinctive and clear boundaries, represent false distinctions. For Little, Somali structures are better understood as projects of changing social and political processes within unequal fields of power (2003: 53). The larger context in which change occurs is therefore what really matters. Accordingly, shifts in power relations are reflected in the region's changing configuration of clan and subclan identities, which in turn are shaped less by rigid alliances and more by the overall political context. The same holds for order.

POLICE

The pre-1991 Somali police force, which had a reputation for impartiality and excellence (Hills 2000), had ceased to exist as a coherent organisation by the time Barre fled Mogadishu in January 1991. A few officers stayed at their posts, and one tall, distinguished policeman directed donkey carts, camel trains and Land Cruisers armed with machine guns throughout the worst violence (Huband 2001: 299). But most did not, and the few remaining policemen disappeared when bandits armed with bazookas arrived on the streets at midday or dusk (Huband 2001: 283).

Precisely what happened to the police during this period is unclear; most probably destroyed their uniforms and returned to their clan areas, and there are no reports of senior police officers acting like the group of generals who established an action committee in January 1991. An interim government in Mogadishu tried to re-establish a police force for internal security, using guerrillas, but it proved impossible to disarm the populace. Protection rackets flourished and intense factional fighting broke out repeatedly, resulting in further destruction, hunger, intimidation and extortion. Drug trafficking and prostitution increased, NGO drivers stole food, and UN food stores, peacekeepers and aid workers were attacked. Some form of order undoubtedly existed during these years, but quite what the indicators were is impossible for outsiders to tell.

RESURRECTION

Most international plans for Somalia's future included the formation of a state police force; attempts to resurrect and restructure the Somali Police Force (SPF) were invariably driven by external prompts. A typical development involved the arrival in Mogadishu in January 1993 of three police consultants (from France, Germany and Italy) at the request of the UN, prompted by the USA. Equally typically, the mission was delayed because France and Germany disagreed about its remit, though the USA continued to press for a new force, arguing that 2,400 of the SPF's 3,500 officers could be rehabilitated.[3] The argument for this 'indigenous solution' was based on a judgement that the old force was never totally under Barre's control, and was made up of older men 'wise and careful in their behaviour' who were 'still widely respected in the country' (*Indian Ocean Newsletter* 1993: 561). This seems unlikely. Whatever the case, a Somali police force officially began operations in Mogadishu in February 1993, for the first time in two years, with more than 2,000 of all ranks taking part in general relief activities such as the distribution of assistance, helping food convoys and collecting arms.

Ganzglass says the police were well trained, disciplined and generally non-tribal. If this was the case then he is right to suggest that the nucleus for a Somali police existed. Certainly General Ahmed Jama, the last commandant of the SPF, had suggested to Mohamed Sahnoun (the UN secretary general's special representative for Somalia) in 1992 that the police should be used to maintain law and order in the sectors of Mogadishu where the population accepted them.[4] But such proposals were premature because, as a UN consultant noted, without 'government revenue there is no security. Where there is no security it is difficult to generate revenue' (Ganzglass 1996: 115). Also, policing was essentially about clan, rather than national, politics. Indeed, the contention surrounding it was not about ethnic power so much as state power itself, which the clans saw as a source of revenue.

Although Sahnoun resigned before any of these ideas were put into practice, it is unlikely that such policing represented more than isolated examples. The police in Mogadishu could not, for example, function throughout the city, which was, in any case, divided into war zones. Despite this, various attempts were made to introduce conventional policing. In late 1992, General Ahmed Jama, for one, suggested an incremental approach that involved the police being re-established in areas under the control of the American-led Unified Task Force (UNITAF). His ideas appealed to the US special envoy (Robert Oakley), who wanted to start organising the police by district and region, without addressing the more controversial and difficult problem of combining such commands into a national force. The means through which Jama proposed to achieve this was a police committee in Mogadishu to which each faction would nominate police officers. In fact, an arrangement was brokered between faction leaders, and by March 1993 Mogadishu had a 3,000-strong force (plus 2,000 in the remainder of the UNITAF zone), and police began arresting criminals again after a two-year gap.

This represented a positive step forward, with the subcommittee agreeing selection criteria, such as two years' service with the Somali National Front (SNF) , some literacy, and the assurance that candidates had not committed any significant offence (Thomas and Spataro 1998). It was intended that the force should be paid from the operational funds of the second UN operation in Somalia after May 1993, for Security Council Resolution 814 of March 1993 had requested UNOSOM II to 'assume responsibility for the consolidation, expansion and maintenance of a secure environment throughout Somalia'. In practice, however, there was no budget (officers were paid in food) and no planning, and no thought was given to expanding the concept of the police committee to the rest of the country. So, in the absence of a national government, it remained merely one force among many. It was an essentially factional arrangement to which UNITAF became a part, as Ahmed Jama recognised when he refused command of the Mogadishu force in January 1993.

International authorities continued to emphasise the need for a future national force, even if the political will to fund and support it was lacking. Thus Security Council Resolution 814, crafted largely by the USA, laid out the tasks required to establish long-term order and stability. It mandated the UN to undertake the re-establishment of national institutions and assist in the re-establishment of the Somali police. The UN even sent a small technical team to look at an auxiliary security force which, it was claimed, had 4,000 members from the SNF capable of dealing with short-term requirements for order. (The SNF was at that time an armed militia consisting of Barre loyalists and remnants of the National Army.) The UN team, which met three former SPF commandants and the Mogadishu police committee during their three-week visit, concluded that a national force should be established at its pre-civil-war level of 18,000–20,000 men, monitored by and assisted by a 500-strong UN CIVPOL.

But these recommendations existed in a vacuum. The UN secretary general took no further action, no CIVPOL team was sent, and no decision was taken regarding the source of funding for the proposed 5,000-strong force with its notional budget of US$12.6 million for an initial six months. It was never clear who would ensure officers were paid. UNITAF had used food from relief agencies in lieu of salaries, though UNOSOM I eventually made some funds available for equipment, uniforms and salaries. But this still left the force without uniforms, transport and stations. There was nothing unusual about this in Africa but the result was the 'preposterous situation of an open air arms market in Mogadishu existing under UNITAF, and armed guards of NGOs serving as security personnel during the day and moonlighting as bandits at night, while UNITAF struggled to find funds for batons, berets and whistles for the police' (Ganzglass 1996: 135).

BAIDOA

Despite the situation in Mogadishu, there were temporary pockets of policing excellence and conventional order in other Somali towns. That enforced by Australian troops in the Bay region was operationally the most successful.

The Australians arrived in Baidoa with a comprehensive civil-affairs programme and quickly set up an auxiliary police force to deal with the entrepreneurial banditry plaguing Baidoa, using former members of the SNF whose names were vetted by the police committee in Mogadishu (Kelly 1997, 1999: 33–64; Patman 2001; Zaalberg 2006). Aware that his operation in Baidoa would fail unless a secure environment for the distribution of humanitarian aid was established, the Australian commander took on the role of a military governor in a counterinsurgency-style operation: Australian forces were placed above the clansmen instead of among them. Security was maintained by their constant and visible presence, with relentless patrolling on foot and in armoured personnel carriers, static security positions, and rapid-reaction forces. The Australians trained an auxiliary police force to deal with local banditry, and restored a functioning legal system based on the 1962 Somali penal code. Later, they set up a criminal intelligence department (CID) of former CID officers, which was considered exceptionally effective. Police equipment (which came from UNITAF) included typewriters, stationary, VHF radios, uniforms, batons, whistles and transport, and training was given to the 25 per cent of the force who were armed. Other units were set up throughout the Bay region once those in Baidoa were established, and the police

MAKING THEIR OWN RULES **159**

station was rebuilt in the same compound as a court and small prison. By such means security and a degree of public order were ensured. This was sustained by the 1,100 French UN troops that replaced the Australians in May 1993, and by the Indians who succeeded them. But sustaining an orderly environment depended on the presence of determined internationals (all three contingents had practised 'total immersion'). Consequently, although Baidoa represented a UN success story until 1994, 260 Somali police could not stop militias moving back into the region once the internationals left, for police remained at the mercy of factional leaders, militias and UNOSOM politics.

Even allowing for the differences between Mogadishu and Baidoa in terms of size and clan composition, the contrast between the two cities is significant. The Australians, recognising that Somalia was a heavily armed society characterised by coercive and volatile forms of order, used measured force to restrain local warlords, but unlike US forces they also employed a coherent strategy to deal with the humanitarian and socio-political symptoms of violence. Nonetheless, the order they enforced was based on their superior military skills and resources, and for that reason could never be more than a temporary and localised arrangement.

ORDER AND POLICING

The relationship between order and public policing in Somalia was complex. Policing was shaped by the collapse of the central state and its institutions, compounded by the fact that, though new social groups emerged, traditional cultural patterns (based on kin, elders and Islam) were eroded, and there was no authority or leader capable of sustaining the order (the agreed set of rules) a police institution needs. Faction leaders exploited clan animosity and resources for their own purposes, and, though Somalis seemed willing to pay taxes at the local level (where immediate results were visible), the resources needed to fund state police could never be collected. Looting further reduced the resources available, but it was the centrifugal nature of clan politics that ultimately overwhelmed efforts at public policing. In other words, indigenous order prevailed over international forms. Factional leaders intimidated local communities, and, although their resources and activities were on a comparatively small scale, there was sufficient consensus among powerful men and the communities concerned to ensure that a context-specific form of order prevailed.

One reason why this situation proved remarkably stable despite consistently high levels of insecurity was that Somali leaders had a vested interest in fragmentation; their power base depended on conflict and mobilisation. Businessmen might have benefited from stability, as might the political class of former civil servants, high-ranking officers, and ministers whose place was within the state apparatus. But the status and wealth of many would have dropped with 'peace'. Too many factions and individuals profited from Somalia's economy of plunder and extortion rackets for the situation to be challenged; many businessmen would have lost out if trade were opened up to newcomers, while national reconciliation would have meant clans losing property. Centrifugal forces were stronger than centripetal influences.

The order that emerged represented an adaptation to insecurity and the fragmentation of the state. It was based on local districts developing informal systems and mechanisms which provided minimal security and social support. As such, it was in many respects successful, for by 1995 Mogadishu had a variety of overlapping and fluid local authorities, ranging from militias to clan elders, mafia-like rackets and fundamentalist mosques, all of which provided forms of private policing. They reflected a 'mosaic of fluid, highly localized polities' (Menkhaus and Prendergast 1995: 25) in which security and judicial systems often overlapped. Thus in 1993 the Medina neighbourhood of Mogadishu used a neighbourhood watch system (a crime-prevention scheme in which residents blew whistles if armed outsiders were seen or crime suspected), while paying local armed youths to serve as private security forces. Elsewhere policing ranged from Kismayu's grey-uniformed, truncheon-wielding police led by a former officer in Barre's CID who supported General Mohammed Hersi Morgan, son-in-law and leader of the SNF, to the councils in Baidoa which ran small local forces. This situation offered sufficient stability and predictability to allow businessmen to set up private telephone exchanges, passport offices, and franchises for the export of goats and fruit. Elsewhere, as in the self-proclaimed republic of

Somaliland, clans and subclans had recourse to their own traditional structures, with heads of lineage groups expanding into the vacuum left by the collapse of Barre's administration. However, traditional systems of governance rely primarily on the moral authority of lineage and clan leaders, and the power of such systems to prevent crime and violence was limited.

Fundamentalist mosques imposing sharia law through the use of armed young men in clan areas provided another scheme. In north Mogadishu, sharia authorities were established, with the consent of local faction leaders, to perform basic governance tasks within their area of control. This often happened where faction leaders were unwilling to ensure security. Sharia authorities then gained popularity because they were able to deliver security. Those in Mogadishu performed policing functions, converting armed Toyota trucks (known as technicals) into police vehicles, and sanctioning court decisions in the areas of north and south Mogadishu managed by sharia law. Amnesty International described the punishments imposed by Islamic militia as inhuman and degrading (Amnesty International 1996: 273–4), but execution as a form of punishment was retained by all existing court systems in Somalia, whether secular, Islamic or traditional and clan-based. In other words, an order existed that was based on agreed rules.

Similar patterns developed in other urban areas. In Somaliland, the town of Hargeisa saw a district police force of 300 recruits formed in late 1992 to deal with looting. By 1994, the police force numbered about 400, but funding and a lack of resources were significant problems, tying the police closely to sections of the town. Local people paid for the force in kind rather than cash (using, for example, rice, oil and powdered milk), and the force had its first vehicle (a loaned second-hand Toyota) from one of a group of volunteers supplying food to Hargeisa jail,[5] so its loyalty was to the elders of the region rather than to the self-proclaimed government. But local businessmen evidently welcomed it, for they ran a small electricity grid using two bulldozer engines and gave free power to police stations, courts, mosques, ministries and main streets. Fourteen years on, the police continue to operate, but there is no reliable tax base, and the only assistance they ask for is guns (Private communication 2008a).

One reason why this system endured was because, as Menkhaus and Prendergast noted,

> Collectively this web of radically privatized, quasi-vigilante security arrangements provides reasonable deterrents to crime – for those who can afford them, and who hail from sub-clans with adequate power to reinforce the deterrent factor ... However imperfect this security system may be, it is and will remain far superior to any police force in coming years. (Menkhaus and Prendergast 1995: 25)

Another reason was that the tax revenues that could pay for police were collected by militias and distributed by factional leaders as a form of patronage; gunmen naturally remained loyal to their warlords, rather than to the various governments based in Kenya. The policing that ensued was sometimes little more than routine extortion, but its development suggests a grey area linking extortion and taxation which falls into the general theories about state-building proposed by commentators such as Charles Tilly and Mancur Olson. A third reason was that no one wished to change it. Admittedly, by 2002 the then transitional government was so concerned by the proliferation of armed bandits in Mogadishu that it deployed nearly 2,000 police and military to tackle the problem. But since it allocated only $5,000 to the operation (an AK-47 assault rifle cost $200 at that time) the results were at best temporary (BBC 24 January 2002). This situation continued until the summer of 2005, when the four most powerful warlords agreed to set up a united force, dismantle the roadblocks, withdraw some of the technicals, and stop banditry. But order remains based on violence, plunder and militiamen. Mogadishu's levels of security can be gauged from the estimated 34,000 people who fled the fighting of early 2007, or the reputed 400,000 who left as the government attempted to pacify an insurgency during the Ethiopian-led offensive in April that year.

The extent to which this matters is difficult to judge. In 2004, for example, DFID (which currently supports a development of law enforcement capacity through a UNDP Rule of Law and Security programme) noted that the lack of a central government had only limited effect on daily life because 'local authorities' filled the vacuum. It observed that not only are other African countries in parts as violent and chaotic, but also that in Somalia 'Ordinary life is sustained by a rather vigorous economy based on pastoral and agro-pastoral livelihoods, and on trade. Commercial infrastructure and institutions are functional and relatively sophisticated. Service delivery is undertaken by a mixture of NGO and commercial interests' (DFID 2004).

This is a further demonstration that order depends on the existence of an agreed set of political and social rules. When they are present, order can be said to exist regardless of institutional collapse and violence. For this reason, developments in Mogadishu convey a sense of cultural coherence that is lacking in other post-conflict cities. This is noticeably so in West African cities such as Monrovia, where policing is institutionalised but lacks political and societal roots.

MONROVIA

It is as difficult to define the post-conflict period in Monrovia as it is in Mogadishu, for Liberia's civil war consisted of three wars lasting from 1989 to 2003, with renewed fighting in 1992, 1993 and 1996, and multiple instances of intense conflict in the years since (Ellis 1999). But there the similarities end, for the fragmented, personalised, superficial and corrupt order that re-emerged in Monrovia owed more to the activities of Liberia's small Americo-Liberian elite and the presence of international peacekeepers than to clan or tribal loyalties. Indeed, it is arguable that the uncertainty that resulted was due primarily to the weakness of Liberian traditions and social organisation (Huband 2001: 152).

The order that emerged was shaped by what had gone before, and by what took place during the war, when Liberia's distinctive (and arguably dysfunctional) traditions disintegrated (Huband 2001: 148–9). Major trends coalesced around Charles Taylor. Elected president in 1997, he ran the country as his personal property by using intimidation, patronage and corruption – but this was expected of him. Liberian politics was, and is, 'intensely personalised and mercenary'; it is organised around 'the elevation to power of individual candidates, supported by networks of people who stand to personally benefit' (ICG 2002: 18). Similarly, Taylor's invasion of northern Liberia in late 1989 was probably motivated by his determination to end the domination of the Krahn (the tribe to which Samuel Doe, his predecessor, belonged), rather than tribal rivalry as such; for Doe had favoured the Krahn throughout his decade-long presidency (Huband 2001: 146–7).[6] Personal pathology, ignorance, indiscipline, and the presence of thousands of teenagers and young boys, often high on drugs or alcohol, meant that the rules and guidelines tacitly agreed by Taylor and his adversaries were easily exploited.

Monrovia showcased the results. Half a million Liberians lived in Monrovia when war began, and some 59.5 per cent of Liberia's 3 million population lived there when it ended (UN DESA 2005).[7] Monrovia was ruined for most of the period, but its population rose or fell according to the fighting. In April–May 2003, for example, several thousand people were reportedly killed and more than half of the 1.3 million then living in the city fled when Taylor's rebel National Patriotic Front of Liberia (NPFL) fought for its control. ECOMOG lost control of the situation for six weeks, but people returned once its forces re-established themselves.

Life in wartime Monrovia can be gauged from the reports of journalists such as Mark Huband, who lived there in 1990. He watched as troops from the government's Armed Forces of Liberia (AFL) executed suspected sympathisers of Taylor's NPFL on street corners, on the beach and at an airstrip on the edge of the city (Huband 2001: 144–5). Army discipline fell apart as Monrovia divided into government- and rebel-held areas, and tribal loyalties deepened the divisions. People stayed at home during the fighting, emerging only to pray in churches and beg for food when it slackened. They spoke of needing to go to work, 'but that was only because nobody any longer knew what normality was' (Huband 2001: 146). Telephone cables drooped across the streets, and on the few occasions that the electricity supply was switched on, blue sparks leapt out of houses as junction boxes exploded.

Taylor was elected president in 1997, but conflict continued and the order that resulted yo-yoed between insecurity and appalling abuse. Sexual violence, torture and arbitrary arrest by teenage soldiers were commonplace, and all of Monrovia's prisons were destroyed and emptied. On the other hand, by 1999 the situation was sufficiently

-time curfew (from 02:00 to 05:00) to
ersary of Liberian independence. Again,
nt ECOMOG for control of the city in
at businesses, government buildings, banks,
this made little difference to most of the
t had running water or electricity for at least
a de   duced to scavenging for food. When Taylor
finally lost co   Monrovia, the two separate groups of drugged
teenagers who by then controlled much of the country fired heavy
artillery into any remaining office blocks and looted buildings such
as the brewery (*The Economist* 5 March 2005).

Taylor left Liberia in August 2003, when Nigerian and US troops
arrived, and two months later Gyude Bryant was inaugurated as chairman of the National Transitional Government of Liberia (NTGL),
which was set up to organise elections and was recognised by all factions involved in the conflict. US forces left in September/October but
the UN launched a major peacekeeping mission (UNMIL) involving
more than 1,000 international police and 15,000 UN troops, making
it the largest peacekeeping force in the world; it cost some $800
million a year. In early 2004, donors pledged more than $500 million
in reconstruction aid. A new 3,500-strong UN-trained police was to
replace (or augment) the existing and discredited police (Gompert
et al. 2007), and training at the new National Police Academy began
as a matter of urgency.

Monrovia was calm, even if violence was never far below the
surface. In October 2004, Bryant imposed a curfew after fighting
(prompted by a religious dispute) spread through the city overnight,
but the roadblocks controlling it were manned by disciplined Bangladeshis, whereas formerly militiamen had stretched human intestines
across roads as a signal to stop. By 2005 Monrovia's population had
risen to some 900,000, primarily because of the arrival of internal
refugees, but also because the presence of international forces ensured
a degree of order and stability. Liberia's first peacetime presidential
elections took place in October 2005, when the successful candidate
Ellen Johnson-Sirleaf narrowly defeated George Weah in a second-
round run-off. Johnson-Sirleaf was officially sworn in as president
in early 2006.

NEW ORDER

In June 2006, in a symbolic recognition of Liberia's post-c .
the UN Security Council eased a ban on weapons sales to the
In July Johnson-Sirleaf switched on generator-powered street lights
Monrovia, which had been without electricity for fifteen years, and in
August 15,000 former child combatants were inducted into schools. By
then, Monrovia was, on balance, peaceful, with small traders operating
everywhere, yellow taxis clogging the potholed streets, and police
visible on the main roads. Even so, anecdotal evidence suggests that
most people felt insecure. They feared the activities of street boys,
ex-fighters, political militias, secret societies, machete gangs, and the
internal refugees squatting in unoccupied or burnt-out buildings (cf.
Bøås and Hatløy 2008). Meanwhile the police (who were disarmed
for three years after the 2003 peace agreement) were ineffectual
and dependent on UNMIL. Indeed, the UN was arguably the only
organisation in the country that functioned. Based on data collected
in 2006, Mehler and Smith-Höhn found that urban respondents
regarded UNMIL as the best guarantor of personal safety, followed
by the police (Mehler and Höhn 2007: 54). But the UN's policing
role was at best temporary, and its ability to shape fundamentally the
emergent order was negligible. The role of UNPOL was to advise,
and its unarmed officers did not have authority to arrest or detain.
The International Armed Police (UNPOL's armed unit) provided
support when armed protection was needed, but this applied only
in the case of certain crimes on certain occasions; it did not cover
the innumerable cases of armed robbery.

THE ROLE OF THE NPF

The part played by the Liberian National Police Force (NPF) in
managing the emergent order reflected broader ambiguities and tensions. Above all, its politicised nature, recruitment practices, societal
environment and weak leadership shaped its role.

Liberia's police had long been politicised. Taylor's practice of filling
it with untrained loyalists and ex-fighters who acted as representatives
of their respective factions was never seriously challenged. In 1997,
for example, the Taylor government's refusal to implement measures
whereby recruitment would reflect a more equitable ethnic and geo-

graphical balance led to the USA withdrawing its support for police training, but this made little difference. The end of the war meant that approximately 40,000 former militiamen had to be disarmed, so moving as many as possible into the police made sense from Taylor's perspective.[8] It also ensured that brutality and indiscipline remained common, as did the police's reinforcement by special units. The police's structure soon resembled the security apparatus built by Taylor in his NPFL.

Taylor also filled important posts with relatives, such as Joe Tate. Until he was killed in a plane crash close to Monrovia in 1999, Tate, a cousin of Taylor and a member of his militia, and reputedly guilty of numerous human rights abuses, was police commissioner. Indeed, this practice continues: Johnson-Sirleaf personally chose not only the inspector general but also appointments to the next two levels down. What is more, she appointed her relative Fumbah as director of the National Security Agency, and her cousin Ambullai Johnson as minister of internal affairs.

The police in this way reflect the ambiguous nature of the new order. Signs of conventional order and normality are introduced, only to be undermined or subverted by the realities of everyday life. For the state, and recognisable forms of state-based order, barely exist in Monrovia, let alone outside it. In 2005, for instance, 600 new recruits began policing Monrovia's chaotic traffic. The city centre was regularly brought to a halt by huge traffic jams, so the gesture was significant. Initially the new police (dressed in new uniforms) did not look for bribes. Indeed, one new policeman said that, as well as keeping the traffic moving, his job included persuading pedestrians to cross the road safely (BBC 12 January 2005). But this did not last. Indeed, there was arguably little reason why it should when one of the first acts of the all-party government formed under the 2003 Accra peace agreement was to spend millions of dollars on four-wheel-drive vehicles at the official price of US\$37,000 each. A threat to stop foreign aid was averted only after Bryant promised that the vehicles would remain government property (*Africa Confidential* 2005). Meanwhile police wages were sufficient for little more than a bag of rice. The police's presence outside Monrovia was minimal. In the south-east, for example,

Maryland County had 23 policemen (of whom 16 had received training) for a population of 100,000.

Weak leadership compounded the problems confronting the police, who are themselves divided and lacking in skills, resources and institutional capacity; not only were institutions destroyed by the war but so too was the education system. Johnson-Sirleaf set the tone when she included in her transitional team former police director Paul Mulbah, who had used Taylor's Anti-Terrorist Unit (ATU) and the LNP's Special Operations Division (SOD) to brutalise political opponents. The flawed leadership style of her inspector general, Beatrice Munah Sieh, a former career officer and schoolteacher in the USA, exacerbates the problem. When in July 2007, Munah Sieh was inadvertently held under siege as dozens of LNP officers fought the Seaport police guarding the main port in Monrovia (LNP officers had gone to investigate fuel theft), she pulled out a handgun and demanded the LNP and UNMIL secure her release. The resultant stand-off lasted several hours, leaving traffic gridlocked (*The Analyst* 2007).

The capacity and/or willingness of the new police force to address Monrovia's problems was, inevitably, limited. Not only was police reform, like DDR, to some extent driven by the urgent need to 'satisfy' the needs of ex-combatants (Jennings 2007; cf. Bøås and Hatløy 2008; Ellis 1999; Ebo 2005), but also the vetting and recruitment procedures laid down for the new police included strict criteria that meant many new officers were untrained 18-year-old ex-fighters. This, combined with the lack of public electricity, and the state of Monrovia's roads (and the police's unwillingness to leave the main roads), ensured that the police were at best ineffective. Officers avoided entering alleys and shanty towns, and in 2006 the government admitted they could not cope with the activities of machete gangs: people were asked to form vigilante groups (BBC 19 September 2006).

In this way, the police reflected Liberia's fragile, insecure, politicised and unequal order. Access to electricity and potable water illustrates the point. Lack of electricity is not in itself problematic (it is normal in the region), but the fact that only politicians, senior government officials and successful businessmen – and the hotels and restaurants they frequent – can buy the generators needed to ensure supplies is indicative of the unreconstructed nature of Liberian order. Similar considerations apply to police standards. In fact, lack of resources and training is the normal state of affairs in Africa: Liberia has only one forensic laboratory, but the same is true of Nigeria, Africa's biggest and most populous country. Liberia has no pathologists, toxicologists, ballistics specialists, fingerprint specialists or forgery experts, but neither have many of its neighbours. There is a fingerprint laboratory, but the lack of fingerprint kits means that officers play cards instead (Baker 2007a). Perhaps because of this, people do not look to the police for security.

ORDER MINUS SECURITY

Monrovia shows that order does not necessarily require security: Monrovia is now more orderly than it has been for many years, yet crime has increased. It seems that Monrovia has settled into a post-war order, whereby legacy issues shape emergent threats, and the dominant types of crime are increasingly those seen in most big cities. As Baker has noted, many LNP commanders are aware of the adverse effect of war on crime: 'we have drugs since the war – youth drugged themselves up to fight … Since the war every burglar has a weapon – a screwdriver, knife. Most don't have arms. Or they use pretend guns.' When asked what were the main crime problems they faced, LNP commanders agreed on 'theft, aggravated assault, armed robbery, rape, domestic violence and drug trafficking' (Baker 2007a).

It is impossible to provide hard evidence for such conclusions. Statistical evidence of crime rates is, as in most if not all African cities, limited and misleading; under-reporting is common, there is no systematic recording, and different agencies collect (and keep) information. Even so, Baker found that public complaints in 2007 consistently related to labour disputes (no payment or unfair treatment), house invasions by twenty-strong gangs, police brutality, rape and disputes about family inheritance or land. The cumulative result is that

> large numbers of the population are fearful every night of burglary; large numbers experience petty (though not petty to them) theft regularly; large numbers live where the police are not able or willing to

patrol; large numbers endure child abuse, domestic violence, rape and labour exploitation without redress; few bother with the emergency 911 service because of its unreliability. (Baker 2007a)

At the same time, feelings of alienation and abandonment have intensified. Indeed, to paraphrase Huband's assessment from 2001, it seems that the collapse of the state has left individuals isolated and uncertain, and without strong cultural values to support their understanding of the world (Huband 2001: 152).

The result is a pervasive fear among poor people (which means most of the populace). Baker's respondents told him that '"We are frightened of thieves breaking into our homes and stealing and raping us.... We are abandoned" (three women 20–30, New Kru Town, approximately a mile from the Ministry of Justice).' An elderly man from New Town said, 'after war our security was dissolved ... There are arrests but no judging. Criminals arrive back again' (Baker 2007a).

The UN tried to alleviate insecurity by using armed UN soldiers, accompanied by unarmed Liberian police officers, to conduct nightly random vehicle searches. IG Munah Sieh characterised the squadrons preparing for night patrols as biblical Davids taking on the Goliath-like criminal gangs (BBC 19 September 2006). But this did little to make people feel safe, for the patrols were temporary and police seldom left the main roads. Monrovians tried to manage the situation with their own night-time roadblocks, *ad hoc* check points and small-scale security arrangements.[9] As elsewhere in Africa, people relied on watch teams armed with 'rubber guns', catapults and sticks embedded with nails to confront robbers Baker 2007a).

Police and policing thus reflect an order shaped most strongly by continuities. Police reform was constructed by UNMIL as a quick fix for a desperate post-conflict city. It was based on money and experience gained by the UN in Bosnia, and its appropriateness and sustainability were always questionable. Conflict was soon replaced by ordinary crime and a pervasive sense of insecurity and uncertainty, and 'normality' is now based on localised responses to insecurity and ineffective policing. Yet Monrovia's order seems relatively passive. Contrast the situation in Kinshasa, capital of the Democratic Republic of Congo, whose inhabitants – Kinois – have hustled their way to an order that exists in parallel with that of state institutions. There is, however, nothing romantic about either development.

KINSHASA

The context in which Kinshasa's order emerged was as brutal as Monrovia's; the peace agreement of 2002 ended a four-year war that killed nearly 4 million civilians, either as a direct result of fighting or through starvation, disease or abuse. The post-conflict period in both countries was fragile; both host large UN peacekeeping forces and both elected new governments (2006 saw the DRC's first democratic elections for forty years). Both governments face huge challenges, but those confronting the Joseph Kabila are especially dangerous, as sporadic fighting by militia and government soldiers in the eastern part of the DRC threatens to reignite war, and dangerous legacy issues remain. In particular, many of the thousands of child soldiers used in the war will never be rehabilitated; they represent an alienated reserve of readily mobilised fighters. This situation is exacerbated in the DRC – as in Liberia – because half the population is under 18 years old, with 20 per cent between 15 and 24 (IRIN 2007a: 54).

Many such youths live in Kinshasa, the second biggest city in sub-Saharan Africa after Lagos, and the second largest French-speaking city in the world. Kinshasa's downtown area has skyscrapers, foreign-owned supermarkets and reliable electricity and water. It also has the attention of politicians: the provincial assembly has approved a five-year plan that involves a $1.5 billion revamp of the city. But the downtown's paved boulevards lead to the dirt roads and sprawling neighbourhoods where most of the city's 7 million inhabitants live. There is no formal sector – or formal order – in such areas. The transport infrastructure has collapsed, as have those of health and education, and supplies of electricity, water and food are erratic. Kinshasa has avoided much of the conflict that plagues eastern towns such as Bunia and Kisangani, but the city, like the state, is largely dysfunctional. Kinshasa has much in common with post-conflict cities, even if it was to some extent insulated from the DRC's wars.

HUSTLING TO SECURITY

How, then, do Kinois cope in an environment marked by chronic insecurity, shortages, corruption, institutional collapse and violence? How do people survive in an 'ethos of predation' (McGaffey and Bazenguissa-Ganga 2000: 40)? The answer is that they do so by hustling. Lemarchand describes this as a system involving 'peddling, wheeling and dealing, whoring and pimping, swapping and smuggling, trafficking and stealing, brokering and facilitating, in short making the most of whatever opportunities arise to avoid starvation' (Lemarchand 2002: 395). Building on this interpretation, three recent studies suggest that several forms of order are juxtaposed; typically, political order founded on power gained during war is paralleled by a secondary order based on people's responses to state failure or dysfunction.

In *Reinventing Order in the Congo*, Trefon and his contributors do not address security or policing as such, but they offer a social anthropology of the survival strategies that Kinois develop in order to fulfil their food, water, health-care and psychological needs in the face of state collapse. Their thesis is that have invented an order that entails 'juxtaposing opportunities and interests, capitalising on old alliances and creating new networks' (Trefon 2004: 2). Life is so precarious that most people survive by fending for themselves even as they are forced to depend on each other. Consequently, everyone and everything is subject to bargaining or 'getting by'. First apparent in the early 1990s, bargaining, Trefon argues, is a 'people's initiative having nothing to do with Weberian political order with its functioning bureaucracy, democratically elected representatives, tax collectors, law enforcement agents and impartial judicial system'. Like their peers in Mogadishu and Monrovia, Kinois do without security, leisure and representation. Nonetheless, the state remains omnipresent, and state and state-like actors continue to dominate social relations.

Similar themes emerge in Simone and Abouhani's edited volume on survival in urban Africa, which observes that as livelihood becomes more informal, so too does the logic and form of governance (Simone and Abouhani 2005: 10). This insight shapes Omasombo's account of order in one of the DRC's oldest towns, Kisangani, which (in contrast to Kinshasa) was badly affected by the war and became a symbol of the state's collapse (Omasombo 2005: 96–119). Strategically important but cut off from Kinshasa, whose river transport is its only link with the outside world, Kisangani's natural resources (mainly diamonds and timber) were subject to large-scale plunder. The diamond economy was extremely lucrative, but the town's apathetic inhabitants earned little from it. Compared to Kinshasa it looked like a village. By 2001, its factories had closed, its river port was destroyed, and traces of fighting were everywhere. So too were petty thieves, street children and 'successful guys'. People relied on bicycles, carts, home-made canoes and trekking for transport, on forest products for fuel and food, and on their physical strength for their livelihood and, no doubt, security.

A third account emphasises the critical personal element. Based on their study of traders operating between the DRC and Congo-Brazzaville in West Central Africa, and Europe, McGaffey and Bazenguissa-Ganga found that people created their own order when formal institutional structures collapsed. They relied

> on the trust of personal relationships to compensate for the absence of a functioning legal and judicial apparatus to sanction contracts; creating their own system of values and status, their own order amidst disorder; and evading a venal bureaucracy and an oppressive state by operating in the second economy to find opportunities to better their lives. (McGaffey and Bazenguissa-Ganga 2000: 2)

By second economy they mean 'activities that are unmeasured, unrecorded and, in varying degrees, outside or on the margins of the law, and which deprive the state of revenue'.

Using Clyde Mitchell's definition of personal networks as a set of linkages which exist simultaneously on the basis of specific interests and persist beyond the duration of a particular transaction, they imply that personal networks represent order (McGaffey and Bazenguissa-Ganga 2000: 12). Although they do not discuss order as such, they refer to what I define as order when they speak of 'the recognition by people of sets of obligations and rights in respect of certain other identified people'.

But perhaps the existence of several forms of order is only to be expected, given the legacy of Mobutu's Zaire, and the unchanged nature of political power. For, rather than being a monolith, the state under Mobutu was a 'complicated congeries of only imperfectly controlled organizations and institutions, each motivated by different imperatives' (Schatzberg 1988: 69). Policing disintegrated, and the (usually unpaid) police rarely referred to regional, let alone national, objectives; police squads were often hired to settle personal vendettas. Zaire was replaced in 1997 by the Democratic Congo of Laurent Kabila, whose police had a more coherent profile. But this was only because Kabila was concerned primarily with issues related to law and order; Kinshasa was destabilised by unpaid soldiers and the presence of 30,000 refugees from fighting across the river in Congo-Brazzaville. Local priorities were clear: 'The local Berci polling firm found that 70 per cent of citizens approve of the government's rapid intervention police squads, which ruthlessly pursue robbers' (*Africa Confidential* 1997: 1).

POLICING DRC

What part do police play in the emergent order? As individuals out of uniform they hustle as much as their neighbours. They not only form part of the networks Trefon identifies, but also may contribute to organisations that offer localised justice or commercial guarding; that is, that mimic or replace the police. It is likely that when they are home they are residents, rather than police, and do not see themselves as part of a state institution (Jensen 2007: 115–6). However, when they are in uniform their contribution relates primarily to the formal political order.

The need for an effective police force capable of providing security was recognised by an order in council of January 2002. This created the Congolese National Police (PNC) from the DRC's five police forces (state police, urban police, gendarmerie and civil guard, and the 'police' used by belligerents during the war) and an amalgam of militia, pensioners and officers' widows and orphans. The number of police in Kinshasa at the time was not known, but there are currently some 103,800 officers in the PNC as a whole, including 5,200 women and approximately 5,200 'inactives' (that is, widows and orphans) (Private communication 2007d). The PNC is (like all African forces) an essentially urban institution that focuses on the control of strategically significant urban sites and roads (Private communication 2007e).

Police are gatekeepers to the processes international authorities hope will lead to stability and conflict prevention in the DRC and central Africa more generally. Maintaining order in Kinshasa was recognised by the United Nations Mission in the DRC (MONUC) and international representatives as a key element in ensuring this. In particular, it was thought that order in Kinshasa would help ensure the success of the electoral process that would strengthen the new order. In other words, public order was seen as a key to managing state-based order. A primary requirement was that the police force – and the term was deliberately retained by the DRC[10] – should be civilianised while being made accountable and effective. Secondary challenges were identified as financing wages, resources and training; developing statutes covering service, ranks, and discipline; limiting the scope of the IG's disciplinary powers; and relating rank to function rather than the reverse.

The police contribution to order is primarily functional, hence a number of countries, including Angola, Belgium, France and South Africa, offered bilateral technical support for training armed response/riot squads using basic CRS-type tactics (Lilly 2005). These include the Police for Rapid Intervention (Police d'intervention rapide, or PIR), which has a mandate to keep public order and fight crime. Significantly, the PNC was both the recipient of training intended to improve its management of order, and also a means for other authorities to manage their own order. This was notably so in 2005 when the EU launched a two-year, thirty-strong mission in Kinshasa (EUPOL KINSHASA). The mission's stated goal was to strengthen stability in Kinshasa by improving coordination between the specialised units (approximately 4,500 men) responsible for public order. The support offered consisted of technical assistance, monitoring and supervision. Also, the mission monitored, mentored and advised the (EU) integrated police unit (IPU) that had been established following an official request by the Congolese government for assistance in protecting state institutions and reinforcing the internal security apparatus. The mission's formal aim was to improve decision-making and supervision in the units maintaining order in Kinshasa by ensuring that they acted in accord with democratic standards (Council of EU 2005); improving policing would – in theory – allow the DRC military to concentrate on its core business. In fact, the mission served politics in both Kinshasa and Brussels. Kinshasa could claim the mission as part of its democratic credentials while the EU promoted it as evidence of the reality of the European Defence and Security Policy, within which it was framed.

Kinshasa was special. This was because it is the country's political centre of gravity, and government ministries and parliament (and Kabila's main political opponent Bemba) are based there. Even so, the city's police confronted the same problems as their colleagues elsewhere. They lacked reliable statistics and could not develop policies for dealing with crime; there were no funds for buying information, and telecommunications and data processing were minimal. Inevitably, officers also acted in much the same way as their colleagues elsewhere. For example, they relied on corruption and harassment to supplement their wages. There were traffic police who in addition to their normal duties claimed to walk children across roads to school, but most people thought they concentrated on harassing motorists for money. Amnesty International accused the police of systematically torturing and killing in Kinshasa during and after the landmark 2006 elections, and units such as the PIR are notorious for violating human rights and handling demonstrations brutally (OECD DAC 2007: 180). This situation reflected another feature Kinshasa's police shared with most of the country: the uneven quality of leadership offered by senior officers. In contrast to the situation in Kinshasa, strong leadership in Lubumbashi in the south meant that its police were more disciplined than those in Kinshasa (Private communication 2007d).

Outside of Kinshasa, insecurity limited the role police could play, and distinctions between the various systems of order were ambiguous. This was notably so in provincial towns such as Bunia, capital of Ituri Province. In 2004, Bunia resembled a Wild West frontier town, and there was no formal role for police. Journalists recorded how after leaving the airport (which was teeming with military) the blue helmets of Uruguayan and Moroccan peacekeepers were just visible behind sandbag barriers protected by barbed wire. A steady stream of people tramped along the dusty road, but it was impossible to tell where they were going (*Independent* 25 May 2004; *Digital Journalist*

2003). The streets were heavily patrolled, and gunfire could be heard nightly, usually between MONUC and local militia groups. (MONUC operated under a Chapter VII mandate of the UN Charter, which authorised the use of 'all necessary means' to protect the force, and secure peace; it was peace enforcement, rather than peacekeeping.) A further layer of order existed at the camp for internally displaced people which had been established on a hillside next to the UN base at the airport after fighting escalated in 2003. The facilities for its 15,000 IDPs were basic, and in 2004 NGOs tried to impose some form of order by allocating plots of land. But the neat rows of huts were a veneer, and while a thriving daytime market sold everything from food to guns, fighting between rival ethnic groups broke out every night.

The PNC thus operates across several forms of order. Perhaps as a result of the consequent tensions, its support for the dominant political order is unreliable even as it harasses the government's political opponents, brutalises detainees, intimidates their relatives, and uses tear gas and live bullets for crowd control. For example, officers stayed in their stations when gun battles between Kabila's supporters and militiamen loyal to opposition leader Jean-Pierre Bemba broke out in Kinshasa in March 2007. It was the army that regained control of the city, patrolling the empty streets and using plastic chairs and bricks to set up roadblocks (it reputedly looted supermarkets, shops and private houses too). The PNC's contribution to order is in many respects reactive and negative, but, on balance, it, like the DRC's other security forces, continues to serve narrow political interests (*The Times* 2007). Kinois, like their fellows in Mogadishu and Monrovia, must make their own rules.

CONCLUSION

Most accounts of post-conflict policing include statements such as 'civil war in Liberia claimed the lives of almost 250,000 people ... and led to a complete breakdown of law and order' (UNMIL 2007: 55). War does destroy order and the police institution, but as the cases discussed here show, some form of post-conflict order usually exists, as it did during war. Just as violence during war may be indicative of a perverse but rational and effective form of order, so too post-conflict environments are orchestrated or manipulated for a variety of purposes.

When elites and societies make their own rules about order and its policing it does not necessarily mean that policing is informal, fluid or non-statist in nature. Indeed, Mogadishu may be an exception, for in most cases parallel forms of state and community-based order and enforcement exist. Typically, points of interface between the systems are informal, relatively infrequent, but also functionally useful. For example, the Americo-Liberian elite in Monrovia exploit formal and informal systems according to their needs; relations are placed in important positions in the police, while guards are hired to supplement inadequate state-sponsored security.

Yet even this range of activities and models does not show the range of possibilities in post-conflict cities, so my emphasis now shifts to two further – and distinct – developments in state enforcement. The first concerns situations in the South where (as in Northern Nigeria) state order incorporates, and police work with, traditional religious-based forms of order, while the second concerns internal policing by Western government forces in an industrialised city – in this case, Grozny.

7

RE-EMERGENT ORDER

This chapter explores the thesis that order and security are influenced by networks of subjugation, most of which pre-date (or coexist with) existing relationships while interacting or intersecting with past or present sources of insecurity and disorder. It argues that pre-conflict forms of order and power relations re-emerge, while rebutting the suggestion that reconstruction – or police reform – is enough to determine post-conflict order.

The exercise of power and the management of order cannot be understood in isolation from the stratifying effects of wartime legacies, ethnicity, religion, personal pathologies and the real or symbolic relationships that influence security and survival mechanisms (Koonings and Kruijt 2007: 10). Networks of subjugation are particularly influential, with most pre-dating (or coexisting with) existing relationships while interacting or intersecting with past or present sources of insecurity and disorder. Such relationships have a marked effect on policing in cities such as Basra and Kabul, but they are equally evident in cities where parallel governance structures are interwoven with populist violence. In some instances, state authorities recognise as legitimate informal sectarian-based policing, and the management of policing is by negotiation and accommodation, while in others state authorities rely on exploitative modes of behaviour. In all cases, continuities are as important as change.

Three aspects of these relationships deserve note. The first concerns situations in the South where state-based forms of order and enforcement work closely with non-state systems, and where liberal norms have negligible influence. I explore this in relation to the policing of two historic cities in Northern Nigeria with experience of intense but short-lived conflict: Kano and Kaduna. The second concerns the policing of a new capital city by new police in a new country that has just emerged from war, and that is subject to pressure from both national and international agencies. Such cases are comparatively rare, but the Southern Sudan capital of Juba illustrates the challenges of developing order and policing from scratch while accommodating pre-existing relationships and trends.

These two examples concern internal policing issues while illustrating the cross-cutting nature of policing, yet they are insufficient. They are, like those in the previous chapter, from Africa, albeit from different regions, so they run the risk of presenting an unbalanced picture of policing which reflects its host society. My third illustration therefore offers a contrast in terms of region, response and development. It concerns internal security operations by a Northern government's conventional forces in a sprawling industrialised city: Grozny.

NIGERIA

The case examples discussed so far concern the aftermath of conventional or civil war. But this approach offers only a partial perspective on the overall challenges of post-conflict cities. In particular, it neglects the possibility of different dynamics operating in deep-rooted communal conflicts that are confined to specific cities or administrative localities. In fact, the dynamics are similar. This is evident in Nigeria, where an empirical state with an established police force repeatedly confronts limited but chronic forms of communal violence. Indeed, it is not the type of conflict that is the distinguishing feature of the Nigerian case so much as the predictable forms that violence and the state's response to it take.

A noteworthy feature of such cases is that communal conflict is merely one of a number of security challenges. Indeed, one of the key features of Nigeria is the scale of the challenges facing the Nigeria Police (NP). The NP's 325,000 under-resourced officers are incapable of effectively policing a country as big, populous, poverty-stricken, divided and volatile as Nigeria.[1] They confront high levels of violent crime, much of which expresses or exploits the political, religious, ethnic and societal tensions that are rooted in Nigeria's poverty, unemployment and competition for land.[2] Nigeria may be Africa's biggest oil producer, yet more than half the population lives on less than US$1 a day, and the government's attempts to benefit from high oil prices on the world market are regularly undermined by corruption and gross mismanagement. Although levels of communal violence are significantly lower than they were in the years immediately after Nigeria's return to democratic rule in 1999, when thousands of people were killed, the potential for open conflict remains serious.

This is most evident in Nigeria's burgeoning urban areas, with their high crime rates. For cities lack the societal cohesion and traditional control mechanisms of rural areas, and it is relatively easy for criminals to find anonymity. Police rarely venture into the unpaved or potholed shantytowns typical of many cities, while tarmac roads make it easy for robbers with fast cars to enter and exit urban areas. Also, little thought has been given to public-order strategy. When confronted with widespread rioting, the police usually respond slowly and then use excessive force indiscriminately. Arrests are made and formulaic inquiries held, but lessons are seemingly not learned.

The relevance of Nigeria here is twofold. First, the violent disorder that resulted from the introduction of sharia law in some northern states in 2000 and 2002 offers a snapshot of the policing of cities experiencing intense but short-lived conflict. Second, although the cities concerned belong to a federal system which pays lip service to democratic forms of police reform, the NP operates in parallel with older forms of policing. Both are legitimate in the eyes of the government and much of the populace.

KANO'S PARALLEL SYSTEM

Kano, the largest and most politically and economically important city in the Islamic Hausa-speaking part of Nigeria, is the administrative centre of Kano state. Its population of approximately 3.8 million makes it the third largest city after Ibadan and Lagos. It is also a flashpoint and symbol of Islamic identity. It is not only a key point on Nigeria's internal migration circuits, but also its southern Christian migrants are kept separated from its Muslim inhabitants (Smith 2006).

Physical insecurity is prompted by poverty, inequality and unemployment, but is exacerbated by violent crime and the clashes called by local media 'urban communal violence' (2006: 53). Many Nigerians distinguish communal violence from the violent crime seen as the work of individuals or gangs whose intent is criminal, rather than ethnic or religious, but in practice it is difficult to separate the two. Communal violence involves mobs of youths armed with machetes, knives, stones and guns, and has led to the death of thousands since 1999 (cf. Hoffman 2007a; Leonardi 2007; Richards 1996). The disputes are usually described as ethnically or religiously motivated; those involved are divided by religious affiliation and ethnic identity, which are exacerbated by urban proximity. But sectarian violence is not unusual in the region. The month before the worst violence in Kano, Jos, a city of some 400,000 and the capital of neighbouring Plateau state, experienced religious clashes.

The key point is that cities such as Kano confront problems similar to those in post-conflict cities, and many of the responses are the same (Imobighe 2003). Social networks, for example, play an influential role. Nigerian cities provide few services, so tasks such as neighbourhood security and coordinating interdependencies between family, kin and neighbours require effort. And territory matters, too; social associations serve as arenas in which the meaning and purpose of specific territories are 'elaborated, defended and reworked' (Simone and Abouhani 2005: 18). Residents work out their relationships through economic activities and through displays of physical force. The critical difference – and the reason why Kano matters here – is that a key to the city's order and policing is to be found in the role of the emir, not the state. The emir personifies relationships that represent a parallel governance structure.

KANO'S EMIR

The NP are tolerated as an army of occupation, and they operate in Kano because the emir permits them to. The first task for a new police commissioner is to visit the emir, though it is difficult for, say, a southerner or a woman to meet him without a personal introduction (Private communication 2007a). The commissioner (who is usually a Muslim) acts as an envoy for the federal government in Abuja, so questions of authority and dignity are paramount; commissioners are advised to wear their uniform at all times; and the NP do not pursue investigations or operations in Kano as they would in, say, Jos. In other words, the NP's role in Kano is reactive: criminals are delivered to them.

A report by Mark Doyle is indicative of the emir's authority soon after the riots of mid-October 2001, in which at least 100 died (BBC 21 December 2001). Doyle recounts how the emir progressed to his throne in a large room, at the far end of which a group of petitioners lay prostrate:

> These men didn't look directly at the emir but talked through lawyers who would, in turn, interpret the emir's subtle signals… His word will become law… One petitioner has a land and cattle dispute – the emir would investigate. A young boy appears who is said to have killed someone – he would be *taken to the police* [my stress]. A third man has paid for electricity but it has not been supplied – the emir's men promised to see government officials about it.

Doyle observes that the emir's power should not be overestimated – the federal government and its oil revenues pay for his budget. Nonetheless, the conservative Islamic power structures of Northern Nigeria mean that he represents a major influence on policing.

The workings of traditional structures are to some extent opaque,[3] but to preserve them the emir must navigate between the various religious, ethnic and political elements fuelling conflict. For example, though the mob that burnt down shops in central Kano was angry about the US invasion of Afghanistan, traders blamed the disorder on Ibos, a mainly Christian ethnic group originating in south-eastern Nigeria. Meanwhile Muslim youths burnt Christian churches and tried to kill their pastors. In reality, such disputes, which have as much to do with land ownership and economic questions as with religion, are exploited by unemployed youths from both sides, who use them to loot. Nonetheless, the dispute over the introduction of sharia (that is, the strict application of Koranic law, which imposes amputation and stoning for certain crimes) lay at the symbolic heart of both the conflict and the order that the emir – and by extension the federal government – sought to uphold. (The police enforced sharia even though the federal government was not wholeheartedly behind the move.) Sharia would, it was claimed, reduce crime rates by outlawing theft, adultery, alcohol, prostitution and gambling. But this did not happen, least of all in Kano's sleazier (predominantly Christian) suburbs.

The rioting led to the imposition of a dusk-to-dawn curfew, and the Kano State Police Commissioner ordered security forces to 'shoot troublemakers on sight' (*Al-Ahram* 2001). He accused 'hoodlums' of hijacking the anti-US protest, and provoking Muslims to attack Christians and loot their shops. This was stopped by the police and security forces' use of tear gas and live ammunition. Police also raided the headquarters of several militant Islamist organisations.

KADUNA

Rioting is not conflict or war as such, yet casualties may be in the thousands. This pattern is also evident in Kaduna, a mixed state capital in north-central Nigeria, where approximately 2,000 were killed in the fighting that followed the announcement of plans to introduce sharia law. Hundreds were killed in February 2000 after thousands of Christians took to the streets to protest, and counter-chants by Muslims quickly degenerated into fighting. Muslim youths patrolled residential areas, operating roadblocks and checking the identities of people entering the area, while Christian youths carrying clubs, axes and petrol cans roamed the empty streets of southern suburbs chanting 'No to sharia law' (BBC 25 February 2000). As in Kano, unemployment and alienation arguably fuelled the violence and looting that led hundreds to seek refuge in Kaduna's army and police barracks and academies (Yusuf 2007). Hundreds were made homeless after houses were torched, and eyewitnesses reported scores of bodies lying in the streets.

The response of the authorities was predictable in that their response was confined to immediate problems. Some 1,000 police and military enforced a curfew that ran from midday to 06:00, and the acting state governor warned that violators would be shot on sight; police opened fire indiscriminately on gangs in the working-class Sabo district. Disorder in December resulted in similarly high casualties; 90 per cent of those taken to hospital had gunshot wounds inflicted mainly by the military (few had machete wounds) (BBC 20 2002). The potential of the disorder was evident from the fact that the authorities established a special rapid-reaction force (mainly from the army) to act at points of confrontation.

Nonetheless, the police response was less brutal than might have been expected. Nigeria is party to all the principal human-rights treaties, but misconduct is rarely investigated, and the NP's rapid-response force, the Mobile Police (Mopol), are known colloquially as 'Kill-and-go' from their trigger-happy approach to crowd control. Corruption and brutality are common, and confession is thought to form the basis of some 60 per cent of prosecutions. Policing is a harsh business in Nigeria. Some officers are convinced of the need for reform, but the public fear and mistrust the police with good reason. Human Rights Watch recorded many cases of torture and death in custody at Kano police HQ during 2003–05 (HRW 2005).

The populace meanwhile rebuilt their lives and homes with the support of their kin and neighbours. But it is difficult to say whether the violence led to greater reliance on non-state vigilantes. Vigilante groups were present in many northern towns, where their main activities were debt collection, crime protection, extortion and armed enforcement. There were also pro-sharia vigilante groups of males aged between 15 and 30, though many such groups were not vigilantes so much as groups operating somewhere between vigilantes, ethnic militias and criminal gangs (Smith 2006: 66). For example, an Islamic vigilante group known as the Hisba later emerged to play a role in policing Kano and other northern cities. It concentrated on stopping drinking and prostitution, but the government evidently regarded its activities as political because in 2006 the then inspector general, Sunday Ehindero (a southern Christian), said in a press statement that its existence undermined national security (*Open Doors* 2006). One reason for this may have been the government's awareness that the Biafran civil war resulted when the state's Christian and Muslin regions turned on each other in the 1960s. Whatever the case, Kano and Kaduna emphasise that order may be sufficiently resilient and multifaceted to accommodate instances of intensive (albeit short-lived) violence. This in turn reinforces my earlier point, which is that order is rarely if ever lost; order submerges during conflict, only to re-emerge later.

SOUTHERN SUDAN

This holds true even when, as in Southern Sudan, the aftermath of war requires the creation of a new police force in a new capital in a new country. This is admittedly a rare occurrence. Though the Eritrean People's Liberation Front (EPLF) created its own police force after the capture of Asmara (the former provincial capital) in 1991, concluding its thirty-year fight for self-determination, the construction of a new police force is atypical, and most 'new' forces are actually improved or reconstructed by international agents (Hills 2000). For such reasons, the case of the Southern Sudan Police is both unusual and representative.

It is unusual in that it was created from scratch by an ex-rebel group in a marginalised region where decades of war between the mainly Muslim North and the animist and Christian South had cost the lives of approximately 1.5 million people and destroyed all evidence of state infrastructure.[4] But the new police force was also regionally representative in that most of its officers were former rebels, it was based in a small ramshackle town, and despite hosting a multitude of international consultants it was seriously underfunded and ineffective.

It was not until July 2002 that Khartoum and the Sudan People's Liberation Army/Movement (SPLA/M) ended war in Africa's largest country, with the government accepting the right of the South to seek self-determination after a six-year interim period, and the SPLA accepting the application of sharia law in the North. A ceasefire and accords on wealth- and power-sharing were signed in January 2005, international donors pledged $4.5 billion in recovery aid, and an autonomous government was formed in October, with former rebels dominating in the new administration and its police.

In early 2006, Juba, the largest and most developed town in Southern Sudan, was declared the regional capital, at which point senior police officers relocated to it from the interim capital of Rumbek, a town of under 100,000 people. Juba (which was handed over to the SPLA in 2005) had been the southern terminus of traffic on the River Nile, and a transport hub for roads to Kenya, Uganda and the DRC, but the roads had been destroyed long ago by bombing and heavy rain, and even in 2007's dry season it took four days to reach from the Ugandan border district of Gulu, 46 kilometres away. On the other hand, as in Mogadishu, reconstruction meant a business opportunity: the trade in 4x4 vehicles from Uganda grew steadily from 2006 (*Monitor* 2007).

Juba was not the new government's first choice. It was a strategic site that saw much fighting during the second civil war, but in 2005 its estimated population of about 160,000 lived in what was little more than a collection of mud houses and half-derelict buildings prone to flooding. All available regional resources had been directed towards the war effort, and Juba's 1 kilometre of paved road had been laid fifty years earlier. Most reports from that time refer to other sites for the capital; Ramciel, for example, was favoured even though it was a stretch of sandy scrub days away from central Southern Sudan. Juba is thus atypical of post-conflict cities, but also typical of towns to be found across the geographical south.

Policing Juba is not technically difficult, though Sudan is highly militarised, the ten states are very big, disaffected elements in the Armed Forces (SAF) occasionally cause trouble, and the town's inhabitants never supported the Dinka-dominated former rebels who form the police and government. But disorder is relatively low-key. For example, in December 2006, joint integrated units in the SPLA fired indiscriminately on their way to the Ministry of Defence to protest against the non-payment of their wages. This was dealt with by a dusk-till-dawn curfew, checkpoints and a promise of payment. There is more concern over fighting, raids and crime in the surrounding areas spilling over into the town; disputes over water, grazing and land resources are common. This situation probably owes much to the police's concentration in Juba, the training offered at Juba's Buluk training school, and the presence of UN advisers and bilateral donors supporting procedural police reforms and training. In June 2007, for instance, UNPOL trained twenty-nine officers in tactical operations such as bus entry, vehicular high-risk stop, 'close quarter battle' and ladder entry (*Juba Post* 1 June 2007, 29 June 2007). Several weeks earlier, thirty-four riot police officers had completed the crowd-control module of a special weapons and tactics (SWAT) course designed, it was said, to enhance the police's efficiency, and to build an 'amiable auxiliary unit capable of quelling civil upsurges in a democratic setting'. However, the picture is more nuanced than this suggests.

The new political order Juba represented appeared fragile in that it lacked many formal institutional structures, physical insecurity was high, and automatic weapons were easily available even if water, electricity and agricultural implements were not. As a result, 'banditry, violent cattle raids, theft of children, and inter-tribal conflicts persist as a backdrop to the ongoing North–South tensions' (Refugees International 2007). Life expectancy is 42 years, three out of four Southerners are illiterate, and food prices in Juba are double those in the North; Juba has limited access to trade or agricultural land and must rely on supplies flown in from Khartoum or driven (or bicycled) from Kenyan and Ugandan border towns. Some displaced people returned, but conditions across the South were sufficiently bad for aid agencies to suspend aid to returnees in an effort to dissuade them from moving back. The legacy of war was reinforced by the destruction of the region's physical infrastructure, customary law and traditional authority structures. State police had long been seen as the enemy of the South, a situation that was not helped by the illegal fines that rapidly became the police response to the new government's inability to pay them. Consequently, by 2007 there was a marked discrepancy between the Government of Southern Sudan (GOSS)'s vision of order and that promoted by international advisers and consultants.

Two years after 2005's Comprehensive Peace Agreement was signed by North and South Sudan, Sudan still lacked the most basic state institutions, including a reliable police force. However, this was not a sign that order was necessarily or inherently fragile. It is true that the base from which Southern Sudan started meant that almost any form of reconstruction was a developmental advance. But development and institutional capacity are not necessarily the same as order. In practice, as its policing shows, Southern Sudan's order resulted from, and reflected, Sudan's cultural and political continuities.

SOUTHERN SUDAN POLICE SERVICE

The challenges of building a new police force (and, by extension, the order it was to manage) were substantial, for the police in Southern Sudan ceased to function during the war, as did the region's prisons. The police and prison infrastructure therefore needed rebuilding, and 20,000 police and 8,000 prison officers required training, while documentation on operating policies, procedures and guidelines was required. New standards of evidence-gathering, forensic analysis, case preparation and presentation at court were also needed (Yiga 2007).

There were additional constraints or influences. First, though the political order introduced by the peace agreement required the creation of a decentralised and civilianised police and prison service, it also placed a premium on senior officers with political, rather than policing, skills. For although the new GOSS was authorised to operate an independent police force, it had to cooperate with the government of national unity in Khartoum. Second, Sudanese policing was strongly militarised and the army was the principal agent of law and order. This affected the position of the new police, which consisted of cadres from the GOSS and the SPLA/M. Both were organised on military lines, but GOSS police had received military training, were literate, wore uniforms, had some equipment and received salaries, whereas the SPLA/M police were ex-rebels, many of whom were working voluntarily or were illiterate. Some senior SPLA/M officers had a policing background but most did not, and few had any idea of standard organisational or rank structures. Third, there was no budget for capital expenditure. In theory, police programmes operating across the South were supported by a $5.3 million grant from a trust fund administered by the World Bank, and supported through a multi-donor trust fund (MDTF) and the GOSS. But in practice the police budget was a revenue budget covering salaries alone. Consequently, in early 2006 the SPLA/M components of the police operated from decaying huts.

The police moved between international and Sudanese forms of order. However, tensions between the two were reduced by international advisers presenting goals such as the reorientation of policing from a military to a civilian-based service as being an essentially technical matter. For the UN police, for example, whose strategic mission is building institutional police capacity in post-conflict environments, the critical issues necessary for facilitating reorientation were identified as establishing command structures between headquarters and the states, standardising training and coordinating field training programmes, staffing Southern Sudan Police Service (SSPS) establishments, standardising procedures, and establishing a strong police culture. This interpretation was reinforced by a 2001 report by the UN secretary general that emphasised the UNDP's need to ensure security and negotiate access in order to promote the creation of 'neutral police [services] broadly representative of the community' (UN Security Council 2001: 4). Thus UNPOL's main role was seen as facilitating training and conducting aptitude tests to select suitable candidates, while UNDP's was to rebuild, renovate and equip selected training centres, hire translators, acquire generators and training equipment, and recruit and support technical advisers.

The British Council and DFID adopted a similar technical approach, providing middle and senior management training and logistical support respectively, while other international consultants advised on the procedural skills required for maintaining police records, filing criminal charges, and disciplining officers (for typical projects, see Reliefweb 2006). In 2007, the ICRC organised a course for 13 officers on the basic principles and application of human rights. Later, three-week courses in Juba enabled several hundred new recruits (among them 45 women) to learn about investigation and evidence-gathering, community policing, traffic awareness, firearms, child rights, human rights and dealing with domestic violence; 34 completed a course on crowd control.

This was unproblematic for the Sudanese. After all, it required UN officials to present a case for increased government funding for policing. Also, senior Sudanese officers were adept at navigating their way through donor rivalry, and the precise emphasis of the various projects always varied according to the advisers concerned. Thus an Italian UN adviser emphasised that the focus should be on responding to 'burglary, terrorism and personal crimes' even though banditry was of greater concern in Juba than terrorism. Romeo Rozales, a UN trainer, said that 'If there are terrorist [*sic*] taking place these police units will be responsible to respond. ... So it is very important for them to learn ... capturing the enemy alive and put them behind bars' (UNIFEED 2005). In contrast, Ugandan UNDP consultants argued in favour of more basic training: 'There are no police structures in Southern Sudan' (*Juba Post Online* 2007), so their work concerned pilot projects for building stations, and teaching basic skills.

Of greater concern to many SSPS officers was that although UN consultants and senior GOSS officers used the language of 'international' policing, their understanding of its terms and objectives were not always the same. Take the case of community policing. The new order specified that a context-specific model was to be developed, and the role of elders and traditional institutions in transitional justice strengthened. Officers were to be registered and vetted, recruitment standards defined, and training needs identified, while gender and child protection desks were to be established. Even Sudan's President al-Bashir announced that it was the responsibility of the Sudanese police (in Darfur at least) to protect civilians (*JDW* 21 March 2007: 18). In order to implement this, UN officers were divided into teams which conducted car and foot patrols with local police and other UN agencies, and monitored local policing and the treatment of detainees in local police custody (UN Bulletin 2006a). However, activities such as monitoring were problematic, for while the term is technical and unthreatening in English (which was the language of the CPA), in Arabic it implies control and spying (FCO 2007: 34).

ORDER IN JUBA

Some aspects of security in Juba improved once the CPA was signed, even if mines and the activities of the Lord's Resistance Army meant that security to the east of the town remained precarious. Roads leading to Juba were opened, there were minimal security checks, and UN and local police conducted daily joint patrols to provide assistance and reassurance, but security around Juba deteriorated sharply, especially in late 2006, when SPLA soldiers launched a series of attacks on civilians. At the same time, the integration of militias and other armed groups into the SAF caused international concern

(OCHA 2006), as did the proliferation of small arms. Not only had local militias held on to the arms they had been given during the war (either for protection or to enable them to act as proxy forces), but also easy access to weapons worsened existing local conflicts over scarce natural resources; attacks on neighbouring villages and cattle raids were the result.

In Juba itself the most immediate result of the CPA was, as expected, a rise in crimes such as burglary, which exacerbated insecurity. This was attributed to GOSS soldiers who had had their war-hazard pay removed. There were also tensions caused by the presence of a large group of young Ethiopian males at a refugee site on the southern outskirts of Juba (though Juba's youths do not appear to have been regarded as a distinct or marginalised group). The most dramatic event of this period – ammunition explosions in a military compound that resulted in many casualties – was probably accidental.

But increasing crime was only one indicator of the fragility of order. By the summer of 2007, Juba's crime rates (of murder and rape especially, but also ethnic clashes in the surrounding areas) had risen sharply, thereby undermining international goals. However, public disorder remained on a small scale, the vehicle trade with Uganda boomed, and large-scale currency forgery was a major concern (*New Vision* 2007a). Despite this, the Legislative Council of Central Equatoria State (the state assembly) regarded the situation as dangerously insecure; when it discussed the security situation, the chairman of the assembly's security committee said that the army, not the police, was dealing with law and order (Miraya 101 FM 26 July 2007). Perhaps for this reason the police remained seriously under-resourced, and recruitment and training were effectively frozen. There was also an increase in incidents involving police brutality, though complaints about corruption (especially among traffic police) were relatively few, beyond the usual imposition of illegal fines. Other issues (such as small-arms proliferation) were regional problems and independent of conditions in Juba.

The international contribution to replacing this indigenous order with a new one was, as ever, uneven. Local police officers were successfully registered, and a number of quick-impact projects successfully implemented; middle and senior managers were trained and a police development committee formed. But some projects were too sophisticated – and reliant on electricity – to be realistic. The SSPS database is a case in point. Launched by the UN in June 2007, the system is designed to help the police plan; it will contain information on personnel, payroll, retirement, promotion, training and discipline, among others. Indeed, UNPOL's public information officer said that the UN aimed 'to get the complete dossier of the southern Sudan police service into a data base system service'. Unfortunately the dossier does not exist (Miraya 101 FM 23 June 2007). More seriously, some UN peacekeepers were accused of paedophilia, and of encouraging prostitution in Juba (*Daily Telegraph* 2007).

In practice, indigenous forms of order dominate. Further, order – along with the SSPS's remit and resources – was shaped by decisions taken by the government of national unity in Khartoum, and by their response to Sudan's series of interlocking conflicts. Its future will be decided by decisions taken in Khartoum as well as in Juba. For example, in October 2007 the SPLA/M accused Khartoum of failing to honour the CPA and suspended for three months its involvement in the national unity government.

In the two years after the CPA, the challenges confronting the SSPS were political as much as functional; political skills were always more important than policing skills for senior officers (most of whom were former rebels) even as the SSPS was under international pressure to create public confidence in public policing. To do this the SSPS had not only to build or reconstruct buildings, equipment and systems, but also to develop adequate management skills (including a capacity for strategic planning), and to decentralise police from GOSS headquarters to state, county and local levels. In other words, law and order had to be seen to exist, even if in practice order was independent of security. But the SSPS had no money. Further, government corruption ensured that the SSPS lacked training, uniforms and regular salaries. For example, the sum supposedly left over from 2006's budget – $498 million – disappeared in three months. Constables, like army privates and GOSS drivers and clerks, theoretically earn $350 a month, but ministers make $5,000 plus the same again in allowances, and are paid on time (*Sudan Tribune* 2007).

GROZNY

The case examples discussed so far concern Southern cities, so a geopolitical counterweight is needed if meaningful generalisations are to be made. This is best found in the sprawling industrialised Chechen city of Grozny.

Grozny is in many respects unique, not least because the war that began in 1994 was technically an internal security operation, fought on Russian Federation territory against bandits, criminals, mercenaries and terrorists. Moscow referred to its operations as internal counterterrorist operations aimed at restoring constitutional order, and Ministry of Internal Affairs (MVD) troops played the main role, for Chechnya had become a centre for drug and weapons trafficking, and the Chechen drive for secession and an alternative order was viewed by Moscow as a direct threat to the integrity of the Russian state. Yet Grozny has much in common with the other cases discussed here. The conflict and its aftermath was brutal, with atrocities against prisoners, the wounded and civilians marking every phase, while distinctions between the various post-conflict phases were always ambiguous.

Conflict continued for some years after full-scale operations ceased. The first battle for the city occurred in January 1995, the second in August 1996, and the third in January 2000, but the rebel core was displaced rather than crushed, and the notion of 'post-conflict' was effectively meaningless. In the summer of 2002, for example, President Putin insisted that the 'military phase' of operations was over, yet 70,000 troops were still stationed in the region (*Moscow Times* 2004: 2). By 2004 heavy fighting was rare yet clashes continued, with dozens of Russian casualties reported each month, and reconstruction had barely begun.

As a visiting Médecins Sans Frontières manager noted in 2005, the war not over, the number of deaths remained constant, and the Russian presence was unchanged. What had changed was the methods used. 'Cleansing' operations were more targeted, and several of the Chechen factions that emerged during the war had turned against each other, with a consequent increase in insecurity (MSF 2005).

As in West Africa, the post-conflict order was rooted in power relations that either pre-dated the conflict or were dependent on it. Chechens had made money from drugs, counterfeiting and hostages long before 1995, and the multimillion-dollar ransoms paid for some hostages had created private armies even before Russian operations began. Arms had always been plentiful. The Kremlin-backed government was weak, discredited and divided, and hawkish generals, rebels and gang leaders on both sides shared an interest in continued conflict. Many of the armed groups had no interest in peace, let alone in claiming power in a Chechen state they did not believe in, preferring a continuation of sporadic violence that allowed them to consolidate their own local power.

THE MOST DESTROYED CITY IN THE WORLD

The results were evident to Eric Bouret, a French photojournalist, who was overwhelmed by the destruction he saw in 2000; entering the city, 'it was as if I was hit by an apocalyptic vision' (Bouret 2000). Five years later, Grozny still resembled Berlin in 1945. It was

> a wasteland of abandoned rubbish, stray dogs and half-bombed, half-inhabited apartment blocks, with washing strung across the shell holes and decorated by giant posters of its then first-deputy prime minister (and now president) Ramzan Kadyrov. ... Along with embezzlement, money is commonly raised by pilfering oil, trading stolen military kit, and ransom. Drunken Russian soldiers still murder people, but Kayrov's militia are thought responsible for many of the mass kidnappings, torture and killings. They clash with federal troops and with the Chechen police, and answer only to him. There is rarely redress for their victims. (*The Economist* 3 December 2005: 41)

An especially harsh winter made living conditions even more difficult. Some 36,000 returnees were housed in temporary accommodation centres without electricity in which only electric heaters were permitted. Health and sanitary conditions were appalling. Tens of thousands of Grozny's 1994 population of 490,000 had lost everything, and malnutrition, child mortality and epidemics were at record levels.

The order that permitted these conditions was brutally and corruptly repressive. That the rubbleisation of Grozny was followed by a period of restoration work under the governments of Khadzhiyev and Zabgayev that was marked by large-scale embezzlement indicates its nature. Continued violence (including that between the head of the new Chechen Republic administration, Akhmad-hadji Kadyrov, and his first deputy, Gantamirov), wartime legacies and inadequate federal financing for social and economic programmes further undermined the chances of stabilisation, but those trading in people, weaponry, petroleum products and drugs often did very well. In other words, the post-war order was to some extent the result of the economic and institutional devastation, violence and degradation caused by war, but also it reflected the order embedded in Chechen society.

Chechnya had long been seen as a deeply criminalised society, though most of Grozny's Chechen and elderly Russian inhabitants were intent only on survival. In Grozny, as in Kinshasa, a combination of innovative enterprise, endurance and hard work ensured that survival imperatives dominated everyday life. Also, as the Russian deputy commander of a riot police unit sent to the town of Ivanovo in 2000 noted, 'Chechnya is not all uniform, but has many different places, individual actors, and social groups that create a dramatic cacophony of post-war reality' (Tishkov 2001: 37f). Yet 'common for all was neglect of rules set by the state and by the cultural tradition, also self-deception resulting in a sharp conflict between illusions and real life' (Tishkov 2001: 37f).

KEY INDICATORS

Grozny's order reflected that existing before and during the war, even as it was shaped by the contingencies associated with post-conflict insecurity and power relations. Six key indicators of the re-emergent order deserve note.

First, the revival of street markets is an empirical indicator not only of transition to the post-conflict phases, but also of an order's nature. Traders quickly re-emerged after the third battle of Grozny to operate amidst the rubble, and by the summer of 2000 most things were available in the central market. The number of traders was large because anyone who owned, acquired or stole anything immediately tried to sell it, if only to feed themselves. Inevitably, the markets, like the order they represented, operated according to known (albeit criminal in Russian eyes) rules. The tax officers who tried to regulate trading activities lacked protection from the wholesale traders who intimidated and blackmailed them, while the few policemen patrolling the markets were ineffective. At the same time, the new military and civil administration was full of large-scale embezzlers who had learnt from the sophisticated shadow economy that existed under former president Dudayev in the early 1990s (Tishkov 2001).

Second, order was based on martial law, brutality, vested interests, political subversion and organised crime. The indicators marking its re-emergence (for each of these elements was well established) divided into those associated with Moscow's vision of order and those associated with Chechen politics and culture. The imposition of Russian order, for example, was marked by the formal declaration by Russian military and political leaders on 15 April 2000 that the fighting stage of the counterterrorist operation in Chechnya had ended. This marked a legalistic and operational shift whereby the MVD and the Federal Security Service (FSB) became responsible for suppressing a guerrilla war. However, the move was offset by the inability of the MVD, OMON (the special police forces) and SOBR (special rapid response units) to prevent guerrilla or terrorist acts. Negative aspects of the wartime order re-emerged to manifest themselves in, for example, the special 'cleaning' operations that led to an increase in civilian casualties, refugee flows and support for guerrillas.

Third, the economy was effectively criminalised, and groups and individuals profiting from instability flaunted their gains. They included traffickers in people, arms, drugs and oil (most of whom were linked to specific clans), and any factional leaders with access to federal resources or international humanitarian aid. On the Russian side, high-ranking officers and officials had a vested interest in continuing instability because it increased their political influence over budgets.

A fourth indicator was the dysfunctional Russian legal framework in Chechnya, which tolerated OMON and SOBR contract-based subunits arbitrarily killing and robbing civilians (Reliefweb 2001). Legitimate formations kidnapped and trafficked thousands in a 'filtration' system; people detained at roadblocks and during cleaning operations disappeared. Indeed, brutality was explicit in the law governing the role of the military, police and security service units operating in Chechnya. This stated that anti-terrorist units were exempt from liability for damage to the 'life, health and property of terrorists' (HRW 2001: 26).

Appointments were a fifth, overtly political indicator of the instability characterising the new order. A relevant case concerned the appointment by Moscow of the head of a provisional administration, Ramzan Kadyrov (his father Akhmad-hadji had been killed in May 2004), and his repudiation by pro-Russian Chechens. That Chechnya's political elite seemed unable to establish their own leader was equally significant. The resultant instability suggested either that Chechens were unfit to govern, or that security operations remained necessary.

The style of policing represents a sixth indicator, not least because restoring law and order in Russia is a national security issue. However, the signals were mixed. In 2003 officers in the new Chechen police earned monthly salaries of 20,000–30,000 roubles, but this was cut to 10,000 (around $380) in 2005 on the basis that security had stabilised (*Prague Watchdog* 14 March 2007). Policing remains a corrupt and repressive activity.

POLICE

Grozny was policed by a number of military and paramilitary units. They included troops from the Ministry of Defence, the FSB, the Ministry of Justice's riot units, and the Ministry of Internal Affairs' militarised forces, which included riot police such as OMON and SOBR. Many of these troops were essentially light infantry trained to deal with civilians as much as with enemy troops. As such, they were the key component of forces deployed to post-conflict environments within Russia (Stepanova 2002). Regional police were also sent to Chechnya as temporary riot police. In contrast, Chechen police (many of whom had served in Chechnya previously) staffed regular police departments. They were weak, ineffective, usually lacked weapons, vehicles and equipment, and were not directly involved in 'anti-terrorist' operations.

In November 2002, the regional department of the Russian Interior Ministry was transformed into an autonomous Chechen police under the new Chechen Interior Ministry. The move was designed to strengthen the administration of pro-Moscow leader Kadyrov, and to relieve the federal Interior Ministry of its responsibilities in Chechnya. It was part of the process of Chechenisation, which entailed transferring primary responsibility for reimposing order from Moscow to pro-Moscow Chechen forces. The new police force was to have 12,000 men (equivalent to the number of officers being withdrawn from Chechnya), though this figure was negligible in comparison with the 80,000 army troops that remained. Significantly, the new force was distrusted by both Chechens (who feared that it be would be more brutal, corrupt and vulnerable to infiltration by rebels or radical Islamists than its Russian equivalent) and by Moscow. Anatoly Kulikov, the former Russian interior minister who commanded in Chechnya during the 1994–96 war, said the police should be restricted to investigating crimes like cattle theft.

According to the new Chechen interior minister, the police's goal was to restore trust in the Interior Ministry so that Chechens saw the police as their defenders, but it was not long before the police acted as part of Kadyrov's power base. Various attempts were made to curb abuse between 2004 and 2006 (for example, officers were forbidden to wear masks or drive unmarked or darkened vehicles), but such measures made little difference. According to the government website (chechnya.gov.ru) on 10 January 2006, Kadyrov's criticism of the police was confined to the traffic police for routinely failing to stop suspicious vehicles, and even this was offset by his claim that the percentage of crimes solved had risen. Putin then reinforced the message when, in January 2006, he told journalists that 'Chechnya's law enforcement system is becoming very effective ... Chechen law enforcement bodies are practically assuming the bulk of the responsibility for law and order' (Radio Free Europe 1 February 2007). He attributed this to their 'knowing local customs and local conditions and reacting more subtly to processes in society'. But not all public comment was as complimentary. Major General Mikhail Shepilov, deputy commander of the Joint Group of Forces in the North Caucasus, stressed the police's 'unjustifiably low' record of solving serious crime, and their failure to crack down on illegal weapons, extortion, bribery and economic crimes. He singled out for special censure collusion between the police and Chechen rebels (Radio Free Europe 2007). But this was probably inevitable, given that rebels were recruited into the police, partly because it provided them with an alternative source of income, but mainly because it counterbalanced their recruitment to Kadyrov's rivals. In other words, Kadyrov co-opted some of his potential adversaries just as Moscow co-opted Kadyrov to impose order and crush the remaining separatists.

In this way, Moscow transferred the responsibility for reimposing order to Chechnya's pro-Moscow police at the same time as policing was effectively Chechenised. The order the police managed was the result of imposition, complicity and negotiation. It reflected the power relations structuring Chechen politics and society.

CONCLUSION

This chapter has considered the parallel and legitimate systems of order and enforcement in cities affected by various forms of communal and/or internal violence in three distinct geopolitical regions. None of the countries concerned can be compared to, say, the DRC or Somalia, but cities such as Kaduna, Juba and Grozny offer a salutary reminder that state capacity remains a significant indicator of the re-emergence of order. In each of the cities discussed here, state authorities either never lost or quickly regained physical and political control over the population and territory of the city concerned. Even the GOSS in Juba, which started from a very low base, was well placed to perform minimal state functions.

Also, developments in each city emphasise that legal security and the rule of law mean whatever the strongest agents say, and all forms of political transition and reform must be assessed in relation to their calculations. Institutional capacity as such means little to power brokers, and notions such as reconstruction and development mean at best the development of funding capacity; health, education and infrastructure are secondary to political order. This may seem short-sighted or iniquitous, but it suggests alternative perspectives that Western analysts must engage with if they are to understand (let alone influence) developments in post-conflict cities. It means that analysts must go beyond merely identifying hardliners or spoilers. Also, they must acknowledge that state police and criminal justice systems are not necessarily the central agents of order and social control.

8

CHALLENGING ORTHODOXY

I began this book by arguing that although insecurity is widely cited as the main problem confronting post-conflict cities, order is the more significant issue. Even so, the two are to some extent co-dependent; both are the result of processes of negotiation, accommodation and coercion, and are structured through relations of power. This idea has been explored by reference to a range of cities, for only by noting the range of possibilities can we identify the rationalities, dynamics and structures that give this subfield its distinctive patterns.

Post-conflict cities differ in location, culture, population, regime, significance and experience, and the range of contextual factors and outcomes makes direct comparison of questionable value. Yet all share certain features. Commonalities include the fragmented, localised and temporary nature of security provision, and the ineffectiveness of public police. And cities are special, for their history is known and they are to all intents and purposes the state. For such reasons, cities offer a laboratory where competition between emergent trends and social continuities can be mapped. They act as a unit of analysis in which the variables and dynamics involved in the production of order can be identified and traced.

Consider the problem of the sequence of order and security. Security is commonly seen as the precursor for order. This is arguably so in Baghdad, but elsewhere (especially in Grozny, Kabul and Mogadishu) insecurity is a dominant feature in the emergent order. Compare Kigali or Sarajevo, where order submerged during conflict, only to re-emerge in contextually predictable patterns regardless of the levels of security. Or contrast Kinshasa, where chronic insecurity has resulted in the development of a coherent socio-economic order operating beneath the level of state institutions. In Kano, however, order and security are effectively synonymous.

The processes and manoeuvres involved in the production of security are significant, as are its multiple levels and meanings, and these have been discussed in relation to cities such as Basra and Monrovia. Additionally, developments in such cities show that security is a means rather than an end. They emphasise that security is as much a means to power and aggrandisement as it is to stability, personal safety and democratisation. And they offer a salutary reminder that there is as yet no coherent and comprehensive understanding of security capable of incorporating into one definition the practices of the EU or Canada with those of Vladimir Putin or Mohammed Aideed, let alone the needs of a Russian pensioner living in Grozny or a Somali widow in Mogadishu.

Based on the experiences of a range of cities, my answer to the questions posed in Chapter 1 – how does order re-emerge, how is it structured, and how is it managed – are as follows: order typically submerges during conflict, re-emerging to reflect the patterns of domination, subjugation and power relations that are prompted by, or facilitated through, insecurity. The management of order is for this reason about the management of security, and the management of both is by omission as often as it is by commission. Security makes sense at many levels, but its dominant meaning is based on physical security. It is a means, not an end, and its provision typically involves a mixed economy in which state police (indigenous and international) are supplemented by local voluntary groups such as militias, mosques or neighbourhood watchmen, and by commercial security or guarding companies.

SUMMARY OF FINDINGS

Cities consist of multiple relationships displaying some form of order. They would not otherwise survive. However, the often cataclysmic effect of conflict on the buildings, infrastructure and social cohesion associated with those relationships ensures that societal trends sometimes emerge after wars in ways that would previously have been inconceivable. London in 1918 or Tokyo in 1945 offer compelling examples (Marwick 1965). Further, cities are nowadays commonly subject to social engineering projects. These often result from international or substate interventions designed to achieve regime change and reconstruction (or, less frequently, humanitarian goals), and usually involve some form of police reform.

Most of these projects refer to the need for security and stability, rather than order, but, as this book has shown, order is the fundamental factor. Contra Thakur, order is a prerequisite of law, not the other way around (Thakur 1982). Of course, terms such as 'order' oversimplify the complex dynamics of transition (Lemarchand 1994: 584), but it is clear that order is essentially (to paraphrase Wendt) what strongmen make of it. State institutions are not essential for order, but order's most accurate indicator is state police, and what they do or do not do. Ironically, order and police are factors over which external agents have little meaningful influence, because:

- the re-emergence of order is determined by pre-existing relationships of power and subjugation;
- order is dependent on agreement regarding its rules, and is managed by negotiation as well as coercion;
- societal norms, and legacy and structural issues determine policing;
- police institutions are resilient.

KEY FACTORS AND INDICATORS OF ORDER

Despite what donors would wish, order depends on what went before. In other words, order is a reconfigured complex of interlocking structures, processes and relationships that are composed of old elements and habits, only some of which will be revised and reoriented by new pressures and new or modified contexts. It depends on agreements on rules, behaviour and predictability, and is managed by coercion, adaptation, accommodation and negotiation.

Order and security are interwoven, but while security facilitates order, order is necessary for meaningful security. In other words, security is best understood as a process and a variable within order, rather than as its end. Both are dynamic processes, which are influenced by networks of subjugation, most of which pre-date (or coexist with) existing relationships while interacting or intersecting with past or present sources of insecurity and disorder. In other words, personalities, politics and contingencies determine when and how order re-emerges. Above all, order and security are literal rather than theoretical constructs in post-conflict cities: they mean whatever the strongest man says. For this reason alone, it may not be possible to develop a comprehensive understanding of security that integrates state, factional and personal security.

The best indicator of order is its policing, and its most significant marker is the presence or absence of state police. Many associations and factional groups offer policing, but the role of state police is qualitatively different in its symbolic power, residual position and regulatory potential (Crawford 2006: 137).[1] Police are thought to facilitate control and monitoring, signal credibility for international and national regimes, and offer benefits and sanctions that may ensure the loyalty or acquiescence of a populace. Police resources (and their parent ministries) are desirable prizes for local strongmen. But police are a significant indicator primarily because their policing is shaped by the social realities of the host society: corrupt, brutal or criminalised cities produce corrupt, brutal and criminalised police. As Marenin has noted, police violence and abuse are often a form of legitimate and delegated public power (Marenin 1996: 310). Legacy issues matter, too, for they often mean that certain police cannot operate in certain areas, or that certain ethnic groups have never been recruited. So do contingencies; the killing of a police chief or station commander changes the behaviour of his officers, some of whom may seek revenge, while others run away.

In practice, this means that the level of insecurity influences policing. High levels during conflict mean that officers disappear, while high levels in the post-conflict phase mean that officers stay in their stations (though those in Ba'athist Iraq always stayed there, and high unemployment means that policing is a desirable job despite its dangers). But the fundamental factors shaping public policing relate to the resilience of the police institution.

RESILIENCE

The cities discussed here present two apparently contradictory features. On the one hand, police disintegrate or dissolve when the political processes on which their organisation and activity is predicated fragment. The police's function and role reflects the political patterns representing order, so the destruction of the pre-conflict order means that the police system breaks down and its agents disperse. On the other hand, the police institution is remarkably resilient, and usually re-emerges relatively early in the post-conflict period. There are always exceptions, but individual officers or small groups often return to work once it is safe to do so. The reopening of stations signals the re-emergence of the institution, which in turn marks the initial adaptation of the police to post-conflict circumstances, and the re-emergence of order. This occurs partly because the police fulfil a functional need, partly because it is what international and national authorities or strongmen want for reasons of legitimacy, expedience or prestige, and partly because most inhabitants simply want someone to stop looting and crime. Most people think in terms of a police force unless (as in the case of Albanians in Mitrovica) there are good reasons why they should not.

Despite this, the emergence or imposition of new or adaptive forms of order means that police may be pressured into adopting new procedures and habits. For example, officers from the pre-war force may be purged, thereby offering job opportunities to ex-fighters who might otherwise be unemployed; the police are often used to integrate fighters into society. Much depends on the alternatives open to national or international authorities, but officially recognised militias or ex-fighters are often incorporated into the police. The point at which factional militias become part of a police force is, however, often difficult to identify because it may be camouflaged. This trend implies that most cities will see the re-establishment of a police force because police are considered useful and controllable

TABLE 8.1 Adaptive role of the police

POLITICAL PHASE	FUNCTION
Strong central government	Public police role includes: order maintenance; regime representation; regulatory activities; conventional duties.
Fragmentation	Limited police role. Influence devolves to local big men. Police supplemented by informal policing (e.g. militia, mosques).
Collapse	Localised enforcement by armed groups.
Immediate post-conflict (1–3 months)	Deployment and/or enforcement gap. Localised policing arrangements. Individuals/police institution re-emerges.
Medium post-conflict (3 months–5 years)	Public police supplemented by informal policing groups. Police perform conventional duties.
Long-term post-conflict (5–10 years)	Police perform conventional duties. Revert to former (corrupt/harsh) habits.

in a way that militaries are not. Armies are regarded as particularly untrustworthy; their senior officers form part of ruling elites, while junior ranks are unreliable, intervening in politics, abusing human rights, or siding with rebels when it suits them. Also, they often affect everyday life in a way that police do not. Police are for such reasons seen as a desirable attribute of governments.

And police are adept at accommodating and manipulating unavoidable political pressures. This does not mean that policing is unchanged, for conflict often destroys the system of didactic transfer shaping police work. Many police skills are learned on the job, and knowledge is commonly handed down, but this breaks down during civil wars as stations are destroyed and officers targeted. It crumbles still further when undermined by peace agreements brokered by international agents intent on reform. This happened in Freetown, for example. Many Sierra Leonean officers died during the war, and although Commonwealth advisers later offered basic training, there were too few of them to allow junior officers to follow the usual process of learning from their seniors.

Police adapt to change (superficially at least) remarkably easily (as shown in Table 8.1). Policing in the aftermath of conflict often involves a redistribution of power, but this is only problematic when international organisations seek to reform police on democratic lines, as in Bosnia. Elsewhere it is less significant, especially when one party achieves outright victory. The reason is that police are content to be used; they rarely have an ideological stake in the political regime of their country. Regardless of rhetoric or regime, senior officers rarely build power bases comparable to those of the military. Some seek to preserve the appearance of a degree of operational and 'professional' autonomy, but most are unable or unwilling to operate as independent political actors. Typically, they are adjuncts to groups that control resources more directly. Basra offers multiple illustrations of this.

In all cases, the imperatives of accommodation and survival dominate the working lives of officers; hence some Iraqi officers patrolled with US marines even as others disappeared. Despite this (and despite the fact that officers are despised or feared and policing is often provided by local groups), the resources associated with the police institution make control of the police a desirable political prize. Most strongmen value the police as a potential resource, and aspire to the legitimising prestige it attracts. So do occupation forces, though this can be a double-edged sword. International forces must engage with local realities if they are to efficiently manage a populace, but this can (as the British discovered before they withdrew from central Basra) lead to complicity and appeasement; that is, to weakness rather than pragmatic accommodation.

The function and role of the police thus mirror political developments. Even when politics and policing are localised or fragmented, a residual national system is retained in the form of individual memories and aspirations. Embedded fragmentary tendencies may dominate in Mogadishu, and the police in south-central Somalia may be one of three Somali public forces,[2] but centripetal pressures did not prevent the emergence of a centralised police system in the past, and there is no reason why they should not in the future. This suggests that political contingencies and leadership are on occasion as influential as social issues.[3]

POLICING CHANGE

What, then, is the role of the police in the post-conflict city, and how does it relate to order? I suggest that police manage (rather than achieve or create) order, for while (to paraphrase Tilly) policing arguably belongs on the same continuum as war-making, banditry, piracy and gangland rivalry (Tilly 1985: 170), police are better at reproducing order than producing it. This is a topic on which police studies has much to say, and the theory of police in change offered by Marenin is relevant (Marenin 1996: 313–25). Extrapolating from his work, the basic elements affecting policing in the city can be formalised as contingent reproduction, agency and autonomy.

Change, like order, security, police, policing and the state itself, is reproduced or created. Just as states do not exist in isolation – the idea and functions of the state are reproduced each day – so there are no order and no police in isolation. There are only the decisions of strongmen to manipulate or respond in predictable and/or acceptable patterns, and for the police to do their jobs in routine, accepted and habitual ways. Second, police are only one of a number of actors in cities, and are rarely independent; they function under various political and empirical constraints. Third, police in post-conflict cities are usually inadequately trained, resourced and motivated, and the policing they provide is selective, sporadic and corrupt. They tend to have fluid group structures, limited administrative capacity, and inadequate technical capacity. Consequently, they offer little in the way of security, and are supplemented by informal and self-help initiatives.

Assuming that the host culture tolerates discretion, officers may take decisions potentially affecting the management of order. Constables may decide to avoid leaving a main road, mid-ranking officers may select priorities or choose organisational structures according to kin or individual preferences, while senior officers may act at the behest of their patron. All forms of policing depend on coercion, so police also accommodate locally acceptable levels of force, protection and infrastructure. Personal, family and group instincts and identities dominate at the expense of Western state-based notions of law and order. This implies, too, that some people will always be excluded. City-wide order may be possible, but security for all is not.

This interpretation of the police role, with its stress on contingencies and social possibilities, is reinforced by the literature on police culture and institutional change.

POLICE CULTURE

There is an extensive literature on a police subculture that reflects the values and beliefs of its parent society while containing characteristics that are unique to the police (Kappler et al. 1994; Reiner and Newburn 2000). It emphasises the entrenched and resilient nature of police culture, and the consequent difficulty of reform, and it has value here because it offers insights into the management of functional order, and whether or not a common constabulary ethic is identifiable. Also, it flags up potential differences between conventional and post-conflict policing. This matters because we do not know if what applies in Anglo-American policing is also true of police in Basra, Grozny and Kinshasa.

Most of today's ideas about police culture draw on the work of three influential authors working on policing in the US, UK and Australia: Skolnick, Reiner and Chan. Skolnick's classic (1966) study of patrol work in the USA was the catalyst. He found that culture developed and was transmitted as a means of coping with three fundamental features of policing, which he characterised as danger, authority and efficiency. He argued that these elements interacted with the paramilitary character of the police institution 'to generate distinctive cognitive and behavioral responses' that he referred to as the police 'working personality' (Skolnick 1966: 42). Reiner later expanded Skolnick's characterization by defining police culture as a patterned set of understandings which helps officers cope with the pressures and tensions of everyday policing (Reiner 2000: 86). He maintains that its key features include a sense of mission (the police exist as the thin blue line between order and chaos); cynicism and pessimism (this may result from working with the dregs of their society, but it also expresses the feeling that morality is being eroded) (Reiner 2000: 90); and suspicion of people and places (Reiner 2000: 88–92). Feelings of solidarity, of them and us, reinforce the culture (Reiner 2000: 92–3). Chan questioned Reiner's account on the basis that it assumed that individuals are passive recipients, did not explain cultural variation, and had little to say about the structural (social, political, economic) conditions of policing (Chan 1996, 1997, 2001; Chan et al. 2003).

The value of Chan's approach is enhanced here by the use she makes of Bourdieu's notion of field, which she defines as a 'social space of conflict and competition, where participants struggle to establish control over specific power and authority, and, in the course of the struggle, modify the structure of the field itself' (Bourdieu and Wacquant 1992; Chan 2001: 118). Chan's original study was based on the policing of minority groups in Australia, but her general argument applies to post-conflict cities. As this book shows, police culture is indeed shaped by its political context (the dominant concept of order), by the social and economic status of those policed (and of the police themselves), and by government (or strongmen's) policies. The elements Chan and Bourdieu identify as significant reflect the power relations that result from competition for resources. They include support networks, knowledge and capacities, and symbolic assets such as reputation and legitimacy (Chan et al. 2003: 36–8). Chan argues that the relative force, position and strategic orientation of the police in the power games that result depends on variables such as the volume and composition of their tokens (Chan 2001: 119).

Chan argues that the police negotiate this field according to a 'habitus', or 'a system of dispositions' or a feel for the situation (Chan 2001: 119) that integrates 'past experience and enable[s] individuals to cope with a diversity of unforeseen situations' (Chan 1996: 115). Drawing on the work of organisational theorists (Sackmann 1991), Chan argues that this habitus is shaped through the transmission of different forms of cultural knowledge, which include: axiomatic knowledge (such as the police mandate), dictionary knowledge (categories used to place people and events), directory knowledge (generic guidance for routine situations), and recipe knowledge (guidance for specific situations, such as keeping out of trouble) (Chan 1997;

Chan 2003: 30–34). Chan's variables are based on settled and liberal conditions, and would not have applied in, say, Freetown in 1998, but they offer a framework for thinking about police, even as they emphasise the need for more comparative analysis.

ASSESSMENT

The resilience of the police and the skill with which officers manage or manipulate external pressure for change are evident from the record of international interventions: reform programmes are temporary in effect, and while they may make an immediate impression (as in Freetown), standards and procedures usually drift back to those prevalent before the intervention. This is true even in the special circumstances of Bosnia, the geopolitical position of which has made it a centre of EU and NATO attention for some fifteen years. This trend becomes stronger as time passes and international attention moves (as it must) to other cities; Namibia's police are rarely mentioned nowadays, whereas their reform was once regularly cited as a success story. This is not to argue that police reform cannot make a difference, or should not be attempted. Rather, it is to suggest that similar patterns of manipulation and response are identifiable across a range of cities.

This interpretation is reinforced by the selective and ethnocentric approach offered by many donors. In promoting the social engineering necessary for democratic policing, donors such as the UK state that 'a police force must reflect the communities it serves' at the same time as they insist that it does not (FCO 2007: 30). Reform is advocated for Basra and Sarajevo precisely because their police reflect the dominant local – and in liberal eyes undesirable – ethnic balance and social norms. Indeed, rather than engaging with social realities, the FCO's statement that this 'may take a generation to achieve' reflects its idealism; it proposes nothing less than the creation (that is, imposition) of a multi-ethnic force with a high proportion of women officers. Sustainable reform, as many criminal justice texts note, does indeed take a generation or more, but it does so because the hardest thing to change is the mindset or culture of officers in a Kabul or Monrovia (Grozny rarely figures in English-language accounts). Change may be desirable for a host of reasons, but it is dishonest to ignore the ideological imperatives and unsubstantiated assumptions and assertions driving so much of current policy. Further, the bureaucratic and technical means employed cannot overcome the divisions common to post-conflict cities. Terms such as 'security', 'stability' and 'sustainable development' are not synonymous with order.

RESEARCH AGENDA

Despite considerable literature on state formation and reconstruction, systematic analysis of the emergence of order, security and policing in post-conflict cities is in its infancy (Bajraktari et al. 2006). In particular, while much is known about the consequences of conflict and war economies, most of the analyses relevant to policing are driven by today's policy requirements, or are rooted in an uncritical liberalism; nuanced theoretical analyses are missing, as are ethnographic studies.

Most research on policing post-conflict cities adopts a normative or culturally specific standpoint, and is rooted in a specific understanding as to what police should look like. Similarly, policing usually refers to the activities of international militaries or the attempts of UN or EU police to reform a repressive indigenous police. Existing relationships and practices are assessed according to culturally specific normative, ideological or technocratic objectives such as ethnic and sexual parity, local partnerships, and adherence to international human rights legislation. Police building has become a 'piecemeal, incremental, administrative and technical exercise' (Ioannides 2007: 372), even though it requires a notoriously conservative and resilient institution to change cherished practices and beliefs.

Many police are undeniably corrupt and brutal, as are the societies that permit their functioning, but current approaches consistently fail to acknowledge the complex social and urban environment in which police live and work. The result is inaccurate assessments and unrealistic policies that contain a challenging research agenda. For example, there is no comparative framework for understanding how policing, order and security are (re)constructed and contested; the structural relations of power, order and security, and their functional expression, have yet to be located in the context of post-conflict cities. We know that security may be ghettoised as subgroups move in or out of areas, but there is little analysis of the different policing dynamics this leads to. We do not know how popular expectations influence policing, and there are few if any studies of policing from the perspective of indigenous police. Similarly, there is as yet no systematic and comparative study of police responses to the political pressures exerted by, say, NATO, the EU or the UN.

Police forces are resilient and conservative organisations, so it may be that reform is little more than a tactical compromise on the part of senior officers in the face of unavoidable political pressure. In which case, certain patterns of manipulation and response should be identifiable. On the other hand, war often facilitates social change; it induces a sense of crisis that breaks traditions, and disrupts or dislocates the existing order (Marwick 1965), so meaningful shifts in police culture and procedures may also be identifiable. Even so, change is usually balanced by continuities: peace settlements rarely establish a new order; rather, they result in friction, discontent, and adjustment or manipulation. This line of enquiry has yet to be explored. In a similar vein, despite the attention now paid to local ownership, civil society, and the dispersal of security provision to corporations and community-based organisations, we have yet to determine the ways in which a city's inhabitants interpret or assess the daily practices of security governance. Notions of transition and transferability need questioning, as does the relationship between international programmes and local ideas and practices.

So, too, do basic facts. The primary location of power and influence on order and security in cities remains the strongman or big man, who is usually a politician or a warlord with political ambitions. He may be a Paddy Ashdown or a Paul Bremer, a Mohammed Aideed or a Charles Taylor. The order such men enforce (or attempt to enforce) is unambiguous, even when temporary. However, order is much more precarious when a leader is perceived to be weak or reliant on external forces: Karzai was chosen as Afghanistan's president precisely because he was weak, while Sierra Leone's Kabbah lacked a secure indigenous power base and was vulnerable to challenges from the army. The analytical implications of this have yet to be assessed. More long-term assessments are needed too. For example, most commentators say that reform takes at least ten years, yet there are no comparative studies assessing the statement's truth. Systematic and/or nuanced comparative assessment is missing; there are only studies of specific missions, and few of them evaluate change in the longer term.

One further issue deserves note. Police act in a pluralised field of security delivery, and the governance arrangements that result are increasingly framed in terms of networks. Of the texts available at the time of writing, Wood and Dupont's edited volume is particularly relevant because it addresses the meaning of security, the role of the state in the provision of security, and policing as a public good (Wood and Dupont 2006). Loader and Walker's contribution, for example, suggests that it is states or their functional equivalent that are best able to engage in the 'instrumental ordering work *and* in the … cultural production of social identity' (Wood and Dupont 2006: 193, their stress) on which long-term stability in the post-conflict city arguably depends. However, none of Wood and Dupont's authors addresses the transferability of their insights to the situations encountered in a Basra, Kano or Grozny. Wood, for example, notes that police have adopted the language of other institutional actors, particularly those in the realm of business, in negotiating their place within the wider field of security governance. But she neglects to note that many more incorporate those of the military. There are also a number of analytically separable but linked tensions running through our understanding of the policing of post-conflict cities, and many fundamental questions have yet to be asked, let alone answered.

UNRESOLVED ISSUES AND TENSIONS

From a liberal perspective, the nature of security is arguably the most significant unresolved intellectual issue and source of empirical tension in post-conflict cities. However, this is less problematic if we accept that security has multiple meanings and is characterised by movements, processes and relationships. It is unhelpful to focus either on the individual or on the state, and is more productive to consider how people and authority interact. Hence the importance of analysing power relations.

Inevitably, different interpretations result in tension. It means, for example, that international authorities and local people often value individual life or property differently: in January 2004, British troops in Basra allowed looting, rather than fire on rioters, whereas Basrawis thought that the troops thereby failed to do their duty of ensuring the security of both life *and* property (Stewart 2007: 295). The consequences of this can easily undermine the preferred order. Additionally, the broad definitions of security favoured in the West fail to address the understanding of security (or order or stability) in the parts of the world to which they are usually applied. The application of, say, human security as a policy is plausible only when the stakes are not high or where there is prosperity; its promotion would be thought weak or incomprehensible by the strongmen of Grozny and Kabul. Thus, at a meeting between the UN and the governor of Afghanistan's Kandahar province in December 2002, the UN's officials spoke of building a civil society and a state, but the governor talked only of securing power in a continuing conflict (Personal communication 2006).

Even if security and developmental concerns are linked – which I doubt – they cannot be disassembled into a simple temporal sequence. The merging of conventional security and development that aims to broaden our understanding of life in post-conflict cities has normative, and also analytical, value, but it ignores the unpredictable violence common to many cities while assuming that the police should manage it. And it ignores also that protection, crime prevention and community policing are not what most police do, especially in the South: police are usually predators rather than protectors.[4] In other words, police cannot solve the social problems that human security prioritises or act as moderating agents even if they wanted to. Consequently, there are always tensions between attempts to create security and attempts to ensure Western-style political reconstruction. Reconstruction is difficult without security, but heavy-handedness in pursuing security alienates people, and makes them less willing to support or tolerate reform and reconstruction.

This has implications for the role played by the police. It means, for example, that simplistic paradigms about the beneficial effects of democratisation are difficult to translate into policing that increases safety citywide. Indeed, there is little evidence to show that democratic policing is effective. In practice, the constellations of power at local and national (and, indeed, international) levels shape the processes of institutional reconstruction in such a way as to limit its effects. And while the presence of a reformed police force is generally thought desirable, a police presence cannot of itself build security or dispel uncertainty. Indeed, a heavy security presence can be counterproductive. A heavy police presence on the streets usually combines with rumours about its purpose to fuel feelings of insecurity. Further, there are never enough police (let alone trained police) in cities, yet the numbers of police deployed does not seem to affect significantly the levels of security or types of order. This reflects ambiguity regarding the extent to which the police create or re-create order. It is often argued that police re-create social order, but the application of this insight to fragile cities remains unproven.

This book has argued that security is a dependent variable in the re-emergence of order, and its presence or absence may be manipulated to produce specific patterns of order. Nevertheless, the relationship between security as a means and as an end (and the role of the police therein) is complicated, especially when security is defined broadly. For example, institutions are favoured because they are visible and conform to donors' expectations, but they are not necessary for order or security; institutions alone cannot ensure security or order. As Stewart notes, the Taliban provided both, yet he walked for 600 miles through Afghanistan without staying in a village with electricity or a salaried civil servant (2007: 55). Also, establishing citywide security requires more than merely managing looting and crime. Indeed, the cases cited here suggest that it also requires people to have adequate food, shelter and protection. Nevertheless, as the Gaza operations of the United Nations Relief and Works Agency for Palestine Refugees in the Near East (UNRWA) show, this cannot be a complete answer. Indeed, its unintended consequences may in the longer term exacerbate insecurity.

Gaza has no real economy, yet between 1950 and 2007 its population rose from 240,000 to 1.5 million. This was made possible by UNRWA's policy of treating every Gaza resident as a refugee; UNRWA provided housing, schooling and health care to every newborn child.

The security consequence of this internationally approved programme is the chronic insecurity that results from the presence of Gaza's unemployed youths. As a Hamas adviser to the Palestinian prime minister told Cairo's *Al-Ahram* newspaper in May 2007, the main problem in Gaza is the inability of Fatah and Hamas 'to control their men in the streets' (*Financial Times* 13 June 2007). But managing such youths is a security challenge for many IGOs and governments. Recent UN statistics forecast that by 2030, 60 per cent of the world population will live in cities, and as many as 60 per cent of urban residents in Southern cities will be aged under 18 (IRIN 2007a: 34).

Other unresolved issues include the following:

- Most reforms are successful only in the short term, and the medium- to long-term implications of international interventions have yet to be systematically assessed. Further, the way in which the various phases relate to each other is unknown. For example, there is little evidence to show that cities that have undergone reconstruction in a segregated manner (such as Beirut) are significantly more secure or stable compared to others (such as Sarajevo) where former enemies have been encouraged to mix. The success of such programmes arguably depends on the continued presence of international forces, but the political implications of that are unacceptable to Western governments.

- The difference between war-related insecurity and crime-related insecurity is indistinguishable, especially in the early months. Both offer business opportunities to criminals, and to the officers and politicians who manage them in an informal extractive sense. Both thrive when accommodated by the local populace. Any attempt by reformers to place crime prevention at the forefront of policing strategies is likely to be obstructed by the legacy of war economies.

- Initial feelings of optimism are soon replaced by anxiety and, in some cases, a sense of despair and abandonment. This is partly the result of destruction and dislocation, but also because conflict is more often frozen than terminated, too much is expected of international organisations, politics continues as usual, and uncertainty abounds. All were evident in southern Lebanon in

2007. A year after Israeli bombardment displaced a million people, Lebanon's public infrastructure was much improved, with projects paid for by the government in Beirut, and in the south by Iran. However, the level of discontent was high because international aid pledged to rebuild houses was not dispersed, leaving some 200,000 IDPs: the Lebanese government kept the money pledged by Saudi Arabia in Beirut's banks as a means of pressurising Hezbollah into disarming.

• The networks people use to make sense of such developments are unmapped. Baghdad's inhabitants can watch broadcasts by Al Jazeera, the BBC and CNN, but rumour (as in Kinshasa's *radio trottoir*) is probably more influential, acting as a source of information about security threats and political developments. Rumour is not necessarily based on empirical evidence, but it is a potentially useful source of information about political trends and dangers. Further, the fears it expresses are often rational: Baghdad shopkeepers are kidnapped, and Palestinian refugees in northern Lebanon have been caught up in the conflict between Hezbollah and Israel.

• The North–South experience of police reform dominates today's debate, and there is as yet no analysis of the South–South experience, or of the ways in which norms, values and procedures are transferred between indigenous police officers and police agencies: we know more about Portuguese assistance to Angolan police than Angola's assistance to the DRC. Above all, we do not know why certain processes and norms travel across societies and others do not.

ORTHODOXY REVISITED

The cases discussed in this book challenge the liberal orthodoxy outlined in Chapter 3. Not only are its policies based on inaccurate analyses and unproven assumptions, but also Western models of policing do not adapt well to Southern environments. Local conditions and norms reassert themselves, and security institutions that lack popular legitimacy survive. The establishment of a secure environment does not of itself guarantee the success of police reform, but neither does the inability to establish a secure environment guarantee failure.

In other words, police reform is, like the notion of the rule of law, something of a cargo cult. Its application may be appropriate, but the phrase is too often used as a panacea for situations that require a more strategic and long-term approach (Stromseth et al. 2006: 65).

In fact, democratic-style policing is of limited appeal in the post-conflict city, where the behaviour of police is based on pragmatic day-to-day calculations of personal survival. There is evidence of a common police ethic in post-conflict cities, but it is not the one discussed by Sheptycki (2007: 31–72). Some UN police may display a 'structural continuity between the dynamics of security-threatening situations across a broad range of national and transnational contexts and a real sense of the value of a common policecraft in repairing these situations' (Loader and Walker 2007a: 264), but indigenous police do not. For them policing is a dangerous job that provides (typically irregular) wages, or the means to support their extended family, and it usually requires the use of physical force to achieve its aims. Police have much in common throughout the world, but they must be understood in terms of the environment in which they operate.

Given the number of unresolved issues and tensions, it is easy to be cynical or dismissive about idealistic projects intended to create a new order. Yet such projects may, regardless of their flawed nature, make a genuine difference to order and security (Hills 2008).

Sierra Leone, a small country, started from such a low base that almost anything represented reconstruction.[5] In 2005, three years after the eleven-year war finally ended, the UN's Human Development Index ranked it at 176 out of the 177 countries surveyed (UNDP 2005). Donors focused much of their efforts on Freetown, where the government's presence was evident and police were visible; that is, the conventional indicators of order were present. At the same time, Freetown was a source of potential insecurity, not least because its population was swollen by ex-fighters crowded into former hotels (Hoffman 2005), by unskilled young people from rural areas living on the streets, and by older migrants living in corrugated-iron shanties, who put pressure on land and local services. Public expenditure and urban projects were paid for by foreign grants, but most people were too busy surviving to care who funded reconstruction. Given these circumstances, police reform illustrates both democratic good practice in building a new order based on security for all, and the challenges to be overcome. The best account of the three phases of reform is that of Horn, which is based on his time as leader of the Commonwealth Police Division Task Force (CPDTF) (Horn and Olonisakin 2008).

Horn found that many of the lower ranks of the 6,500-strong police genuinely wished to change their poor public image, but they lacked the skills and equipment needed to fulfil donor expectations. General-duty officers did not have torches, batons and handcuffs, let alone stationery, fuel or reasonable accommodation, and the few serviceable vehicles available had been annexed by senior officers for their personal use. At the same time, most police believed that donors would provide all the expertise and materiel required to restructure, rehabilitate and equip the SLP. Consequently, donors and aid organisations were constantly presented with extensive shopping lists, and courted by government ministers and officials (Private communication 2008b). An early UK proposal to donate a fleet of vehicles had to be revised when it became clear that their maintenance would take most of the police budget, yet Sierra Leonean officials continued to request 4x4 Land Rover-style vehicles and heavier vehicles, regardless of their fuel and maintenance costs. In the circumstances, it was not surprising that officers responded to incidents slowly, and that their investigations were often incomplete. Nor was it surprising that government ministers lived in luxury. In other words, the state of the police was, as ever, an accurate indicator of its government's real priorities and interpretation of order.

The challenge confronting CPDTF advisers was how to manage simultaneously the short- and long-term challenges of reconstruction (the emergent order), and how to pay for it. Practical projects intended to demonstrate visible progress were quickly implemented. For example, as part of the emergency post-conflict response, the CPDTF's initial budget of $900,000 was used to buy bicycles, vehicles and a basic radio communication system. Drugs were supplied to the police hospital too, for many officers had malaria, and taking care of them improved their health, morale and effectiveness. Also, a mission statement was published which symbolically broke with the past and offered a vision for the future. It was publicly legitimised when presidential approval for a policing charter was secured in 1998. But these achievements were lost when the RUF attacked Freetown in January 1999; police stations were torched, files lost, vehicles destroyed, and 250 officers murdered, together with approximately 375 of their families. Police became invisible. Freetown was full of vehicle checkpoints, but they were once again manned by soldiers, armed members of the civil defence forces, or youths acting independently.

In the event, the reform programme that began again in 1999 was seen as relatively successful; a new philosophy of policing was introduced, and police capacity and skills were built. But it was not many years before traffic police were once again asking for money from the drivers of commercial vehicles, and by 2007 Freetown's order and security were again shaped by pervasive petty corruption, patronage, mismanagement, social exclusion and the military's questionable loyalty to the government. It was, however, minimal compared to what had gone before.

This situation raises the question of 'normalisation', which is arguably more significant than the legitimacy internationals prize (cf. Lin 2007). The goal of police reform and reconstruction varies from regime support to regime change to social engineering, but achieving such goals (legitimate or otherwise) requires something approximating to normality; that is, to relatively stable and predictable patterns that conform to accepted rules. So far as West Africa is concerned, the key empirical indicators are arguably the presence of police on the main roads in urban centres, and, later, the appearance of traffic police. Police may be purged, and new recruitment practices and standards introduced, but public confidence generally requires the police to be seen in the vicinity of their stations, or about daily tasks such as traffic duties.

Traffic police are key, not because they perform an essential task (though traffic control is as desirable in the potholed and crowded streets of Freetown as in the vehicle-choked streets of Baghdad) so much as because they are among the most visible of police: they act as a political signal that normal forms of order are emerging. In Freetown, their presence at checkpoints meant that the rebels and civil defence forces had lost influence. Similarly, in Monrovia in

2006, much was made of the introduction of a set of working traffic lights near the port. The fact that the lights are usually out of order (Monrovia does not have regular electricity supplies) mattered less than their status as the first new lights to be erected since the war began. Above all, normality returns when police demand bribes from drivers, for traffic police are among the first and easiest of police to corrupt. The re-emergence of market traders and taxi drivers is equally significant, especially when taxi drivers are prepared to work at night.

CONCLUSION

One thing is clear about post-conflict cities. Security is the critical variable shaping early developments, but it is a means to an end: order. And some form of order emerges even in a Mogadishu. For cities comprise myriad relationships and opportunities; they consist of people, associations and infrastructures interacting in such a way as to form identifiable and predictable patterns. Such patterns may be undesirable, but they can be manipulated. As such, they represent a political resource that can be managed to the advantage of specific groups. This applies as much to IGOs and NGOs as to indigenous elites.

The links and balances between the various elements vary, and order, like security, may be fragmented, localised or temporary, but it exists; vacuums are rare. The key to understanding this dynamic is to be found in power relations, for order and security are subject to, and are shaped by, coercion, negotiation and manipulation. Both are best understood as an interaction, which is (ideally) managed by various policing groups, of which state police are the most significant. From this it follows that policing styles develop in response to circumstances, rather than legal–rational institutional imperatives.

Different constituencies have different objectives and criteria, but the international ideal remains a disciplined apolitical organisation of trained officers that protects citizens and their goods. Unfortunately, the reality is different. Billions of dollars have been poured into projects promoting reconstruction and democratic policing since the end of the Cold War, yet remarkably little has been achieved in terms of fundamental and lasting change. Police may or may not be brutal, corrupt and ineffective, but their culture and organisational resilience ensure that they can adapt to, or subvert, most unavoidable external pressures. And they are the coercive resource that political interests (indigenous and international) use to reinforce their power and impose a particular morality or ideology. Reformers forget at their peril the social realities of policing, the multiplicity of ways in which order is reproduced, and the multidimensional nature of security.

The account offered here affects the academic and policy-relevant debate in three main ways. First, the multiple rationalities evident in the production of order and security obstruct the development of a single comprehensive account integrating conventional and new forms of security. Second, the conflation of order, security and development is questionable, resting as it does on assumptions concerning the existence of progressive phases. Despite circumstantial evidence that 'security from violence is fundamental to ... sustainable economic, social and political development' (OECD DAC 2004), there is no simple process or analytical link between security and the order and development thought to result from security. Assessment of the linkage is made more difficult by the frequent emergence of an informal order coexisting with formal institutional arrangements. Third, confidence-building and credibility are key. Failure to identify the optimal point at which conventional Western techniques for control can be combined with indigenous methods results in political failure. The critical points of interface and transition (which vary according to context) have yet to be identified.

Ultimately, order is a matter of perception; it only makes sense as an aspect of social processes and relationships. There are no clear theoretical or empirical answers to the question of how order emerges, but this book offers a plausible explanation for the complex and often contradictory tendencies associated with it.

NOTES

CHAPTER 1

1. Before the war Ato had been a representative for the US oil company Conoco. Shadow or wartime economies also re-emerge (Berdal and Malone 2000: 43–68; 69–91; Reno 1995).
2. Estimates of future urbanisation are based on the observation that in Europe and the Americas the urban percentage of total populations has stabilised at 75–85 per cent.
3. Classical authors of urban sociology, such as Georg Simmell and Louis Wirth, caught this element of urban life by defining urbanism in terms of the density and diversity of human interaction and institutions, anonymity, the breakdown of traditional community and its replacement by 'society' (Andrusz 1996).
4. Only in Africa has urbanisation been accompanied by marginalisation and indebtedness, rather than economic growth and diversification. Case studies of the impact of globalisation and urbanisation on selected African cities (including Kinshasa) are to be found in Rakodi 1997.
5. There is no consensus on what fragility means. DFID defines fragile states as poor countries unable or unwilling to use domestic and international resources to alleviate poverty, while USAID defines them as lacking the capacity and legitimacy to deliver public goods (which may include policing). The World Bank has its own classification of 'low income countries under stress'. I use the word descriptively because there are a range of countries that might be described as subject to significant levels of stress. These include countries that are resource-rich but ruled by rapacious elites or with inadequate institutional capacities, as well as those characterised by fragmented power structures. Compare Bøås and Jennings 2005,

who emphasise that different actors have different interests. We should therefore ask, for whom is the state fragile, and how?

6. This interpretation owes much to Giddens's theory of structuration (Giddens 1984).

7. This was true even in the 1960s, when attention focused on the role of militaries in modernisation and development.

8. Youths are teenage boys or young men. I deal with the role played by men because in cities such as these, only donors consider women and girls significant (cf. Meintjies et al. 2001).

CHAPTER 2

1. Between 1945 and 1993, two-thirds of the negotiated settlements ending ethnic conflicts and civil wars that had lasted for a minimum of five years failed to produce lasting peace (Licklider 1995).

2. For a typology of looting, see MacGinty 2004.

3. For a review of urbanisation in developing countries and the major theories guiding global urban studies, see Kasarda and Crenshaw 1991.

4. I distinguish between comparative policing and the more recent emphasis on transnational policing, much of which is concerned to develop the idea of a common constabulary ethic. For comparative policing, see Mawby 1990. For transnational policing, see Goldsmith and Sheptycki 2007.

5. Donors argue that sustainable policing requires a revenue basis, but this is only partly true. Conflict usually results in informal and illegal economic activities, so tax collection (usually regarded as a primary indication of state capacity and legitimacy) is difficult; the tax base is narrow and dependent on, say, trade taxes. Further, most Southern police have always operated on a limited or irregular revenue basis.

6. This section is based on Hills 2000, 2002, 2006.

7. This is seen as the future. In July 2007, a NATO planning team worked with the Iraqi National Police authorities to adapt the European Gendarmerie training model to Iraqi needs (US Central Command 2007). For alternative policing styles, see Ashraf 2007; Zaalberg 2006.

8. For example, in 2002 a British employment tribunal forced DynCorp to pay £110,000 compensation to the UN investigator it sacked for reporting police trainers involved in an illegal sex ring in Bosnia. None of the trainers involved was prosecuted. In 2007, the USA's special inspector general for Iraq reconstruction criticised both DynCorp for billing the State Department for $4.2 million in unauthorised work related to the construction of a camp for police trainers in Iraq, and the State Department for paying DynCorp (*Dallas Morning News*, 31 January 2007).

9. For a different perspective, see Caygill 2001. Caygill argues that the 68-day war in Kosovo in 1999 was a struggle between two rival policing forces and conceptions of policing; the Serb police operated to restore order in their sovereign territory while the international 'police' (i.e. NATO) sought to exercise their new strategic concept. Kosovo, he says, marks

the shift of NATO from a military to a police organisation, whereby war masqueraded as a police action, and police operations pretended to be war.

10. The aim of police was originally regulatory, and was only incidentally concerned with crime. It was not until the late eighteenth century that Patrick Colquhuon developed a model of crime control capable of coping with rising crime in London and other big English cities.

11. Contrast Alpert and Dunham's statement that the use of physical force is an extraordinary and rare event with the realities of policing in the USA, let alone in Nigeria (Alpert and Dunham 2004; HRW 2005).

12. This may reflect the relative unimportance of crime prevention. Policing tends to be specific whereas crime control is generalised.

13. This is not refuted by Sheptycki's argument that policing is no longer a set of practices embedded in the sovereign nation-state. Indeed, the structures that support his view of transnationalised, fragmented and greatly differentiated policing remain statist – witness Interpol, UN civilian policing etc. (Sheptycki 2002; Goldsmith and 2007).

14. 'Rule of law' is shorthand for a specific form of democratic security governance. It is an operational goal, which is believed to be what protects a populace from arbitrary violence and criminality. It is expressed through formal structures (such as the police and judiciary) and processes (elections and courts), but it does not refer to order as such. By 2004 it had become 'a principle of governance in which all persons, institutions and entities ... are accountable to the laws that are ... consistent with international human rights' (Smith et al. 2007: 6).

CHAPTER 3

1. By accountability Bayley means 'the processes whereby the behaviour of police is brought into conformity with 'international standards', rather than (as he originally argued) 'the requirements of the encapsulating society' (1985: 160).

2. It is about commercial opportunity too. A feature of police reform has been its profitability for companies such as the US-based DynCorp and the UK-based Atos Consulting. But the market for protective security is more lucrative. In early 2003, the UK-based security company Armor Group commissioned a survey to measure the global market for protective security and security training. The estimated market was of US$900 million per annum. The exercise was repeated in 2007, by which time the estimated value of the market was $2.5 billion (*JDW* 30 May 2007: 34).

3. Take the case of minority recruitment in Bosnia. The UN assumed that by making officers from different ethnic groups go through the same training an *esprit de corps* would develop (Celador 2005: 367); officers would represent the interests of the Bosnian state, rather than their ethnic group, and would treat all citizens equally. This has yet to happen.

4. For relevant literature, see Marenin 1998. Indigenous police, like police in Western democracies, are expected to repeatedly legitimise themselves (Waddington 1994: 93). Describing police objectives as ethnically representative or as crime fighters does not describe what they do or what they are, but it offers a mandate that confers legitimacy.

5. It is difficult to distinguish between corruption, begging and supplementing inadequate wages when (as in Sierra Leone in 2001) constables received about $21 a month plus allowances. This was less than the cost of a bag of rice, the staple food.

6. This is partly because, as Klockars noted, 'in police circles there is a model of what an ideal police agency should look like called "the professional model". It envisions [an agency] organized along military lines, highly centralised, strictly disciplined, exceptionally efficient, technologically sophisticated, free from the influence of partisan politics, and staffed by officers of honor and integrity' (1985: 120).

7. Judges do not see themselves as part of the security sector, while donors do not wish to be tainted by prisons. Iraq offers numerous examples of the consequences of this. Further, prison issues may yet destroy US hopes of a relatively smooth exit from Iraq, for the US must also transfer 23,000 predominantly Sunni prisoners from its custody to the Shia-dominated Iraq government (*Financial Times* 16 July 2007).

8. This section is based on a series of personal discussions, reports and unpublished presentations by UN Police Division officials, 2006–07.

9. Countries that are technically at peace can experience gang warfare sufficiently intense to warrant the deployment of UN stabilisation forces. Haiti is such as case.

10. As Murray notes regarding Afghanistan,

> The US practice of outsourcing recruitment and management of police advisers for international police missions has been questioned in many quarters, and the use of DynCorp as the contracting agent has been particularly criticized. Police and retired police contracted by DynCorp vary in quality and have been accused of scandalous personal behaviour in at least one mission. The profit motive also makes DynCorp vulnerable to charges, even from its own personnel, of making very low bids to gain contracts, thereby compromising the quality of the service delivered. The difficulty for the United States is that the federal government has no general policing resources at its disposal to commit to international missions. All the federal law enforcement agencies, including the FBI, are specialist organizations that do not carry out basic policing duties. Moreover, given the long-standing constitutional and administrative practices of the US government, outsourcing is the way it delivers a significant number of its programmes. (Murray 2007: 125)

For a discussion of the difficulties of the US government in fulfilling its international policing responsibilities, see Serafino 2004.

CHAPTER 4

1. There are three branches to the Iraqi Police. The Iraqi Police Service is responsible for the day-to-day patrolling, the National Police is a gendarmerie based in Baghdad, while the Supporting Forces include the remaining police organisations.
2. Electricity is critical in a country where temperatures reach 50°C.
3. Contract values are high. In 2003, DynCorp received $50 million for the first year of a contract to create a new Iraqi police force (CSC 2003: 41).
4. More damaging than the failure by different US departments to agree on the core police mission was the failure to rehabilitate the Ministry of Defence, which managed and administered the police (Rathmell 2007).
5. Compare the inaction of Australian troops and police in Dili in 2006 as approximately 1,000 residents looted a government warehouse. Contrast Portugal's Republican National Guard (GNR) gendarmerie, which, with firearms and clubs, stopped the looting in an hour.
6. This section is based on Hills 2004.
7. Compare British troops in Maysan. They did not stop looting because, unlike Iraqis, they believed life to be more important than property (Stewart 2007: 291, 295–6).
8. For the influence of militia groups on appointments, see Stewart 2007: 282–6.

CHAPTER 5

1. The agenda did not shift to the broader remit of nation-building and financial sustainability until the EU took over the UNPOL mission in 2003 (Wisler 2007).
2. It was worth their while. Approximately US$4 billion was committed to finance civil aspects of the agreement in the years 1996–99 (Johnson 2000: 1).
3. Basic training included patrol duties, use of firearms, use of force, criminal investigation, forensic evidence collection, traffic control, defensive tactics, first aid, legal training, and interviewing techniques. Specialised courses (including senior-level management, criminal investigations and emergency response driving) were introduced later.
4. Perhaps for this reason Richard Monk (a former IPTF commander) questioned 'the requirement for a strong police quotient in peacekeeping operations' (*International Police Review* 2000; BBC 4 August 1999).
5. Compare the situation in Kosovo 1999–2000 where senior French and American officers were accused of improper ties with gangsters and war criminals (*Indigo Intelligence Newsletter* 2001: 1).
6. This was a confederation of minority ethnic Tajik and Uzbek Afghans opposed by the majority Pashtun tribes in the south, from which the Taliban draw support.
7. Under the Bonn agreement of December 2001, which mapped out Afghanistan's future, Afghan units were to withdraw from Kabul and

other urban centres where international troops were deployed. The reasons were political in that operating in unsafe areas outside urban centres would risk casualties and undermine Western acceptance of the operation.

8. ISAF in Kabul considered police training to be part of its role, but its contribution was confined to practical training during joint patrols.

9. LOFTA was a mechanism managed by the UN Development Programme (UNDP) for channelling multilateral aid to the police. It covered salaries, the procurement of non-lethal equipment, the rebuilding of police facilities, and training. It was supposed to run from 2002 to 2006, but it was never solvent because pledged aid was either late or never arrived.

10. Political calculations played a part in determining priorities. For example, in early 2006 the training pillar was converted to gender support. This was a pragmatic move to attract the American and German money known to be available for gender projects (Murray 2007: 110; Hodes and Sedra 2007: 62–71).

11. In 1991, 300,000 of Rwanda's 8 million population lived in Kigali (Joint Evaluation 1991). In 1996, the population was some 358,000, and in 2000 it was 603,000; 56 per cent of the population was aged below 20, with women constituting 52 per cent of Kigali's population (Rwandagate 2006).

12. It goes on to say: 'the major security threat in the world generally and Rwanda in particular is bound to take the form of terrorism' (Rwanda National Police Website 2007). That is, the police say what they think influential governments want to hear.

CHAPTER 6

1. For a timeline and information on public and social sectors, see UNDP 1998.

2. For the social linkages and strategies used by traders, see Little 2003: 87.

3. This section is based on Hills 2000: 145–7.

4. Somalia had long experience of tight links between politics and former police officers. Barre, for example, had been a policeman, and General Mohamed Abshir, chairman of the Somali Salvation Democratic Front, whom the USA regarded as a potential president of Somalia, had been police chief to President Egal of the self-proclaimed republic of Somaliland.

5. The individual concerned also supplied food to Zairean jails. *Africa Report*, January/February 1994, 36–8.

6. Liberia's war prompted the debate regarding the drivers of contemporary war. See Berdal and Malone 2000; Ellis 1999: 214; Huband 2001: 142; ICG 2002.

7. For background, see Ellis 1999.

8. In 2001, it was front-page news when the then police director (Paul Mulbah) apologised after officers from the Special Operations Division

flogged fifty bus drivers and passengers who refused to pay bribes at a checkpoint (BBC 5 July 2001). Mulbah blamed the incident, which he described as unacceptable, on 'a few bad apples' and on the poor training of the ex-combatants who had been recruited into the police

9. For alternative non-state arrangements, see Baker 2007b.

10. In francophone countries, 'force' is commonly understood to refer to the institution, rather than to an instrument of repression.

CHAPTER 7

1. Nigeria's area is 923,768 square kilometres, and its population approximately 130 million. Precise figures are not known because issues of ethnic and electoral balance and the allocation of federal revenue mean that population figures are controversial.

2. Bloomfield and Reilly identify two elements at the centre of such conflicts. The first is identity, which they define as 'the mobilisation of people in communal identity groups based on races, religion, culture, language'. The second is distribution, which refers to the sharing of economic, social and political resources in a society (Yusuf 2007: 241).

3. The work of anthropologist Murray Last on the Sokoto caliphate is a notable exception.

4. The conflict was separate from that in Darfur, which is only one of many insurgencies challenging the Khartoum government.

CHAPTER 8

1. The debate may be followed in Wood and Dupont 2006. For example, Marks and Goldsmith draw on South Africa's experience to argue that, 'notwithstanding the ... potential of community-based governance structures ... the state is, philosophically and practically speaking, best placed to manage and deliver security' (Wood and Dupont 2006: 5). Loader and Walker are even more explicit: 'the state's place in producing the public good of security is both necessary and virtuous' (Wood and Dupont 2006: 167).

2. The self-declared autonomous state of Puntland has a force, as does the self-declared but internationally unrecognised state of Somaliland.

3. So too is funding, as the following examples make clear. In June 2008, Somali police pay was twelve months in arrears, while the logistical and financial costs of introducing an African Union police operation capable of supporting police reform for six months was estimated at US$44 million (Private communication 2008a).

4. Hence the problematic nature of making the protection of a populace an integral part of human security. Contrast Axworthy 2001: 4, 6.

5. The nature of the previous order is significant. Stewart notes that Iraq's Ba'athist state was based on a centralised bureaucracy that the CPA could not replace, whereas it was straightforward to create institutions in Sierra Leone (Stewart 2007: 55).

REFERENCES

Abrahamsen, R., and M. Williams (2007) 'Introduction: The Privatisation and Globalisation of Security in Africa', *International Relations*, vol. 21, no. 2.

Africa Confidential (1997) 'Kabila Takes On the UN', vol. 38, no. 19.

Africa Confidential (2005) 'Off-road rage', vol. 46, no. 23.

Afrol News (2007) 'Rwanda Genocide Witnesses Killed', 22 January. www.afrol.com/articles/23900.

Al-Ahram (2001) 'Hunting the Hoodlums', 18–24 October. http://weekly.ahram.org.eg/2001/556/9war1.htm.

al-Khalil, S. (1989) *Republic of Fear: Saddam's Iraq*, Radius, London.

Alpert, G., and R. Dunham (2004) *Understanding Police Use of Force: Officers, Suspects, and Reciprocity*, Cambridge University Press, Cambridge.

Amnesty International (1992) *Rwanda: Persecution of Tutsi Minority and Repression of Government Critics 1990–1992*, Amnesty International, London.

Amnesty International (1996) *Amnesty International Report 1996*, Amnesty International, London.

Amnesty International (1998) *Annual Report 1998: Rwanda*, Amnesty International, London.

Amnesty International (2002) 'Rwanda: Peace Workers Are Victims of Increasing Political Repression', 5 February. www.amnesty.org.uk/news_details.asp?NewsID=13847.

Amnesty International (2005) *Annual Report 2005*, Amnesty International, London.

The Analyst (Monrovia) (2007) 'Liberia: LNP, Seaport Police in Showdown', 10 July. http://allafrica.com/stories/200707100775.html.

Anderson, J. (2006) *The Fall of Baghdad*, Abacus, London.

Andreas, P. (2005) 'Criminalizing Consequences of Sanctions: Embargo Busting and Its Legacy', *International Studies Quarterly*, vol. 49, no. 2.

Andrusz, G., M. Harloe and I. Szelenyi (eds) (1996) *Cities after Socialism: Urban and Regional Change and Conflict in Post-socialist Societies*, Blackwell, Oxford.

Arnson, C., and I. Zartman (eds) (2005) *Rethinking the Economics of War: The Intersection of Need, Creed, and Greed*, Woodrow Wilson Center Press, Baltimore MD.

Ashraf, M. (2007) 'The Lessons of Policing in Iraq: A Personal Perspective', *Policing*, vol. 1, no. 1.

AusAID(2005) *Fragile States and Australia's Aid Program*. www.ausaid.gov. au/keyaid/fragile_states.cfm.

Australian Federal Police (2006) *Submission 16 to Joint Standing Committee on Foreign Affairs, Defence and Trade, Human Rights Sub-Committee: Inquiry into Australia's Aid Program in the Pacific*, Australian Federal Police, Canberra.

Avant, D. (2006) *The Market for Force: The Consequences of Privatizing Security*, Cambridge University Press, Cambridge.

Axworthy, L. (2001) 'Introduction', in R. McRae and Hubert (eds), *Human Security and the New Diplomacy: Protecting People, Promoting Peace*, McGill-Queen's University Press, Montreal.

Ayoob, M. (1995) *The Third World Security Predicament: State Making, Regional Conflict and the International System*, Lynne Rienner, Boulder CO.

Ayoob, M. (1997) 'Defining Security: A Subaltern Realist Perspective', in K. Krause and M. Williams (eds), *Critical Security Studies*, University of Minnesota Press, Minneapolis.

Bajraktari, Y., A. Boutellis, F. Gunja, D. Harris, J. Kapsis, E. Kaye and J. Rhee with G. Peake (2006) *The PRIME System: Measuring the Success of Post-Conflict Police Reform*, Woodrow Wilson School of Public and International Affairs, Princeton NJ.

Baker, B. (2007a) 'Policing in Liberia: Getting the Policies Right', unpublished paper, Coventry University.

Baker, B. (2007b) *Multi-Choice Policing in Africa*, Nordiska Afrikainstitutet, Uppsala.

Baker, B. (2007c) 'Reconstructing a Policing System Out of the Ashes: Rwanda's Solution', *Policing and Society*, vol. 17, no. 4.

Baldwin, D. (1997) 'The Concept of Security', *Review of International Studies* 23.

Barakat, S. (ed.) (2005) *Third World Quarterly: Reconstructing Post-Saddam Iraq*, vol. 26, no. 485.

Barnett, T. (2004) *The Pentagon's New Map*, Putnam, New York.

Bayley, D. (1976) *Forces of Order: Police Behavior in Japan and the United States*, University of California Press, Berkeley.

Bayley, D. (1985) *Patterns of Policing: A Comparative International Analysis*, Rutgers University Press, New Brunswick NJ.

Bayley, D. (1995) 'A Foreign Policy for Democratic Policing', *Policing and Society* 5.

Bayley, D. (2001) *Democratising the Police Abroad: What To Do and How To Do It*, US Department of Justice, Washington DC. www.ncjrs.org/pdf-files1/nij/188742.pdf.

Bayley, D. (2006) *Changing the Guard: Developing Democratic Police Abroad*, Oxford University Press, Oxford.

BBC (1999) 'World: Europe: Police Start Kosovo Patrols', 4 August. http://news.bbc.co.uk/1/hi/world/europe/414936.stm.

BBC (2000) 'Nigerian Mosques Under Guard', 25 February. http://news.bbc.co.uk/1/hi/world/africa/656553.stm.

BBC (2001) 'Liberian Police Sorry for Floggings', 5 July. http://news.bbc.co.uk/1/hi/world/africa/1424502.stm.

BBC (2001) 'Nigeria Road Trip: Kano', 21 December. http://news.bbc.co.uk/1/hi/in_depth/africa/2001.

BBC (2002) 'Kaduna: Nigeria's Religious Flashpoint', 20 January. http://news.bbc.co.uk/1/hi/world/africa/2579825.stm.

BBC (2002) 'Arms Banned on Mogadishu Streets', 24 January. http://news.bbc.co.uk/1/hi/world/africa/1780862.stm.

BBC (2003) 'Iraq Rumour Mill Grinds On', 6 July. http://news.bbc.co.uk/2/hi/middle_east/3049300.stm.

BBC (2003) 'The Perils of Liberian Peacekeeping', 4 August. http://news.bbc.co.uk/1/hi/world/africa/3113009.stm.

BBC (2005) 'Hopes for Liberia's Traffic Cops', 12 January. http://news.bbc.co.uk/1/hi/world/africa/4163001.stm.

BBC (2005) 'Iraq Police Accused of Torture', 27 July. http://news.bbc.co.uk/2/hi/middle_east/4718999.stm).

BBC (2006) 'Vigilantes Take On Liberian Gangs', 19 September. http://news.bbc.co.uk/1/hi/world/africa/5357718.stm.

BBC (2007) 'Most of Baghdad "Not Controlled"', 5 June. http://news.bbc.co.uk/1/hi/world/middle_east/6721689.stm.

BBC (2007) 'Taleban "Shifting Focus To Kabul"', 21 June. http://news.bbc.co.uk/1/hi/world/south_asia/6224900.stm.

BBC (2007) 'Nineteen Die in Rio Slum Battle', 28 June. http://news.bbc.co.uk/2/hi/americas/6247608.stm.

BBC (2007) 'Isolated Gaza a Jail for Its People', 9 August. http://news.bbc.co.uk/1/hi/world/middle_east/6939223.stm.

Beaumont, R. (1995) 'Constabulary or Fire Brigade? The Army National Guard', *Parameters* 25 (Summer).

Berdal, M., and D. Malone (eds) (2000) *Greed and Grievance: Economic Agendas in Civil Wars*, Lynne Rienner, Boulder CO.

Berenskoetter, F. (2006) 'Under Construction: ESDP and the "Fight Against Organised Crime"'. Unpublished paper, London School of Economics. www.lse.ac.uk/depts/intrel/pdfs/EUPU%20challenge%20working%20paper%205.pdf.

Bieber, F. (2005) 'Local Institutional Engineering: A Tale of Two Cities, Mostar and Brcko', *International Peacekeeping*, vol. 12, no. 3.

Bienen, H. (ed.) (1968) *The Military Intervenes: Case Studies in Political Development*, Russell Sage Foundation, New York.

Bittner, E. (1970) *The Functions of Police in Modern Society*, NIMH, Rockville MD.

Bøås, M., and K. Dunn (eds) (2007) *African Guerrillas: Raging Against the Machine*, Lynne Rienner, Boulder CO.

Bøås, M., and A. Hatløy (2008) '"Getting In, Getting Out": Militia Membership and Prospects for Re-integration in Post-war Liberia', *Journal of Modern African Studies*, vol. 46, no. 1.

Bøås, M., and K. Jennings (2005) 'Insecurity and Development: The Rhetoric of the "Failed State"', *European Journal of Development Research*, vol. 17, no. 3.

Bollens, S. (2000) *On Narrow Ground: Urban Policy and Ethnic Conflict in Jerusalem and Belfast*, SUNY Press, Albany NY.

Bollens, S. (2006) 'Urban Planning and Peace Building', *Progress in Planning* 66.

Booth, K. (1991) 'Security and Emancipation', *Review of International Studies*, vol. 17, no. 4.

Booth, K. (ed.) (2005) *Critical Security Studies and World Politics*, Lynne Rienner, Boulder CO.

Bourdieu, P., and L. Wacquant (1992) *An Invitation to Reflexive Sociology*, Chicago University Press, Chicago.

Bouret, M. (2000) 'Witness to Madness'. www.time.com/time/europe/photo essays/grozny.htm.

Bowling, B., and J. Foster (2002) 'Policing and the Police', in M. Maguire, R. Morgan and R. Reiner (eds), *The Oxford Handbook of Criminology*, Oxford University Press, Oxford.

Bremer, B., with M. McConnell (2006) *My Year in Iraq: The Struggle to Build a Future of Hope*, Simon & Schuster, New York.

Broadhurst, R. (2002) 'Lethal Violence, Crime and State Formation in Cambodia', *Australian and New Zealand Journal of Criminology*, vol. 35, no. 1.

Brogden, M., and P. Nijhar (2005) *Community Policing: National and International Models and Approaches*, Willan Publishing, Cullompton.

Brogden, M., and C. Shearing (1993) *Policing for a New South Africa*, Routledge, London.

Bronson, R. (2002) 'When Soldiers Become Cops', *Foreign Affairs*, vol. 81, no. 6.

Brown, J. (2000) 'Combat Cops? The Army as Constabulary: Lessons from Our Past', *Armed Forces Journal* (September).

Brzoska, M. (2003) *Development Donors and the Concept of Security Sector Reform*, DCAF Occasional Papers 4, Geneva Centre for the Democratic Control of Armed Forces, Geneva.

Cain, M. (1979) 'Trends in the Sociology of Police Work,' *International Journal of the Sociology of Law* 7.

Caldeira, T. Pires do Rio (2000) *City of Walls: Crime, Segregation and Citizenship in Sao Paulo*, University of California Press, Berkeley.

Call, C., and W. Stanley (2001) 'Protecting the People: Public Security Choices after Civil Wars', *Global Governance*, vol. 7, no. 2.

Caparini, M., and O. Marenin (2004) 'Police Transformation in Central and Eastern Europe: The Challenges of Change', in *Transforming Police in Central and Eastern Europe. Process and Progress*, LIT, Münster.

Lessons from Timor-Leste and Solomon Islands', *Third World Quarterly*, vol. 28, no. 6.

Goldsmith, A., and J. Sheptycki (eds) (2007) *Crafting Transnational Policing Police Capacity-Building and Global Policing Reform*, Hart, Oxford.

Gompert, D., O. Oliker, B. Stearns, K. Crane and Riley (2007) *Making Liberia Safe: Transformation of the National Security Sector*, RAND, Washington DC.

Goverde, H., and J. van Tatenhove (2000) 'Power and Policy Networks', in H. Goverde, P. Cerny, M. Haugaard and H. Lentner (eds), *Power in Contemporary Politics: Theories, Practices, Globalizations*, Sage, London.

Goverde, H., P. Cerny, M. Haugaard and H. Lentner (eds) (2000) *Power in Contemporary Politics: Theories, Practices, Globalizations*, Sage, London.

Graham, S. (2004) (ed.) *Cities, War and Terrorism: Towards an Urban Geopolitics*. Oxford, Blackwell.

Guardian (2000) 'Uneasy Calm Follows Kosovo Clashes', 22 February.

Guardian (2005) 'Police in Basra Out of Control, Say Chief', 31 May.

Guardian (2007) 'If They Pay We Kill Them Anyway' – The Kidnapper's Story', 27 January.

Guardian (2007) 'Blair Guilty of Capitulating to Sinn Féin – Mandelson', 13 March.

Guardian (2007) 'Welcome to Tehran – How Iran Took Control of Basra', 19 May.

Guardian (2007) '14 Killed in Attack on Police Chief's House', 9 June.

Guardian (2007) 'When Night Falls, the Assassins Gather in Hayaniya Square', 17 November.

Hansard (2006) *Written Answers 10 July 2006: International Development Overseas Projects*. www.publications.parliament.uk/pa/cm200506/cmhansrd/cm 060710/text/60710w1516.htm#06071017000172.

Hansen, L. (2006) *Security as Practice: Discourse Analysis and the Bosnian War*, Routledge, London.

Harris, C. (1957) *Allied Military Administration of Italy, 1943–45*, HMSO, London.

Hartley, A. (2004) *The Zanzibar Chest*, Harper Perennial, London.

Held, D. (1995) *Democracy and the Global Order: From the Modern State to Cosmopolitan Governance*, Polity Press, Cambridge.

Herring, E., and G. Rangwala (2006) *Iraq in Fragments: The Occupation and Its Legacy*, Hurst, London.

Herscher, A. (1998) 'Remembering and Rebuilding in Bosnia', *Transitions*, vol. 5, no. 3. www.haverford.edu/relg/sells/mostar/Mostartransition.html.

Hills, A. (2000) 'The Inherent Limits of Military Forces in Policing Peace Operations', *International Peacekeeping*, vol. 8, no. 3.

Hills, A. (2002) *Future War in Cities: Rethinking a Liberal Dilemma*, Frank Cass, London.

Hills, A. (2003) 'Dissolving Boundaries? The Development Marketplace and Military Security', *Contemporary Security Policy*, vol. 24, no. 3.

Hills, A. (2004) 'Basra and the Referent Points of Two-fold War', *Small Wars and Insurgencies*, vol. 15, no. 3.

Hills, A. (2006) 'Fear and Loathing in Falluja', *Armed Forces and Society*, vol. 32, no. 4.

Hills, A. (2007) 'Police Commissioners, Presidents and the Governance of Security', *Journal of Modern African Studies*, vol. 45, no. 3.

Hills, A. (2008) 'The Dialectic of Police Reform in Nigeria', *Journal of Modern African Studies*, vol. 46, no. 2.

Hinton, M. (2006) *The State on the Streets: Police and Politics in Argentina and Brazil*, Lynne Rienner, Boulder CO.

Hobbes, T. (1962) *Leviathan*, ed. J. Plamenatz, Fontana, London.

Hodes, C., and M. Sedra (2007) *The Search for Security in Post-Taliban Afghanistan*, Adelphi Papers, vol. 47, no. 391, Routledge, London.

Hoffman, D. (2005) 'The Brookfields Hotel (Freetown, Sierra Leone)', *Public Culture*, vol. 17, no. 1.

Hoffman, D. (2007a) 'The City as Barracks: Freetown, Monrovia, and the Organization of Violence in Contemporary West African Cities', *Cultural Anthropology*, vol. 22, no. 3.

Hoffman, D. (2007b) 'The Meaning of a Militia: Understanding the Civil Defence Forces of Sierra Leone', *African Affairs*, vol. 106, no. 425.

Holme, T. Tanke, and E. Barth Eide (2000) *Peacebuilding and Police Reform*, Frank Cass, London.

Holt, V., and T. Berkman (2006) *The Impossible Mandate: Military Preparedness, the Responsibility to Protect and Modern Peace Operations*, Henry Stimson Center, Washington DC.

Horn, A., and F. Olonisakin (2008) 'United Kingdom-led Security Sector Reform in Sierra Leone', in G. Peake, Scheye and A. Hills (eds), *Managing Insecurity: Field Experiences of Security Sector Reform*, Routledge, London.

Horne, A. (1987) *A Savage War of Peace: Algeria 1954–1962*, 2nd edn, Macmillan, London.

HRW (Human Rights Watch) (1995) *Human Rights Watch, Rearming with Impunity: International Support for the Perpetrators of the Rwandan Genocide*. www.hrw.org/reports/1995/Rwanda1.htm.

HRW (1998) *Bosnia and Hercegovina. Beyond Restraint: Politics and the Policing Agenda of the United Nations International Police Task Force*. www.hrw.org/reports98/bosnia/.

HRW (2001) *Background Note on the Russian Operation in Chechnya*. www.hrw.org/reports/2001/chechnya/Disapfin-01.htm.

HRW (2003) *Basra: Crime and Insecurity under British Occupation*. www.hrw.org/doc/?t=mideast_pub&document_limit=80,20.

HRW (2005) *'Rest in Pieces' Police Torture and Deaths in Custody in Nigeria*. www.hrw.org/reports/2005/nigeria0705/.

HRW (2007a) *Killings in Eastern Rwanda*, HRW, New York. www.hrw.org/backgrounder/africa/rwanda0107/.

HRW (2007b) *'There Will Be No Trial': Police Killings of Detainees and the Imposition of Collective Punishments*, HRW, New York. hrw.org/reports/2007/rwanda0707/4.htm.

HRW (2007c) 'Nigeria: Investigate Widespread Killings by Police, Police Chief

Boasts of 785 Killings in 90 Days, 18 November', *Human Rights News*. http://hrw.org/english/docs/2007/11/16/nigeri17361.htm.

HRW (2007d) *World Report 2007*, HRW, New York. www.hrw.org/wr2k7/#nolink.

Huband, M. (2001) *The Skull Beneath the Skin: Africa After the Cold War*, Westview, Boulder CO.

Huggins, M. (1998) *Political Policing: The United States and Latin America*, Duke University Press, Durham NC.

Human Security Centre (2005) *Human Security Report*, Oxford University Press, Oxford.

Huntingdon, S. (1968) *Political Order in Changing Societies*, Yale University Press, Newhaven CT.

Ibrahimi, S. (2006) 'Afghan Police Part of the Problem', Institute of War and Peace Reporting, 6 June. www.rawa.org/police-3.

IBRD (International Bank for Reconstruction and Development) (2000) *The World Bank Annual Report 2000*, World Bank, New York.

ICG (International Crisis Group) (2002) *Liberia: The Key to Ending Regional Instability*, Africa Report no. 43, Freetown/Brussels.

ICG (2005) *Bosnia's Stalled Police Reform: No Progress, No EU*, Report 164, ICG, Brussels/Sarajevo.

Imobighe, T. (ed.) (2003) *Civil Society and Ethnic Conflict Management in Nigeria*, Ibadan, Spectrum Books.

Independent (2004) 'Sex and Death in the Heart of Africa', 25 May.

Independent (2006) 'Return to Kandahar: The Taliban Threat', 21 August.

Independent (2006) 'Operation Sinbad: Mission Failure Casts Doubt on Entire British Presence in Iraq', 8 October.

Indian Ocean Newsletter (1993) 6 February.

Indigo Intelligence Newsletter (2001) 'The West's Questionable Ways in Kosovo', 397, 11 January.

Innes, M. (2004) 'Reinventing Tradition? Reassurance, Neighbourhood Security and Policing', *Criminal Justice* 4.

Institute of War and Peace Reporting (IWPR) (2002) 'New Chechen Police 2002: Chechen Police Plan Raises Concerns', 28 November.

International Police Review (2000) 'Keeping the Peace', May/June.

Ioannides, I. (2007) 'The European Union and Learning from Support for Post-conflict Police Reform: A Critical Analysis of Macedonia (2001–2005)', Ph.D. thesis, University of Bradford.

IRIN (2002) 'Sierra Leone: IRIN Focus on Security Threats', 2 July. www.irinnews.org/Report.aspx?ReportId=32808.

IRIN (2007a) *Youth in Crisis: Coming of Age in the 21st Century*, UN Office for the Coordination of Humanitarian Affairs (OCHA). www.irinnews.org/IndepthMain.aspx?IndepthId=28&ReportId=70140.

IRIN (2007b) 'Africa: Urban Population To Double – UNFPA', 27 June. www.irinnews.org/Report.aspx?ReportId=72956.

IRIN–CEA (2000) 'Rwanda: New Police Force to Replace National Gendarmerie', 11 January. www.africa.upenn.edu/Hornet/irin836.html.

Jackson, L., and J. Wade (2005) 'Police Perceptions of Social Capital and Sense of Responsibility: An Explanation of Proactive Policing', *Policing: An International Journal of Police Strategies and Management*, vol. 28, no. 1.

Jackson, R. (1990) *Quasi-states: Sovereignty, International Relations, and the Third World*, Cambridge University Press, New York.

Jackson, R., and A. James (eds) (1993) *States in a Changing World*, Oxford University Press, Oxford.

Japan Times (2005) 'Iraqi police to get $ 3.3 million in aid', 13 October. http://search.japantimes.co.jp/member/member.html?nn20051013b8.htm.

JDW (2004) 'Stabilising Bosnia', *Jane's Defence Weekly*, 4 August.

JDW (2007) ' Sudanese Conditions Undermine Darfur Peacekeeping Plan', *Jane's Defence Weekly*, 21 March.

JDW (2007) 'Interview: David Seaton, CEO, ArmorGroup', *Jane's Defence Weekly*, 30 May.

JDW (2007) 'US General Warns on Leadership Shortage for Iraqi Security Forces', *Jane's Defence Weekly*, 20 June.

Jennings, K. (2007) 'The Struggle to Satisfy: DDR through the Eyes of Ex-combatants in Liberia', *International Peacekeeping*, vol. 14, no. 2.

Jensen, S. (2007) 'Security and Violence on the Frontier of the State: Vigilant Citizens in Nkomazi, South Africa', in P. Ahluwalia, L. Bethlehem and R. Ginio (eds), *Violence and Non-Violence in Africa*, Routledge, London.

Jentleson, B. (2002) 'The Need for Praxis: Bringing Policy Relevance Back In', *International Security*, vol. 26, no. 4.

JIDR (2000) 'French Army in Profile: From Hollow Force to Hard Core', *Jane's International Defence Review*, June.

JIR (2004) 'Iraq Provides Lessons in Nation Building', *Jane's Intelligence Review*, January.

JIR (2006) 'Police Reform in Afghanistan', *Jane's Intelligence Review*, November.

Job, B. (1992) 'National, Regime, and State Securities in the Third World', in Job (ed.), *The Insecurity Dilemma*, Lynne Rienner, Boulder CO.

Johns Hopkins Bloomberg School of Public Health (2006) 'Updated Iraq Survey Affirms Earlier Mortality Estimates', 11 October. www.jhsph.edu/publichealthnews/press_releases/2006/burnham_iraq_2006.html.

Johnson, H. (2000) 'Bosnia: Crime and Corruption Threaten Successful Implementation of the Dayton Peace Agreement', Testimony to the House of Representatives, Washington DC, 19 July.

Johnston, L. (2000) *Policing Britain: Risk, Security and Governance*, Harlow: Longman.

Joint Doctrine (2007) *Countering Irregular Activity within a Comprehensive Approach*, Note 2/07, Development, Concepts and Doctrine Centre, Shrivenham.

Joint Evaluation of Emergency Assistance to Rwanda (1996) *The International Response to Conflict and Genocide: Lessons from the Rwanda Experience*, Danida, Copenhagen.

Jones, S., J. Wilson, A. Rathmell and K. Riley (2005) *Establishing Law and Order after Conflict*, RAND, Santa Monica CA.

Jones, T., and T. Newburn (1998) *Private Security and Public Policing*, Oxford University Press, Oxford.

Jones, T., and T. Newburn (2002) 'The Transformation of Policing? Understanding Current Trends in Policing Systems', *British Journal of Criminology*, vol. 42, no. 1.

Juba Post (2007) '34 Riot Police Trained in Juba', 1 June. www.k2–media.org/jubapost/go/record.php?cat=16&recordID=43.

Juba Post (2007) 'UN Police Trains SSPSon Tactical Operation Course', 29 June. www.k2–media.org/jubapost/go/record.php?cat=16&recordID=156.

Juba Post Online (2007) vol. 3, no. 20, 1–8 June. www.k2–media.org/jubapost/go/index.php.

Kaldor, M. (1999) *New and Old Wars: Organised Violence in a Global Era*, Polity Press, Cambridge.

Kalyvas, S. (2001) '"New" and "Old" Civil Wars: A Valid Distinction?', *World Politics*, vol. 4, no. 1.

Kappler, V., R. Sluder and G. Alpert (1994) *Forces of Deviance: Understanding the Dark Side of Policing*, Waveland Press, Prospect Heights IL.

Kasarda, J., and E. Crenshaw (1991) 'Third World Urbanization: Dimensions, Theories, and Determinants', *Annual Review of Sociology* 17.

Keen, D. (2005) *Conflict and Collusion in Sierra Leone*, James Currey, Oxford.

Keen, D. (2008) *Complex Emergencies*, Polity Press, Cambridge.

Kelling, G., T. Pate, D. Dieckman and C. Brown (1974) *The Kansas City Preventive Patrol Experiment: A Technical Report*, Police Foundation, Washington DC.

Kelly, M. (1997) *Peace Operations: Tackling the Military Legal and Policy Challenges*, Australian Government Publishing Service, Canberra.

Kelly, M. (1999) *Restoring and Maintaining Order in Complex Peace Operations: The Search for a Legal Framework*, Kluwer Law International, The Hague.

Khan, H. (1965) *On Escalation: Scenarios and Metaphors*, Pall Mall Press, London.

Kitson, F. (1971) *Low Intensity Operations: Subversion, Insurgency, Peacekeeping*, Faber & Faber, London.

Klockars, C. (1985) *The Idea of the Police*, Sage, Beverley Hills CA.

Koonings, K., and D. Kruijt (eds) (2007) *Fractured Cities: Social Exclusion, Urban Violence and Contested Spaces in Latin America*, Zed Books, London.

Krasner, S., and C. Pascual (2005) 'Addressing State Failure', *Foreign Affairs*, vol. 84, no. 4.

Krause, K. (1998) 'Theorizing Security, Formation and the "Third World" in the post-Cold War World', *Review of International Studies*, vol. 24, no. 1.

Krause, K., and O. Jütersonke (2005) 'Peace, Security and Development in Post-Conflict Environments', *Security Dialogue*, vol. 36, no. 4.

Laclau, E. (1996) *Emancipation(s)*, Verso, London.

Lee, J. (1969) *African Armies and Civil Order*, Chatto & Windus, London.

Lemarchand, R. (1994) 'Managing Transition Anarchies: Rwanda, Burundi, and South Africa in Comparative Perspective', *Journal of Modern African Studies*, vol. 32, no. 4.

Lemarchand, R. (2002) 'The Tunnel at the End of the Light', *Review of African Political Economy*, vol. 29, no. 93/94.

Leonardi, C. (2007) '"Liberation" or Capture: Youth in Between "*Hakuma*" and "Home" During Civil War and its Aftermath in Southern Sudan', *African Affairs*, vol. 106, no. 424.

Licklider, R. (1995) 'The Consequences of Negotiated Settlements in Civil Wars, 1945–1993', *American Political Science Review*, vol. 89, no. 3.

Lilly, D. (2005) 'Faltering Reform of the Security Sector Impedes the DRC Peace Process', *Conflict, Security & Development*, vol. 5, no. 3.

Lin, T. (2007) 'Institutional Capacity and Cooperation for Policing Operations: The Australian Experience', *International Peacekeeping*, vol. 14, no. 5.

Little, P. (2003) *Somalia: Economy without State*, James Currey, Oxford.

Loader, I., and N. Walker (2001) 'Policing as a Public Good: Reconstituting the Connections', *Theoretical Criminology*, vol. 5, no. 1.

Loader, I., and N. Walker (2007a) *Civilizing Security*, Cambridge University Press, Cambridge.

Loader, I., and N. Walker (2007b) 'Locating the Public Interest in Transnational Policing', in A. Goldsmith and J. Sheptycki (eds), *Crafting Transnational Policing Police Capacity-Building and Global Policing Reform*, Hurst, Oxford.

Luckham, R. (2003) 'Democratic Strategies for Security', in G. Cawthra and R. Luckham (eds), *Governing Insecurity: Democratic Control of Military and Security Establishments in Transitional Democracies*, Zed Books, London.

Luethold, A. (2004) 'Security Sector Reform in the Arab Middle East: A Nascent Debate', Occasional Paper, DCAF, Geneva.

McCaffrey, B. (2007) 'Strategic and Operational Assessment of Operations in both Iraq and Kuwait – 9 to 16 March 2007', *British Army Review* 142.

McConville, M., and D. Shepherd (1992) *Watching Police, Watching Communities*, Routledge, London.

MacFarlane, N., and Y.F. Khong (2006) *Human Security and the UN: A Critical History*, Indiana University Press, Bloomington IN.

McGaffey, J., and R. Bazenguissa-Ganga (2000) *Congo–Paris: Transnational Traders on the Margins of the Law*, James Currey, Oxford.

MacGinty, R. (2004) 'Looting in the Context of Violent Conflict: A Conceptualisation and Typology', *Third World Quarterly*, vol. 25, no. 5.

Manning, P. (1977) *Police Work*, MIT Press, Cambridge MA.

Manwaring, M., and E. Corr (1996) 'Confronting the New World Disorder: A Legitimate Governance Theory of Engagement', in M. Manwaring and W. Olson (eds), *Managing Contemporary Conflict: Pillars of Success*, Westview Press, Boulder CO.

Marcuse, P., and R. van Kempen (eds) (2000) *Globalizing Cities: A New Spatial Order?* Blackwell, Oxford.

Marenin, O. (1982) 'Policing African States: Towards a Critique', *Comparative Politics*, vol. 15, no. 2.

Marenin, O. (1996) 'Changing Police, Policing Change: Towards More Questions', in O. Marenin (ed.), *Policing Change, Changing Police: International Perspectives*, Garland Press, New York.

Marenin, O. (1998) 'The Goal of Democracy in International Police Assistance Programs', *Policing: An International Journal of Police Strategies and Management* 21.

Marenin, O. (2005) *Restoring Policing Systems in Conflict Torn Nations: Process, Problems, Prospects*, Occasional Paper 7, DCAF, Geneva.

Margry, K. (1999) 'The Battle for Cologne', *After the Battle*, vol. 104, no. 2.

Marks, M. (2000) 'Transforming Police Organizations from Within', *British Journal of Criminology*, vol. 40, no. 4.

Marwick, A. (1965) *The Deluge: British Society and the First World War*, Bodley Head, London.

Matthews, J. Tuchman (1989) 'Redefining Security', *Foreign Affairs*, vol. 68, no. 2.

Mawby, R. (1990) *Comparative Policing Issues: The British and American Experience in International Perspective*, Unwin Hyman, London.

Mehler, A., and J. Smith-Höhn (2007) 'Security Actors in Liberia and Sierra Leone: Roles, Interrelations and Perceptions', in T. Debiel and D. Lambach (eds), *State Failure Revisited II: Actors of Violence and Alternative Forms of Governance*, Institute for Development and Peace at the University of Duisburg–Essen, Duisberg. http://inef.uni-due.de/page/documents/Report89.pdf.

Meintjies, S., A. Pillay and M. Turshen (2001) (eds) *The Aftermath: Women in Post-Conflict Transformation*, Zed Books, London.

Menkhaus, K., and J. Prendergast (1995) 'The Stateless State', *Africa Report*, May–June.

Merlingen, M., and R. Ostrauskaite (2006) *European Union Peacebuilding and Policing: Governance and European Security and Defence Policy*, Routledge, London.

Milbert, I. (2006) 'Slums, Slum Dwellers and Multilevel Governance', *European Journal of Development Research*, vol. 18, no. 2.

Ministry of Foreign Affairs of Japan (2005) 'Grant Aid to Iraq for "Program for the Police Training and Mentoring in Al Muthanna Province"', 14 October. www.mofa.go.jp/announce/announce/2005/10/1014–2.html.

Miraya 101 FM (2007) 'The UN Lauches [*sic*] the South Sudan Police Service Data Base', 23 June. www.mirayafm.org/index.php?option=com_content&task=view&id=1015&Itemid=71.

Miraya 101 FM (2007) 'The Central Equatoria State Expresses Concern over Crime Rates in Southern Sudan', 26 July. www.mirayafm.org/index.php?option=com_content&task=view&id=1242&Itemid=71.

MNF (Multi-National Force–Iraq) (2007) 'Italian Police to Train Iraqi National Police', 20 July. www.mnf-iraq.com/index.php?option=com_content&task=view&id=12933&Itemid=46

Monaghan, R., and S. McLaughlin (2006) 'Informal Justice in the City', *Space and Polity*, vol. 10, no. 2.

Monitor (Kampala) (2007) 'Sudan: Vehicle Trade Booms in Southern Sudan', 25 May. http://allafrica.com/stories/200705241020.html.

Moscow Times (2004) 'Federal Forces and Chechen Police Clash', 25 May. www.

moscowtimes.ru/stories/2004/05/25/013.html.

Moseley, L. (1945) *Report from Germany*, Victor Gollancz, London.

MSF (Médecins Sans Frontières) (2005) 'MSF Article: Return to Grozny', 18 April. www.msf.org/msfinternational/invoke.cfm?obj...EDB23FD&component=toolkit.article&method=full_htm.

Murphy, C. (2005) 'Police Studies Go Global: In Eastern Kentucky?' *Police Quarterly* 8.

Murray, M., and G. Myers (2006) *Cities in Contemporary Africa*, Palgrave Macmillan, London.

Murray, T. (2007) 'Police-Building in Afghanistan: A Case Study of Civil Security Reform', *International Peacekeeping*, vol. 14, no. 1.

Neild, R. (2002) 'Sustaining Reform: Democratic Policing in Central America', WOLA, Washington DC. www.wola.org/publications/security_monitor_policing_ca_10_02.pd.

Neocleous, M. (2000) *The Fabrication of Social Order: A Critical Theory of Police Power*, Pluto, London.

Newsweek (2001) 'How to Put the Pieces Together', 17 December.

New Vision (Kampala) (2007a) 'South Sudan Warns on Money Forgeries', 25 May. http://allafrica.com/stories/200705280429.html.

New Vision (Kampala) (2007b) 'Uganda: Iranian Police to Train Ugandans', 28 September. http://allafrica.com/stories/200709290018.html.

Nichiporuk, B. (2000) *The Security Dynamics of Demographic Factors*, RAND, Washington DC.

Oakley, R., M. Dziedzic and E. Goldberg (1998) *Policing the New World Disorder: Peace Operations and Public Security*, National Defense University Press, Washington DC.

Observer (2005) 'UK Aid Funds Iraqi Torture Units', 3 July.

OCHA (2006) *Humanitarian Update*, 11–17 December. www.unsudanig.org/library/data/sitreps/2006/dec/Sit%20Rep%20for%2011%20–%2017%20Dec%2006.doc.

OECD DAC (2001) *The DAC Guidelines: Helping Prevent Violent Conflict*, OECD, Paris.

OECD DAC (2004) *Security System Reform and Governance: Policy and Good Practice*, Policy Brief, Paris.

OECD DAC (2005) *Security System Reform and Governance*, OECD, Paris.

OECD DAC (2007) *OECD DAC Handbook on Security Sector Reform (SSR): Supporting Security and Justice*, Paris.

Ogata, S., and A. Sen (2003) *Human Security Now*, Commission of Human Security, New York.

Omasombo, J. (2005) 'Kisangani: A City at its Lowest Ebb', in A. Simone and A. Abouhani (eds), *Urban Africa: Changing Contours of Survival in the City*, Zed Books, London.

O'Neill, W. (2005) *Police Reform in Post-Conflict Societies: What We Know and What We Still Need to Know*, Policy Paper 2, International Peace Academy, New York.

Open Doors (2006) 'Vigilantes Becoming Parallel Police Force', 17 February.

www.opendoorsuk.org.uk/news/news_archives/001261.php.

Paris, R. (2001) 'Human Security: Paradigm Shift or Hot Air?' *International Security*, vol. 26, no. 2.

Paris, R. (2002) 'International Peacebuilding and the "Mission Civilisatrice"', *Review of International Studies*, vol. 28, no. 4.

Patman, R. (1997) 'Disarming Somalia: The Contrasting Fortunes of United States and Australian Peacekeepers During United Nations Intervention, 1992–1993', *African Affairs* 96.

Patman, R. (2001) 'Beyond "the Mogadishu Line": Some Australian Lessons for Managing Intra-State Conflict', *Small Wars and Insurgencies*, vol. 12, no. 1.

Peake, G. (2004) *Policing the Peace: Police Reform Experiences in Kosovo, Southern Serbia and Montenegro*, Saferworld, London.

Perito, R. (2003) *Establishing the Rule of Law in Iraq*, United States Institute of Peace (USIP) Special Report 104. www.usip.org/pubs/specialreports/sr104.htm.

Perito, R. (2004) *Where Is the Lone Ranger When We Need Him? America's Search for a Post Conflict Stability Force*, USIP, Washington DC.

Perito, R. (2005) *The Coalition Provisional Authority's Experience with Public Security in Iraq*, USIP, Special Report 137. www.usip.org/pubs/special reports/sr137.html.

Poulton, R., and I. Youssouf (1998) *A Peace of Timbuktu: Democratic Governance, Development and African Peacemaking*, United Nations Publications, New York.

Prague Watchdog (2007) 'Chechen Police Salaries Cut', 14 March. www.watchdog.cz/index.php?show=000000–000002–000001–000185&lang=1.

Private communication (2006) UN official, Stockholm, May.

Private communication (2007a) Nigeria Police assistant commissioner, Abuja, 26 January.

Private communication (2007b) UN consultant, Pretoria, 13 March.

Private communication (2007c) Liberian consultant, Pretoria, 15 March.

Private communication (2007d) UK consultant, Pretoria, 14 March.

Private communication (2007e) UK consultant, 11 May.

Private communication (2007f) B. Baker, 21 March.

Private communication (2008a) UK consultant, 25 April.

Private communication (2008b) CPDTF consultant, 7 May.

Prunier, G. (1997) *The Rwanda Crisis: History of a Genocide*, Columbia University Press, New York.

Radio Free Europe (2007) 'Russia: Who Is Out to Discredit the Chechen Police, and Why?', 1 February. www.globalsecurity.org/military/library/news/2007/02/mil-070201-rferl03.htm.

Rai, M. (2003) *Regime Unchanged: Why the War on Iraq Changed Nothing*, Pluto Press, London.

Rakodi, C. (ed.) (1997) *The Urban Challenge in Africa: Growth and Management of Its Large Cities*, United Nations University, Tokyo and New York.

Rathmell A. (2007) *Fixing Iraq's Internal Security Forces: Why is Reform of the*

Ministry of Interior so Hard? Center for Strategic and International Studies, Washington DC.

Rathmell, A., O. Oliker, T. Kelly, D. Brannan and K. Crane (2005) *Developing Iraq's Security Sector: The Coalition Provisional Authority's Experience*, RAND, Santa Monica CA.

Rauch, J., and E. van der Spuy (2006) *Police Reform in Post-Conflict Africa: A Review*, IDASA, Pretoria.

Refugees International (2007) 'Sudan: Southern Insecurity Threatens Progress of the Comprehensive Peace Agreement', *Bulletin*, July. www.refintl.org/content/article/detail/10091/.

Reliefweb (2001) 'Chechnya Post-Conflict Reconstruction Plan', 2 January. http://reliefweb.int/rw/rwb.nsf/AllDocsByUNID/04e9428f3e9c8ba785 2569c800600ee5.

Reliefweb (2006) *UN Bulletin Southern Sudan: An Overview of UN Activities in Southern Sudan*, 14 September. www.reliefweb.int/rw/rwb.nsf/db900SID/LSGZ-6VJEPT?.

Reiner, R. (2000) *The Politics of the Police*, Oxford University Press, Oxford.

Reiner, R., and T. Newburn (2000a) 'Police Research', in R. King and E. Wincup (eds), *Doing Research on Crime and Justice*, Oxford University Press, Oxford.

Renauer, B. (2007) 'Reducing Fear of Crime: Citizen, Police, or Government Responsibility?', *Police Quarterly*, vol. 10, no. 1.

Reno, W. (1995) *Corruption and State Politics in Sierra Leone*, Cambridge University Press, Cambridge.

Reno, W. (1998) *Warlord Politics and the African State*, Lyne Rienner, Boulder CO.

Reyntjens, F. (2006) 'Governance and Security in Rwanda', in G. Khadiagala (ed.), *Security Dynamics in Africa's Great Lakes Region*, Lynne Rienner.

Richards, P. (1996) *Fighting for the Rain Forest: War, Youth and Resources in Sierra Leone*, James Currey, Oxford.

Richards, P. (ed.) (2005) *No Peace No War: An Anthropology of Contemporary Armed Conflicts*, James Currey,

Rodgers, D. (2004) 'Disembedding the City: Crime, Insecurity, and Spatial Organisation in Managua, Nicaragua', *Environment and Urbanization*, vol. 16, no. 2.

Rwandagate (2006) www.rwandagateway.org/article.php3?id_article=1646.

Rwanda National Police (2007) 'Establishment of Anti-Terrorism Unit in Rwanda National Police'. http://police.gov.rw/sub.php?id_article=5.

Sackman, S. (1991) *Cultural Knowledge in Organizations*, Sage, Newbury Park CA.

Saferworld (2007) 'Conflict-sensitive Development'. www.saferworld.org.uk/pages/conflict_sensitive_development_page.html.

Sayigh, Y. (2007) *Security Sector Reform in the Arab Region: Challenges to Developing an Indigenous Agenda*, Arab Reform Initiative, Amman.

Schatzberg, M. (1988) *The Dialectics of Oppression*, Indiana University Press, Bloomington and Indianapolis.

Schümer, T. (2007) *New Humanitarianism: Britain and Sierra Leone, 1997–2003*, Palgrave Macmillan, London.

Security Dialogue (2004) 'What is "Human Security"?', *Security Dialogue*, vol. 35, no. 3.

Seekings, J. (2001) 'Social Ordering and Control in the African Townships of South Africa: An Historical Overview of Extra-State Initiatives from the 1940s to the 1990s', in W. Scharf and D. Nina (eds), *The Other Law: Non-State Ordering in South Africa*, Juta, Cape Town.

Sen, A. (1999a) *Development as Freedom*, Oxford University Press, Oxford.

Sen, A. (1999b) 'Democracy as a Universal Value', *Journal of Democracy*, vol. 10, no. 3.

Serafino, N. (2004) 'Policing in Peacekeeping and Related Stability Operations: Problems and Proposed Solutions', Report, 30 March, Congressional Research Service, Washington DC.

Sheptycki, J. (ed.) (2002) *In Search of Transnational Policing*, Ashgate, Aldershot.

Sheptycki, J. (2007) 'The Constabulary Ethic and the Transnational Condition', in A. Goldsmith and J. Sheptycki (eds), *Crafting Transnational Policing: Police Capacity-Building and Global Police Reform*, Hart, Oxford.

Sherman, L. (1992) *Policing Domestic Violence*, Free Press, New York.

Short, C. (1998) 'Security, Development and Conflict Prevention', speech at the Royal College of Defence Studies, 13 May.

Sickle J. (2005) 'Stability Operations in Northern Iraq: Task Force Altun Kupri', *Infantry*, vol. 94, no. 1.

Siegel, A. (2000) 'Postconflict Problems', *Marine Corps Gazette* 84 (February).

Sierra Leone Police News (2004) Freetown.

Sierra Leone Web (2001) 'Interview with Police Inspector-General Keith Biddle', 17 June. www.sierra-leone.org/feature061701.html.

Silber, L., and A. Little (1995) *The Death of Yugoslavia*, Penguin, London.

Simone, A., and A. Abouhani (eds) (2005) *Urban Africa: Changing Contours of Survival in the City*, Zed Books, London.

Sinclair, G. (2006) *At the End of the Line: Colonial Policing and the Imperial Endgame 1945–80*, Manchester University Press, Manchester.

Skolnick, J. (1966) *Justice without Trial: Law Enforcement in a Democratic Society*, Wiley, New York.

Smith, D. (2006) 'Internal Migration and the Escalation of Ethnic and Religious Violence in Urban Nigeria', in M. Murray and G. Myers (eds), *Cities in Contemporary Africa*, Palgrave Macmillan, London.

Smith, J., V. Holt and W. Durch (2007) *Enhancing United Nations Capacity for Post-Conflict Police Operations*, Henry Stimson Center, Washington DC.

Stabilisation Unit (2007) 'UK Concept of Stabilisation'. www.stabilisationunit. gov.uk/.

Stanton, M. (1996) 'Riot Control for the 1990s', *Infantry*, vol. 86, no. 1.

Stepanova, E. (2002) 'The Use of Russia's "Gray Area" Forces in Post-Conflict Environments', *CMR Network* 4.

Stewart, R. (2007) *Occupational Hazards*, Picador, London.

Strachan, N. (2007) 'Abu Naji Returns to Al-Kut', *British Army Review* 137.

Stromseth, J., D. Wippman and R. Brooks (2006) *Can Might Make Rights: Building the Rule of Law after Military Interventions*, Cambridge University Press, Cambridge.

Sudan Tribune (2007) 'South Sudan Development Requires Salaries Reduction', 29 April. www.sudantribune.com/spip.php?article21626.

Sunday Times (London) (1996) 'Gang Warfare Rocks Streets of Sarajevo', 10 November.

Sunday Times (London) (1997) 'Bosnia Aid Millions Go Missing', 27 July.

Sunday Times (London) (2007) 'Hamas Fights Crime Clans for Total Control of Gaza', 24 June.

Talbot, J. (1979) *The War Without a Name: France in Algeria 1954–1962*, Faber & Faber, London.

Thakur, R. (1982) 'Liberalism, Democracy, and Development: Philosophical Dilemmas in Third World Politics', *Political Studies*, vol. 30, no. 3.

Thomas, L., and S. Spataro (1998) 'Peacekeeping and Policing in Somalia', in R. Oakley, M. Dziedzic, and E. Goldberg (eds), *Policing the New World Disorder: Peace Operations and Public Security*, National Defense University Press, Washington DC.

Tilly, C. (1985) 'War Making and State Making as Organized Crime', in P. Evans, D. Rueschemeyer and T. Skocpol (eds), *Bringing the State Back In*, Cambridge University Press, Cambridge.

The Times (Johannesburg) (2007) 'State Linked to DRC Deaths', 25 October. www.thetimes.co.za/News/Article.aspx?id=596173.

Tishkov, V. (2001) *Understanding Violence for Post-Conflict Reconstruction in Chechnya*, Centre for Applied Studies in International Negotiations (CASIN), Geneva.

Trefon, T. (ed.) (2004) *Reinventing Order in the Congo: How People Respond to State Failure in Kinshasa*, Zed Books, London.

Udovičkii, J., and J. Ridegway (eds) (1997) *Burn This House: The Making and Unmaking of Yugoslavia*, Duke University, Durham NC.

UN (United Nations) (1997) *Report of the Secretary General*, A/52/568, 5 November. www.unhchr.ch/Huridocda/Huridoca.nsf/TestFrame/621fa8 f1d82f92f4802566670039278?Opendocument.

UN (2006a) 'Southern Sudan: An Overview of UN Activities in Sudan', *Bulletin*, vol. 1, no. 3 (16 February).

UN (2006b) An of UN Activities in Sudan, *Bulletin*, vol. 1, no. 15 (14 September). www.reliefweb.int/rw/rwb.nsf/db900SID/LSGZ-6VJEPT?.

UN DESA (UN Department of Economic and Social Affairs) (2005) *World Urbanisation Prospects 2005*. www.alertnet.org/db/cp/liberia.htm.

UNDP (1998) *National Human Development Report 1998 – Somalia*, UNDP, Nairobi. http://mirror.undp.org/somalia/hdr98.htm.

UNDP (2005) *Human Development Report 2005. International Cooperation at a Crossroads: Aid, Trade and Security in an Unequal World*, UNDP, New York. http://hdr.undp.org/en/reports/global/hdr2005/.

UN DPKO (2003) *Lessons Learned from United Nations Peacekeeping Experiences in Sierra Leone*, Peacekeeping Best Practices Unit, New York.

UN DPKO (2006) 'Functions and Organization of Formed Police Units in United Nations Peacekeeping Operations', Policy DPKO/PD/2006/00060, 9 November.

UN DPKO Police Division (2007) *Portfolio of Police and Law Enforcement Projects 2007*, UK DPKO, New York.

UN FAO (1996) *FAO/WFP Crop and Food Supply Assessment Mission to Rwanda July 1996*. www.fao.org/docrep/004/w2151e/w2151e00.htm.

UNHCR (UN High Commissioner for Human Rights) (2006) *Rule-of-Law Tools for Post-Conflict States: Mapping the Justice Sector*, UNHCR, New York and Geneva.

UNIFEED (2005) 'South Sudan: Police Training'. www.un.org/unifeed/script. asp?scriptId=2373.

Universities of Bonn and Duisberg-Essen (2007) 'State Failure as a Challenge to Peace and Development Policy'. www.state-failure.de/project.htm.

UNMIL (2006) 'UNMIL's Nigerian Police Contingent Decorated with UN Peacekeeping Medals', press release, 16 February. UNMIL/PIO/PR/21.

UNMIL (2007) Background. www.un.org/Depts/dpko/missions/unmil/background.html.

UN News Service (2007) *Sudan: UN Project to Improve Prisons and Police in Southern Sudan Wins Grant*, 24 May. http://allafrica.com/stories/200705250101. html.

UN Population Division (2006) *World Urbanization Prospects. The 2005 Revision*. www.un.org/esa/population/publications/WUP2005/2005WUP_FS5.pdf.

UN Security Council Secretary General (2001) 'No Exit without Strategy: Council Decision-making and the Closure or Transition of United Nations Peacekeeping Operations', Report S/2001/394.

USAID (US Agency for International Development) (2005) *Fragile States Strategy*, USAID, Washington DC.

US Central Command (2007) ' Italian Police to Train Iraqi National Police', 20 July. www2.centcom.mil/sites/uscentcom2/FrontPage%20Stories/Italian%20police%20to%20train%20Iraqi%20National%20Police.aspx.

US Department of Defense (2004) 'Gen. Abizaid Central Command Operations Update Briefing', 30 April. www.defenselink.mil/transcripts/transcript.aspx?transcriptid=2557.

US GAO (US Government Accountability Office) (2005) *Afghanistan Security*, June. www.gao.gov/highlights/d05575high.pdf.

van Creveld, M. (1991) *The Transformation of War*, Free Press, New York.

Waddington, P. (1994) *Liberty and Order: Policing Public Order in a Capital City*, UCL Press, London.

Waddington, P. (1999) *Policing Citizens: Authority and Rights*, UCL Press, London.

Washington Post (2004) 'Iraqi Battalion Refuses to "Fight Iraqis"', 11 April. www.washingtonpost.com/ac2/wp-dyn/A2680–2004 Apr10?language=printer.

Weber, M. (1962) *Basic Concepts in Sociology*. Citadel Press, Secaucus NJ.

Williams, R. (2000) 'Africa and the Challenges of Security Sector Reform',

Security Challenges for the New Millennium, IIS Monograph Series 46, Institute for Security Studies, Midrand SA.

Wisler, D. (2007) 'The International Civilian Police Mission in Bosnia and Herzegovina: From Democratization to Nation-Building', *Police Practice and Research,* vol. 8, no. 3.

Wood, J., and B. Dupont (2006) *Democracy, Society and the Governance of Security,* Cambridge University Press, Cambridge.

World Bank (1999) *Entering the 21st Century: World Development Report 1999/2000,* World Bank, Washington DC.

World Bank (2002) *World Bank Annual Report 2002,* Volume 1: *Year in Review,* Washington DC.

Wright, J. (2006) 'Police Reform in Afghanistan', *Jane's Intelligence Review,* vol. 18, no. 11.

Yiga, F. (2007) 'South Sudanese Case Study', unpublished paper given at conference 'Police Reform and Democratization in Post-Conflict African Countries', 12–15 March, Pretoria.

Yusuf, H. (2007) 'Managing Muslim–Christian Conflicts in Northern Nigeria: A Case Study of Kaduna State', *Islam and Christian–Muslim Relations,* vol. 18, no. 2.

Zaalberg, T.B. (2006) *Soldiers and Civil Power: Supporting or Substituting Civil Authorities in Modern Peace Operations* Amsterdam University Press, Amsterdam.

Zartman, I.W. (1995) *Collapsed States: The Disintegration and Restoration of Legitimate Authority,* Lynne Rienner, Boulder CO.

Ziegler, M., and R. Neild (2003) *From Peace to Governance: Police Reform and the International Community,* conference report. www.wola.org/publications/police_reform_report.pdf.

All websites accessed January 2008.

INDEX